Local Government Property Transactions in North Carolina

Second Edition

David M. Lawrence

INSTITUTE *of* GOVERNMENT
The University of North Carolina at Chapel Hill

Established in 1931, the Institute of Government provides training, advisory, and research services to public officials and others interested in the operation of state and local government in North Carolina. A part of The University of North Carolina at Chapel Hill, the Institute also administers the university's Master of Public Administration Program.

Each year approximately 14,000 city, county, and state officials attend one or more of the 230 classes, seminars, and conferences offered by the Institute. Faculty members annually publish up to fifty books, bulletins, and other reference works related to state and local government. Each day that the General Assembly is in session, the Institute's *Daily Bulletin*, available in print and electronically, reports on the day's activities for members of the legislature and others who need to follow the course of legislation. An extensive Web site (http://ncinfo.iog.unc.edu/) provides access to publications and faculty research, course listings, program and service information, and links to other useful sites related to government.

Support for the Institute's operations comes from various sources, including state appropriations, local government membership dues, private contributions, publication sales, and service contracts. For more information about the Institute, visit the Web site or call (919) 966-5381.

Michael R. Smith	Thomas H. Thornburg	Patricia A. Langelier	Ann C. Simpson
DIRECTOR	ASSOCIATE DIRECTOR FOR PROGRAMS	ASSOCIATE DIRECTOR FOR PLANNING AND OPERATIONS	ASSOCIATE DIRECTOR FOR DEVELOPMENT

FACULTY

Gregory S. Allison
Stephen Allred
David N. Ammons
A. Fleming Bell, II
Maureen M. Berner
Frayda S. Bluestein
Mark F. Botts
Phillip Boyle
Joan G. Brannon
Anita R. Brown-Graham
William A. Campbell
Margaret S. Carlson
Stevens H. Clarke
Anne S. Davidson
Anne M. Dellinger

James C. Drennan
Richard D. Ducker
Robert L. Farb
Joseph S. Ferrell
Susan Leigh Flinspach
L. Lynnette Fuller
Milton S. Heath, Jr.
Cheryl Daniels Howell
Joseph E. Hunt
Kurt J. Jenne
Robert P. Joyce
David M. Lawrence
Charles D. Liner
Ben F. Loeb, Jr.
Janet Mason

Laurie L. Mesibov
Jill D. Moore
David W. Owens
William C. Rivenbark
John Rubin
John L. Saxon
Jessica Smith
John B. Stephens
A. John Vogt
Richard Whisnant
Gordon P. Whitaker
Michael L. Williamson (on leave)

Cover: Panoramic map image of Greensboro, North Carolina, from an 1891 lithograph, courtesy of the Geography and Maps Division of the Library of Congress.

Cover and book design by Daniel Soileau

Printed in the United States of America

Contents

Preface

Local governments are complex business organizations, and like any business organization they frequently must buy and sell property. Governments engaging in property transactions are, for the most part, subject to the same rules and doctrines of law as are private individuals and businesses. But differences reflecting the peculiar characteristics of government exist. Some of these differences are procedural, requiring that governments acquire or dispose of property in specific ways. Others are substantive, limiting governments in the purposes for which they may acquire property, in the property interests they may acquire, in the consideration they may give or accept, or in other often unexpected ways.

The special rules concerning local government property transactions are not always easily accessible to the local government official or attorney. Many result from judicial decisions, and because the dissimilarity between private property transactions and transactions involving governments is uneven and unpredictable, an older case or set of cases may easily be overlooked. Even when the special rules are imposed by statute, it is not always safe to rely entirely on the written law. The statute may have been enacted in response to a case or line of cases, and its meaning will be shaped by that circumstance. Or a judicial gloss on a statute may modify its apparent meaning.

One purpose of this book is to provide access to the special rules that govern property transactions of local governments—to point out the unexpected case law doctrines, the context in which the statutes have been enacted, and the judicial interpretations of the statutes. A second purpose is to assist in implementing some of the rules, especially the statutory procedures for disposing of property.

The book is organized into six chapters, three appendixes, a glossary, and an index. The first chapter is a short introduction to the subject. Chapters 2 and 3 discuss the substantive and procedural aspects, respectively, of acquiring property. Chapter 4 discusses changing the use of property, while chapters 5 and 6 discuss the substantive and procedural aspects of disposing of property. The three appendixes are a set of forms for disposing of property, a list of the major North Carolina statutes discussed in the text, and a list of North Carolina appellate cases discussed or cited in the text. The glossary sets out short definitions of a number of technical terms of property law.

The book omits certain property-related subjects. The statutory procedures governing purchase of personal property are excluded because those are the subject of another Institute book, *A Legal Guide to Purchasing and Contracting for North Carolina Local Governments*, by Frayda Bluestein. The law of eminent domain—the forced acquisition of real property—is also excluded, in part because another Institute publication, *Eminent Domain Procedure for North Carolina Local Governments*, by Ben F. Loeb, Jr., deals with the subject and also because that law is so specialized and complex that it demands a book of its own. Finally, property transactions affecting city streets are also excluded because these too are the subject of an existing Institute publication, *Property Interests in North Carolina City Streets*, by David M. Lawrence.

The primary audience for this book will be attorneys and persons working in the real estate offices of larger units of local government. The discussion assumes, therefore, a knowledge of the basic law of real property: that, for example, the reader knows the difference between a fee simple absolute and a fee simple determinable. Recognizing, however, that other local government officials—managers, finance officers, board members—may wish to use the book but lack an everyday understanding of real property law, the book includes a glossary of real property terms and concepts.

This is the second edition of this book, replacing the 1987 edition. The new edition encompasses statutory changes since 1987 and new appellate cases decided since that date. It also reflects the hundreds of questions I have received during the past dozen years from local officials and others about local government property transactions. My colleague Frayda Bluestein read each of the chapters of the book, and I am grateful to her for the improvements that resulted from her comments and suggestions.

I

Introduction

§ 101. Judicial Deference to Local Decision Making

In the late nineteenth and early twentieth centuries, courts imposed rigid limitations on local governments' capacity to acquire or convey property. Some of these limitations—such as the rule that local governments could not accept devises of real property[1]—reflected that era's judicial formalism. Others—such as the rule that barred local governments from bidding-in property at judicial sales or tax foreclosure sales[2]—reflected a narrow vision of appropriate governmental activities. And still others—such as the rule that required specific legislative authority to convey each parcel of land[3]—reflected courts' distrust of the motives and behavior of local government officials, a distrust that was, unfortunately, sometimes well deserved. Many of these old rules are now forgotten, modified, or overruled by later decisions or changed by statute. But because of that era's judicial attitudes, we should approach any judicial decision concerning local government property transactions from the nineteenth century or first two or three decades of the twentieth century with some skepticism. While not every decision from that time may be ignored,[4] a reader should analyze carefully the policies underlying the decision and the judicial attitude it reflects and decide if they remain consonant with present-day policies and attitudes.

---

1. *See infra* § 305-B.

2. *See infra* § 305-A.

3. *See infra* § 502-A.

4. For example, those involving security interests in local government property are certainly still good law. *See infra* § 206.

The modern judicial approach to local government property disputes recognizes that local officials must be given room in their everyday business operations, including acquiring and conveying of property. Rather than second-guess the local officials responsible for policy making or administration, a modern court is more likely to defer, recognizing that business judgments can differ. Even if the officials' business judgment is bad, and the local government makes a bad business deal, a court usually will not intervene. Only if a local government's decision is an abuse of discretion—unmistakably unreasonable or clearly suggestive of fraud or corruption—will a court intervene.[5]

The 1975 case of *Painter v. Wake County Board of Education*[6] exemplifies the modern approach in North Carolina. The school board intended to exchange one parcel of land for another, and taxpayers challenged the transaction. The taxpayers alleged and offered proof tending to show that the parcel being conveyed by the school board was worth more than twice the parcel it was acquiring. Although the school board denied the allegation, the issue never went to trial because the trial judge gave summary judgment[7] to the school board. On appeal the taxpayers argued that they were entitled to a trial on the dispute about value. The state supreme court disagreed, stating as follows: "If a discrepancy in valuation does exist it bears only on the question of abuse of discretion, and any such discrepancy is only one of the factors to be considered in determining whether the Board has abused its discretion."[8] This standard of abuse of discretion will recur throughout this book.

---

5. Two out-of-state cases illustrate this point. In Marion County v. Terrell, 38 So. 2d 476 (Ala. 1949), the county sold property for $150, although another buyer was willing to pay more than $1,000. A majority of the commissioners voting for the sale did not know of the higher offer, and there was no evidence of collusion between the successful buyer and the commissioner who did know of the higher offer. In these circumstances the court held there was no fraud and the sale should stand. On the other hand, in Heilig Bros. Co. v. Kohler, 76 A.2d 613 (Pa. 1950), the governing board was considering one offer when it received a considerably better second offer. The board ignored the second offer and sold the property to the first offeror. When these circumstances were combined with additional evidence indicating improper procedures, secrecy, and undue haste by the board, the court found an abuse of discretion.

6. 288 N.C. 165, 217 S.E.2d 650 (1975).

7. If there is no dispute as to the facts underlying a legal dispute, a trial is unnecessary and the trial court can decide the case by awarding summary judgment to one party or the other.

8. 288 N.C. at 179, 217 S.E.2d at 659.

§ 102. Most Property Questions Are a Matter of State Law

A. Generally

On the whole, the rules governing local government property transactions are matters of state rather than federal law. If a local government acquires property with federal money under a federal grant program, federal law may require assistance to anyone displaced by the transaction and may affect whether and how the local government disposes of property and what it does with the sale proceeds.[9] Moreover, except for some First Amendment cases discussed in Section B, efforts to inflate property disputes to federal constitutional questions have generally been unsuccessful. Courts have refused to characterize basic landlord-tenant questions as constitutional torts simply because one of the parties is a state or local government;[10] nor have they recognized equal protection claims simply because a local government makes a better business deal with one party than with another.[11]

B. First Amendment Claims

Establishment of religion. The First Amendment to the federal Constitution prohibits governments from establishing religions. Occasionally, plaintiffs have successfully argued that the consideration paid (or not paid) in a property transaction involving a local government and a church or other religious-based entity amounts to a preference for the church or other entity, thereby violating the prohibition on establishing religions. In one case, property acquired for a highway interchange turned out to include a forgotten cemetery. As part of the consideration it paid for uprooting the cemetery, the state Department of Transportation agreed to erect a statue of Christ in a small memorial within the interchange.[12] In a second case, a city agreed to convey city property to a church-affiliated school for one dollar, even though the school had

---

9. *See infra* §§ 307-E, 408-B, *and* 505-B.

10. Stewart v. Hunt, 598 F. Supp. 1342 (E.D.N.C. 1984) (breach of lease by state lessor is not constitutional tort).

11. Bell Enters., Inc. v. Tulsa County Fairgrounds Trust Auth., 695 P.2d 513 (Okla. 1985) (different arrangements with lessees at state fairgrounds are not equal protection violation).

12. Birdine v. Moreland, 579 F. Supp. 412 (N.D. Ga. 1983).

offered $30,000 for the property.[13] In each case the court held that the transactions tended to establish religion and therefore violated the federal Constitution. On the other hand, as long as a local government receives adequate consideration from a church-related entity and does not otherwise give special favors to the entity, the Constitution does not bar entering into property transactions with churches and other religious organizations.

Freedom of speech or association. The First Amendment also prohibits governments from denying the freedoms of speech or association. In *Elrod v. Burns*,[14] the United States Supreme Court held that a local government may not fire or otherwise act against employees because of their political beliefs or affiliations. Twenty years later the court extended these same protections to those who contract with local governments.[15] Before the Supreme Court acted, some of the lower federal courts had already considered extending these protections to lessees of government property, and those cases illustrate how the Supreme Court's rule might apply to property transactions. In one case a city refused to renew its lease of a former firehouse to a museum because one of the museum's exhibits had offended a powerful political community within the city.[16] In another, a city allegedly refused to renew a lease of city-owned parking facilities because the lessee-operator had lobbied against a city bill in the state legislature.[17] If these kinds of allegations prove true, a local government's normal discretion to decide to whom it will lease property or with whom it will otherwise contract is lost because of the government's unconstitutional motivation.

---

13. Annunziato v. New Haven Bd. of Aldermen, 555 F. Supp. 427 (D. Conn. 1982).

14. 427 U.S. 347 (1976).

15. Wabaunsee County Bd. of Comm'rs v. Umbehr, 518 U.S. 688 (1996); O'Hare Truck Serv., Inc. v. City of Northlake, 518 U.S. 712 (1996).

16. Cuban Museum of Arts & Culture, Inc. v. City of Miami, 766 F. Supp. 1121 (S.D. Fla. 1991).

17. Downtown Auto Parks, Inc. v. City of Milwaukee, 938 F.2d 705 (7th Cir. 1991). The trial court and court of appeals actually ruled against the lessee in this case, refusing to extend the employee free speech cases to independent contractors. The Supreme Court noted this case five years later when it did extend the rule for employees to independent contractors, and the Milwaukee case clearly would be decided differently after the Supreme Court decisions.

II

Property Acquisition:
Substantive Limitations

§ 201. Purposes for Which Governments May Acquire Property

In General

Local governments normally derive their authority to acquire property by combining two sorts of statutes. One sort gives a local government general authority to acquire property. The second sort authorizes it to perform a specific activity and, by doing so, implicitly authorizes the government to acquire whatever property is necessary to the authorized activity. The statutes dealing with cities and fire protection illustrate this general point. Section 160A-11 of the North Carolina General Statutes (hereinafter G.S.) makes each North Carolina city a corporate body, authorized to "acquire and hold any property, real and personal, devised, bequeathed, sold, or in any manner conveyed, dedicated to, or otherwise acquired" by it. G.S. 160A-291 authorizes cities to provide fire protection: each city may "establish, organize, equip, and maintain a fire department." The fire protection statute makes no mention of purchasing property for one or more fire stations, yet because of the corporate power statute a city's authority to do so is unquestioned.

Occasionally a local government acquires property intending to lease or sell it to someone else who will actually put the property to its public use. For example, a city acquires property to construct a fire station; when the station is finished, the city plans to lease it to a volunteer fire department.[1] Or a county acquires property planning to convey the property to another county as the first county's contribution to a cooperative arrangement.[2] Normally, this intention to lease or sell property being acquired does not impair the local government's authority to acquire the property. If the statutes authorize the government to undertake the activity for which it is acquiring the property, its method in doing so—directly or through some other entity—is irrelevant to its authority to acquire the necessary property.[3] Of course, if the acquiring government does not have statutory authority to engage in the activity for which the property will be used, then it may not acquire the property simply to act as a commercial landlord. For example, counties and cities do not have authority to sell alcoholic beverages; only local ABC boards have that authority. For that reason, a county or city may not construct or acquire a building solely for lease to the local ABC system.[4]

§ 202. Purposes for Which Governments May Acquire Property

Purposes Not Authorized by Statute

Although a local government usually acquires and holds property only to further those activities for which it has statutory authority, occasionally it may legitimately acquire or hold property for a nonauthorized purpose. This section reviews those occasions.

---

1. Such a transaction was at issue in Township of Willingboro v. Mobil Oil Corp., 388 A.2d 1014 (N.J. Super. Ct. App. Div. 1978), which allowed the township to condemn property for a fire station that would be leased to a volunteer fire department. G.S. 160A-277 authorizes North Carolina local governments to convey land to volunteer fire departments, while G.S. 160A-279 (1994) authorizes conveying a constructed fire house to a volunteer department.

2. G.S. 160A-460 through -464 authorizes cooperation between governments. In Briggs v. City of Raleigh, 195 N.C. 223, 141 S.E. 597 (1928), the North Carolina Supreme Court upheld Raleigh's acquisition of land in order to give that land to the State of North Carolina for use as a state fairground.

3. Township of Willingboro v. Mobil Oil Corp., 388 A.2d 1014 (N.J. Super. Ct. App. Div. 1978).

4. In Lassila v. Wenatchee, 576 P.2d 54 (1978), the city intended to purchase land for reconveyance to a *private* party for *private* use. (This was not being done as part of an urban redevelopment project or an economic development project.) The court held the purchase was invalid.

A. Property Foreclosed for Nonpayment of Taxes or Other Debts

Counties and cities frequently purchase property at foreclosure sales, most often to protect their interests in the unpaid taxes for which the property is being sold.[5] Once it acquires the property, the government normally seeks to dispose of it as quickly as possible, in order to receive the taxes or other debt that the property secured. Sometimes, however, prompt sale is difficult or inadvisable, and the government begins using the property for activities for which it has no statutory authority. It may, for example, become a residential or commercial landlord.[6] Indeed, if no lessee can be found, the government might itself use the property for commercial purposes, concluding that doing so is more prudent than allowing the property to lie idle. These actions are legal: a government need not leave property unused while in government ownership. The courts recognize that proper stewardship permits the government to put the property to productive use while in public ownership and that the use need not always be a public one.[7]

B. Property Not Currently Needed

Governments sometimes construct facilities that exceed current needs or take older properties out of service when the facilities or services they house move to newer quarters. A government might be given property for which it has no current need. In each case some or all of the property is currently unneeded. It is clear that a government may lease such property to a nonpublic user until the property is needed by the government or is sold.[8] (A current application of this doctrine is the lease of space on public buildings or other structures for mobile communication

---

5. Local government authority to purchase property at a foreclosure sale is discussed *infra* § 305-A.

6. Examples of North Carolina cases that involve property purchased through foreclosure and then leased to a private user are Board of Financial Control v. Henderson County, 208 N.C. 569, 181 S.E. 636 (1935) (downtown property acquired as security for deposits in failed bank); Benson v. Johnston County, 209 N.C. 751, 185 S.E. 6 (1936) (residential property acquired at foreclosure sale); Warrenton v. Warren County, 215 N.C. 342, 2 S.E.2d 463 (1939) (hotel acquired through foreclosure of deed of trust).

7. *See* Libby v. City of Portland, 74 A. 805 (Me. 1909) (city may operate farm until it can be disposed of).

8. Cline v. City of Hickory, 207 N.C. 125, 176 S.E. 250 (1934) (rental of space in city hall for movie theater); *cf.* Latta v. City of Durham, 216 N.C. 722, 6 S.E.2d 508 (1940) (rental of city auditorium to movie theater operator).

antennas.) In other states, courts have even allowed local governments to operate donated commercial property directly, until the government needs the property for public uses or decides to dispose of it.[9]

C. Charitable Trust Property

Occasionally, an individual gives, devises, or bequeaths property to a local government under arrangements that indicate that the government is to hold the property as trustee. (For example, a number of years ago one North Carolina town was given property under a trust to provide college scholarships for local residents.) Although no North Carolina cases treat these questions, the general rule nationally holds that a local government is a suitable trustee for a charitable trust.[10]

Although there is some dissent, the more recent cases hold that no specific statutory authority is necessary for a local government to accept property as a trustee.[11] Furthermore, the predominant rule seems to be that the local government need not have authority to perform the function for which the trust is created, as long as that function is compatible with the local government's corporate purposes.[12] A charitable purpose appears to be compatible with a local government's corporate purposes when the charitable purpose can be supported by some level or unit of government, even if not by the specific government named as trustee.[13]

---

9. Libby v. City of Portland, 74 A. 805 (Me. 1909) (farm); Town of New Shoreham v. Ball, 14 R.I. 566 (1884) (residential property acquired by adverse possession).

10. 2 AUSTIN WAKEMAN SCOTT & WILLIAM FRANKLIN FRATCHER, THE LAW OF TRUSTS, § 96.4 (4th ed. 1987) [hereinafter SCOTT]. A city may not, however, be named trustee of a private trust (one that benefits only specific individuals). *Id. E.g.,* Holifield v. Robinson, 79 Ala. 419 (1885).

11. City of Newberg v. Warren Constr. Co., 279 P. 644 (Or. 1929); *see* Treadwell v. Beebee, 190 P. 768 (Kan. 1920). Two cases that suggest that specific authority is necessary are Dailey v. City of New Haven, 22 A. 945 (Conn. 1891) and Fosdick v. Town of Hempstead, 26 N.E. 801 (N.Y. 1891). Both of these cases, however, can be read to involve other issues, and in each the trust in question may have been established for a purpose beyond the city's statutory powers.

12. SCOTT, *supra* note 10; W.S.R., Annot., *Power of Municipal Corporation or Other Political Body to Accept and Administer Trust,* 10 A.L.R. 1368 (1921).

13. *See In re* Carlson's Estate, 358 P.2d 669 (1961), in which the court permitted a town to administer a trust to pay for the medical education of local residents; presumably the town had no statutory authority to use its own funds for this purpose. *Contra* Stowell v. Prentis, 154 N.E. 120 (Ill. 1926) (school directors may not hold land for use as a spring for public water purposes).

Thus, a city might accept trusteeship of a fund for college scholarships, even though counties and the state are responsible for educational funding in North Carolina.[14]

If a local government does hold property under a charitable trust, the terms of the trust dictate the purposes for which the property may be used and the circumstances, if any, under which it might be leased or conveyed. If the trust terms are more restrictive than the normal statutory powers of the government, the trust rules prevail.[15]

§ 203. The Location of Property

A. In General

The decision as to where property will be acquired—that is, where a new facility will be located—is quite clearly one within a local government's discretion. A court will intervene only if a plaintiff can show that a location decision was arbitrary or capricious or in some other way an abuse of discretion.[16] As a practical matter, unless a plaintiff can demonstrate serious irregularities in the acquisition process (such as a significant conflict of interest),[17] a location decision cannot be successfully challenged in court.

B. Extraterritorial Property

When a local government wishes to acquire property located beyond its borders (extraterritorial property), two legal questions arise. First, does any statute specifically permit (or prohibit) extraterritorial acquisitions? Second, if the answer to the first question is no, does the authority to acquire property for an activity include by implication the authority to do so when the property is outside the acquiring unit's boundaries?

---

14. If property is given in trust to a local government and the purpose is not one for which a local government may be trustee, a court may appoint a new trustee so that the trust will not fail. Scott, *supra* note 10.

15. In Kapiolani Park Preservation Society v. City & County of Honolulu, 751 P.2d 1022 (Haw. 1988), the court prohibited the city from leasing a portion of a park, held under a charitable trust, to a restaurant operator. Although the lease was permissible under general city powers, the court held it was prohibited by the terms of the trust.

16. Philbrook v. Chapel Hill Hous. Auth., 269 N.C. 598, 153 S.E.2d 153 (1967) (housing authority has discretion to decide where to acquire sites for housing projects).

17. *See infra* § 210.

For the most part, modern statutes deal explicitly with the acquisition of extraterritorial property. Cities and counties enjoy authority to acquire property for most purposes both inside and outside their borders.[18] School administrative units must locate their schools inside the boundaries of the administrative unit, but they may place other facilities such as administrative offices or bus garages outside the boundaries.[19] Thus, with most acquisitions, the second question does not arise.

Not all statutes, however, deal explicitly with the issue;[20] and in addition no statute specifically addresses the question of whether a local government with express authority to acquire extraterritorial property may do so in another state. When the statutes are not specific, a government— and then, perhaps, a court—must decide if the authority is implicit. By and large, the courts have held that authority to acquire property includes the authority to acquire both inside and outside the boundaries of the local government.[21] They have noted that some facilities, such as parks, benefit a unit's citizens even if the facilities are located outside the unit.[22] Other facilities, such as sewage disposal plants, may only be placed in

---

18. For example, a city may establish and operate (and acquire property for that purpose) any of its enterprises extraterritorially, G.S. 160A-312, as may counties, *id.* § 153A-275. In another example, both counties and cities may acquire property outside their borders for parks, *id.* § 160A-353(3).

19. G.S. 115C-517. Local ABC boards may locate stores only within the county or city that has approved the stores and established the local ABC system. *Id.* § 18B-801(b).

20. For example, the regional solid waste management authority statute, G.S. 153A-421 through 153A-432, does not explicitly authorize an authority to acquire property outside the borders of its member counties [although the statute does imply that an authority might do so as long as it does not use the power of eminent domain; *see id.* § 153A-427(b)]. The mosquito control district statute, *id.* §§ 130A-352 through 130A-358, also does not indicate whether a district may act outside its borders.

21. *E.g.,* Smith v. City of Kuttawa, 1 S.W.2d 979 (Ky. 1928) (authority to own parks includes authority to acquire land for park outside city); Lester v. Mayor & City of Jackson, 11 So. 114 (Miss. 1892) (city may accept devise of land outside city for park); Schneider v. City of Menasha, 95 N.W. 94 (Wis. 1903) (city may acquire land outside city for gravel pit needed for street maintenance inside city). The Virginia courts, however, have disagreed: Duncan v. City of Lynchburg, 34 S.E. 964 (Va. 1900) (city not liable for negligent operation of extraterritorial rock quarry because without authority to own and operate quarry outside city); Donable's Adm'r v. Town of Harrisburg, 52 S.E. 174 (Va. 1905) (city not liable for explosion at extraterritorial rock quarry because without authority to own and operate quarry outside city).

22. *E.g.,* Lester v. Mayor & City of Jackson, 11 So. 114 (Miss. 1892).

certain locations, and therefore a local government may have little choice but to act extraterritorially.[23] As long as the extraterritorial acquisition is reasonable under these or comparable circumstances, courts will normally uphold it.

The statutes authorizing cities to acquire land for and maintain streets have created some confusion about the statutes' extraterritorial application. G.S. 160A-296 authorizes cities to construct and maintain streets, and it specifically limits the authority to inside the city. For that reason, it is generally understood that cities may acquire property for streets only inside the city. The confusion arises from G.S. 40A-3(b)(1), which authorizes cities and other local governments to use the power of eminent domain. The eminent domain statute specifically states that a city may use eminent domain for any listed function, including streets, both inside and outside the city. But if a city cannot construct or maintain a street except within its boundaries, why then is it authorized to condemn for street projects outside those boundaries? The best answer seems to be that a city may use its condemnation power for street projects outside the city only when it is acting by agreement with the state Department of Transportation (DOT). G.S. 136-66.3 authorizes a city to contract with DOT as to which agency will acquire street or highway rights-of-way "in and around" the city. The statute appears to contemplate that the city might, pursuant to the contract, act outside its borders, and that would provide an occasion for the city's using the Chapter 40A authorization to condemn for streets extraterritorially.

County commissioner approval. If a local government intends to acquire property outside its borders, occasionally it might need first to gain the approval of the board of county commissioners of the county in which the property is located. G.S. 153A-15 requires commissioner approval when the acquiring government is wholly or primarily located in a county other than that in which the property is located. That is, if county A intends to acquire property in county B, or if city M, which is in county A, intends to acquire property in county B, county B's board of commissioners must first approve the acquisition. This statute began as a local act for a few counties in the early 1980s, and the General Assembly has added counties to it piecemeal in the years since. While still not statewide in scope, it currently applies to more than eighty of

---

23. *E.g.,* Langley v. City Council of Augusta, 45 S.E. 486 (Ga. 1903) (sewer system); Freeman v. Trimble, 129 N.W. 83 (N.D. 1910) (drain).

the state's counties, and counties continue to be added to its coverage. The original impetus for the statute was the desire of a few counties to block establishment of sanitary landfills within those counties by local governments located elsewhere. The statute is not, however, limited to acquiring property for solid waste projects but rather applies to acquisitions for any purpose. It does not extend, though, to acquisition by all methods. It applies to acquisitions by eminent domain, purchase, exchange, or lease but does not apply to acquisitions by donation, whether by gift or will.

§ 204. Particular Property Interests

In General

Different sorts of North Carolina local governments are authorized to acquire property by statutes that differ notably in their level of detail. For example, compare the statutes authorizing property acquisition by ABC boards, community colleges, and historic preservation commissions. G.S. 18B-701(10) permits local ABC boards to "buy and lease real and personal property"; G.S. 115D-20(3) permits community and technical colleges to "purchase any land, easement, or right-of-way"; and G.S. 160A-400.8 permits historic preservation commissions to "acquire by any lawful means the fee or any lesser included interest, including options to purchase, to properties within [historic] districts or to any such properties designated as landmarks."

The question suggested by these different statutory formulations is whether the differences in detail should be accorded any legal significance. Does the absence of any mention of the power to *lease* as lessee in the community college statute indicate that such institutions have no authority to acquire leaseholds?[24] Does the specific authorization given to historic preservation commissions to acquire options suggest, by negative implication, that ABC boards and community colleges cannot acquire options because they have no comparable specific power?

These kinds of questions occasionally are litigated, and courts normally read statutory authorizations to acquire property generously. North Carolina cases, for example, hold or suggest that the authority to purchase

---

24. This question is even more acute, because community colleges have explicit authority to enter into lease-purchase agreements in order to buy equipment. G.S. 115D-58.15 (Cum. Supp.)

or acquire property includes the authority to acquire a leasehold as well as a fee simple, or a defeasible fee as well as a fee simple absolute.[25] Cases from other states find nonspecific language broad enough to support acquisition of a tenancy in common, of an option to purchase, and of a fee simple subject to an option to repurchase.[26] Therefore the specific language of different statutes probably should not be given substantive weight. A general authority to purchase property includes authority to purchase not only the fee but any other interest. To return to the usual standard, unless an abuse of discretion can be shown, a court will not disturb a local government's business judgment as to the proper interest to purchase.[27]

Interest beginning in future. May a local government enter into a contract under which it agrees to acquire an interest in property at a future date? For example, may it agree to purchase a tract of land three years from now, or lease property for a term beginning in eighteen months? Apparently, yes. No general rule of property law prohibits such contracts,

---

25. Trustees of Watts Hosp. v. Board of Comm'rs, 231 N.C. 604, 58 S.E.2d 696 (1950) (fee simple determinable); *cf.* Wade v. City of New Bern, 77 N.C. 460 (1877) (leasehold). Rogers v. City of Mobile, 169 So. 2d 282 (Ala. 1964) also holds that the authority to acquire property includes implicitly the authority to acquire a leasehold interest in property.

For many years, G.S. 115C-521(d) prohibited a school administrative unit from contracting to construct or repair school buildings unless the school unit owned the property in fee simple. During these years, G.S. 115C-517 simply stated that school units could "acquire suitable sites for schoolhouses and other school facilities." If the general authorization in G.S. 115C-517 did not include implicit authority to acquire sites for school buildings by lease, G.S. 115C-521(d) would have been unnecessary. (The General Assembly clarified the matter in 1997 by specifically authorizing school units to lease buildings for schools, although any new construction must still be on land owned in fee simple. G.S. 115C-530 [Cum. Supp.].) *See infra* § 205-A.

26. Ragsdale v. Hargraves, 129 S.W.2d 967 (Ark. 1939) (tenancy in common); Mattingly v. Charlotte Hall Sch., 377 A.2d 496 (Md. Ct. App. 1977) (option to purchase); Municipal Sec. Co. v. Baker County, 65 P. 369 (Or. 1901) (tenancy in common). *See* Amick v. Richland County, 255 S.E.2d 855 (S.C. 1979) (fee simple subject to option to repurchase).

27. *See, e.g.,* Jackson v. City of Madison, 107 N.W.2d 164 (Wis. 1961) (within city's discretion to construct building on land owned by state and available to city only by revocable permit). *See also* City of Charlotte v. Cook, 348 N.C. 222, 498 S.E.2d 605 (1998), in which the North Carolina Supreme Court held that when a city brought an eminent domain action to condemn for a waterline, the city could condemn an easement or the fee at its discretion.

as long as they do not run afoul of the Rule Against Perpetuities.[28] And no cases have been found that suggest that local governments may not act in the same way as any other purchaser of property in this context.

§ 205. Particular Property Interests

Statutory Limits

A. School Buildings

G.S. 115C-521(d) limits the authority of local boards of education to acquire the full range of property interests for school purposes. The statute provides that "local boards of education shall make no contract for the erection of any school building unless the site upon which it is located is owned in fee simple by the said board." Two points should be made about this requirement and one question raised.

First, the statute is not an absolute bar against a board of education's acquiring less than fee interests in land. By its own terms, the statute applies only to school *buildings.* Thus a school board may lease land for a playground, acquire an easement for an approach road to a school campus, or construct a parking lot on land subject to a life estate.

Second, the statute is not even an absolute bar to leasing buildings for school uses. The statute prohibits contracting to *construct* buildings on land not owned in fee. A school board may lease an existing building, as is specifically recognized and regulated by G.S. 115C-530.

Finally, it is unclear whether the statute's requirement of *fee simple* ownership means only a fee simple absolute or whether it also includes a defeasible fee.[29] Boards of education have often held land in one or another form of defeasible fee,[30] but the predecessor statutes to G.S. 115C-521 were more open to that form of ownership than is the present statute. From 1901 to 1923 the school law simply required that school

---

28. David A. Thomas, *Rule Against Perpetuities,* 3 THOMPSON ON REAL PROPERTY § 28.06 (D. Thomas ed. 1994). The *Rule Against Perpetuities* is briefly summarized in the glossary.

29. *Defeasible fee* is explained in the glossary.

30. Two cases in which the school board held property in a defeasible fee are Lackey v. Hamlet City Bd. of Educ., 258 N.C. 460, 128 S.E.2d 806 (1963), and Duplin County Bd. of Educ. v. Carr, 15 N.C. App. 690, 190 S.E.2d 653 (1972). In both cases the property was acquired before 1955, which was when the current statutory language was enacted, and the current language was therefore inapplicable to the acquisitions.

buildings be constructed on sites "donated to or purchased by" the school board,[31] while from 1923 until 1955 the statute required that sites be "owned by" the school unit.[32] It was only in 1955 that the present fee simple requirement was inserted into the law.[33] That change in wording might have been intended as a clarification of prior law or as a change of prior law, but no legislative history exists to tell us which. Nor has the state supreme court considered the current language since its enactment.[34]

A fee simple defeasible is a fee simple title, which tends to support a broader reading of the statute. It may be that the statute intends to distinguish between property held in fee and property held by lease, and in that case a fee simple defeasible would qualify. Furthermore, a school may currently own property in fee simple defeasible that was acquired before 1955; a narrow reading of the statute would bar the unit from contracting to construct any buildings or additions to buildings on the property—an illogical result. On the other hand, the phrase *fee simple* normally refers only to a fee simple absolute; if a fee simple defeasible is also meant, one might expect it to be explicitly mentioned. Furthermore, one might argue that the General Assembly did not wish school units to face loss of their investment in buildings, even if the property were no longer needed for school purposes; with a defeasible fee, that could occur. Perhaps this latter sort of reasoning led the South Carolina Supreme Court, in what is apparently the only case interpreting a comparable statute, to hold that a requirement of fee simple ownership meant fee simple absolute.[35] The arguments in favor of a broader reading seem persuasive, but the South Carolina case demonstrates that no definitive answer is currently possible.[36]

---

31. Act of March 11, 1901, ch. 4, § 48, 1901 N.C. Pub. Laws 60.

32. Act of March 3, 1923, ch. 136, § 64, 1923 N.C. Pub. Laws 329.

33. Act of May 26, 1955, ch. 1372, § 1, 1955 N.C. Sess. Laws 1527, at 1586.

34. The supreme court decided one case under the 1923 statute, Conrad v. Board of Educ. 190 N.C. 389, 130 S.E. 53 (1925), but it did not seek to define the phrase "owned by."

35. Beach Co. v. Charleston County Sch. Dist., 207 S.E.2d 406 (S.C. 1974).

36. If a school administrative unit's attorney decides that the statute requires a fee simple absolute, the school unit could seek local legislation from the General Assembly creating an exception to the statute if that were necessary.

If a school unit acquires a fee simple defeasible in property and a court later holds that G.S. 115C-521 requires that it hold a fee simple absolute, the court's holding would not convert the unit's interest into an absolute fee. *Beach Co.*, 207

B. Lead Regional Organizations

In apparent response to the 1978 case of *Kloster v. Region D Council of Governments*,[37] which held that a COG could own property or construct buildings with the specific permission of its member governments, the 1979 General Assembly prohibited COGs from constructing or purchasing buildings, or from acquiring title to real property.[38] Therefore councils of governments may hold only a leasehold interest in real property.[39]

The state has designated eighteen local government planning regions and has designated a *lead regional organization* (LRO) in each region. Most of the LROs are structured as councils of governments but not all of them are. A few are organized as regional planning and economic development commissions under G.S. 153A-391 or G.S. 158-14. These latter organizations do enjoy statutory authority to acquire and hold real property for office purposes, pursuant to G.S. 158-11. This is one way in which they differ from councils of governments.

§ 206. Particular Property Interests

Security Interests

Security interests[40] in property owned by a local government technically should be discussed in the chapters on property disposition, because unless the security interest is assumed upon acquisition of the fee, it is an interest conveyed rather than acquired by the local government owner. Nevertheless, security interests are frequently created near or at the time property is acquired, and for that reason they are discussed at this point.

S.E.2d 406. A conversion would amount to a taking of the reversionary interest for which compensation must be paid.

37. 36 N.C. App. 421, 245 S.E.2d 180 (1978).

38. G.S. 160A-475(8).

39. COGs do not have explicit authority to lease property, but they must have space for their offices.

40. *Security interest* is explained in the glossary.

A. Mortgages and Deeds of Trust

1. The General Rule

In 1896 the North Carolina Supreme Court held that a local government may not mortgage its property without statutory authority, and that the general statutory authority to "sell or lease" the unit's real property is not sufficient.[41] The court reasoned that the statute permitting sales assumed that the selling government would receive full value for any property sold. It was possible, however, for a local government to mortgage property for less than full value yet lose the property if the mortgage lien were foreclosed. In a later case, the court made clear that this was a rule of statutory interpretation; if the General Assembly gives clear authority to do so, a local government may give a mortgage or deed of trust on its property.[42]

Although the rule of these two cases is old, it is generally assumed to remain good law. Therefore, before agreeing to convey (or accept) a mortgage or deed of trust on local government property, the parties to the transaction must be able to point to specific authority for the security interest. That kind of authority remains the exception rather than the rule in North Carolina. The most broadly applicable and widely used authority to give a security interest is found in G.S. 160A-20, which permits counties, cities, and several other specified local governments to enter into contracts to finance the purchase, repair, or construction of property and to give a security interest to the financing party in the property being acquired, repaired, or built.[43] Two somewhat narrower statutes permit school administrative units to give security interests in automobiles, school buses, mobile classrooms, photocopiers, and computer hardware and software, when the property is purchased through installment financing agreements,[44] and permit community and technical colleges to

---

41. Vaughn v. Commissioners of Forsyth County, 118 N.C. 636, 24 S.E. 425 (1896).

42. Brockenbrough v. Board of Water Comm'rs, 134 N.C. 1, 46 S.E. 28 (1903).

43. The statute also applies to water and sewer authorities; metropolitan sewerage districts; sanitary districts; area mental health, mental retardation, and substance abuse authorities; regional natural gas districts; regional transportation authorities; regional public transportation authorities; nonprofit corporations or associations operating or leasing public hospitals; hospitals that operate under Article 2 of former G.S. Chapter 131; two school administrative units; and a few airport authorities or commissions. G.S. 160A-20 (Cum. Supp.)

44. *Id.* § 115C-528.

purchase equipment through installment financing agreements and give security interests in the equipment.[45] Under all three statutes, repossession of the property subject to the security interest is the seller or lender's only remedy if the local government, school unit, or college defaults on the installment financing agreement; the statute prohibits entry of any deficiency judgment against the government, unit, or college. G.S. 159I-30(b1) grants counties and cities a comparable power to give a security interest in property financed with special obligation bonds; this authorization is limited to solid waste projects, however. The other statutory authorizations to give a security interest apply to special purpose agencies: ABC boards,[46] hospital authorities,[47] industrial facilities and pollution control financing authorities;[48] regional solid waste management authorities;[49] regional sports authorities;[50] and facility authorities.[51]

2. Acquiring Property That Is Subject to a Mortgage or Deed of Trust

Although no North Carolina case is on point, and few are nationally, the general rule denying local governments the power to give a security interest on government-owned property probably bars a local government, without specific statutory authority, from acquiring and then holding property that is subject to an existing mortgage or deed of trust.[52] (If the local government acquires property subject to a mortgage or deed of trust and then promptly retires the security interest, so that it holds the property free of such an interest, the concerns expressed in this paragraph do not apply.) Two statutes, however, when read together appear to give such authority in narrow circumstances. As noted in the preceding discussion, G.S. 160A-20 permits counties, cities, and certain other units or agencies of local government to acquire property and give a security interest in the property to secure any loan made to finance the acquisition. The statute also prohibits the entry of any deficiency judgment against the local government if the security interest is foreclosed and the sale proceeds are inadequate to retire the mortgage or deed of trust. The state's antideficiency statute, G.S. 45-21.38, generally prohibits

---

45. *Id.* § 115D-58.15 (Cum. Supp.)
46. *Id.* § 18B-702(b).
47. *Id.* §§ 131E-23(a)(6), -27, and -32.
48. G.S. 159C-12.
49. *Id.* § 153A-427(a)(12).
50. *Id.* § 160A-479.7(a)(12).
51. *Id.* §§ 160A-480.4(12), -480.8(c)(2) (Cum. Supp.).
52. Ironwood Waterworks Co. v. Trebilcock, 58 N.W. 371 (Mich. 1894).

entry of a deficiency judgment against mortgagors under a purchase money mortgage or deed of trust on real property. (A purchase money mortgage or deed of trust is given by the vendor of the property to secure the unpaid portion of the purchase price.) If a local government were to acquire real property and assume a purchase money mortgage or deed of trust on the property, its position would be identical to that of a local government that acquired real property under G.S. 160A-20 and gave a purchase money mortgage or deed of trust to the vendor of the property. For that reason, the combination of G.S. 160A-20 and G.S. 45-21.38 should be adequate authority for assumption of a purchase money mortgage or deed of trust on real property. This is narrow authority, however. It does not include local governments or agencies that are not covered by G.S. 160A-20. More importantly, it does not include mortgages or deeds of trust that do not run in favor of the original vendor of the property, because the antideficiency statute does not apply to these other mortgages or deeds of trust.

If the local government does not assume the mortgage or deed of trust but merely acquires the property subject to the security interest—that is, it acquires only the equity of redemption[53]—the policy concerns that underlie the general rule on security interests come directly into play; indeed they are even more keenly felt. The local government holds property that it can lose at any time if the mortgagor defaults. No consideration would flow to the government upon such a loss, because the loan that the security interest secures was made to the mortgagor and not to the government. For that reason, a local government almost certainly may not, without specific statutory authority, acquire property subject to a mortgage or deed of trust.

3. Security Interests in Leaseholds of Government Property

If a local government leases property to another party, the general rule prohibiting giving security interests in government property does not bar the lessee from giving a mortgage or deed of trust on her leasehold interest.[54] If the leasehold mortgagor should default, all that would be foreclosed would be the leasehold. The local government's fee interest would be unaffected, as would its rights as lessor.

---

53. *Equity of redemption* is defined in the glossary.

54. Department of Culture, Recreation & Tourism v. Fort Macomb Dev. Auth., 385 So. 2d 1233 (La. Ct. App. 1980). *But see* Paerdegat Boat & Racquet

B. Statutory and Common Law Liens

The general rule, at least as old as the rule on mortgages discussed just above, is that the property of a local government is not subject to common law or statutory liens[55] unless specifically made so by statute.[56] North Carolina's courts have applied this rule to the lien normally held by judgment creditors, when the judgment is against a local government,[57] and to the lien normally held by a person supplying labor or materials to a construction project, when the owner of the project is a local government.[58] A person holding a judgment against a local government may only seek mandamus for payment of the judgment debt.[59] Because the normal construction liens do not protect laborers or materialmen on public works projects, G.S. 44A-26 requires the contractor to furnish the local government owner a payment bond as a condition of contract award; the payment bond protects the laborers and materialmen.[60]

In some states courts have held that the above rules do not apply to property held in a local government's *private* capacity.[61] In this context, private property is property not held for any corporate purpose; it is not the same as property held in a proprietary, as opposed to governmental, capacity in tort law.[62] As a practical matter, this sort of private property normally includes only property acquired through property tax or special assessment foreclosures or surplus property held for sale. In one case, the

---

Club, Inc. v. Zarrelli, 443 N.E.2d 477 (N.Y. 1982) (court does not allow mechanic's lien to be placed against leasehold of publicly owned property).

    55. *Lien* is defined in the glossary.

    56. 10 Eugene McQuillin, Law of Municipal Corporations §§ 28.57, 28.58 (3d ed. rev. vol. 1999). The rule also protects government moneys. *See* P.H.V., Annot., *Municipal Funds and Credits as Subject to Levy Under Execution or Garnishment on Judgment Against Municipality,* 89 A.L.R. 863 (1934).

    57. Gooch v. Gregory, 65 N.C. 142 (1871).

    58. Morganton Hardware Co. v. Morganton Graded Sch., 150 N.C. 680, 64 S.E. 764 (1909); *see* American Bridge Div. United States Steel Corp. v. Brinkley, 255 N.C. 162, 120 S.E.2d 529 (1961). A list of cases affirming this rule is found in Noland Co. v. Trustees, 190 N.C. 250, 252, 129 S.E. 577, 578 (1925).

    59. Gooch v. Gregory, 65 N.C. 142 (1871).

    60. American Bridge Div. United States Steel Corp. v. Brinkley, 255 N.C. 162, 164, 120 S.E.2d 529, 531 (1961).

    61. *E.g.,* State *ex rel.* Courter v. Buckles, 35 N.E. 846 (Ind. Ct. App. 1893); Beadles v. Fey, 82 P. 1041 (Okla. 1905).

    62. The Florida Supreme Court defined *private* property in this context as property "unconnected with any public function resting upon the municipal government." City of Coral Gables v. Hepkins, 144 So. 385, 387 (Fla. 1932).

North Carolina Supreme Court noted this exception to the general rule but refused, for the most part, to follow the exception.[63] Only if mandamus for payment of the debt were unavailable because the local government had already reached a constitutional or statutory rate limit on property taxes would property held by the government in its private capacity be subject to execution. Rate limits were often reached in 1890 when this case was decided, but that is no longer true today. For that reason, even this modest potential liability of a local government's property to lien foreclosure is obsolete.

A potentially practical question is whether the lien, say a judgment lien, never attaches to local government property, or attaches but lies dormant while the local government owns the property. If the latter is the case, the lien holder might be able to enforce it once the government had conveyed the property to a private party. There is precious little case law on this point nationally (and none in North Carolina), but the single case located by the author, as well as the policy considerations discussed below, suggest that the lien never attaches and therefore cannot be enforced against subsequent owners of the property. In a California case, a judgment creditor sought to levy on a writ of execution against property that was owned by the local government judgment debtor at the time of the judgment. The local government had either just conveyed the property or was just about to (the court is unclear on this point), and the trial court granted the government's motion to quash the levy. In affirming, the California Supreme Court wrote:

> If prior to the levy of the execution the municipality had fully conveyed all its interest in the property levied upon, the [judgment creditor] would have no right to impose an execution upon such property in the hands of third persons. . . . If the municipality had not completed the transfer of its title at the time of the attempted levy of said writ, it would for that reason be entitled to appear in the action in which such execution had been issued in order to move to quash the levy thereof which, having been made, was impeding its transfer of the property to the purchaser thereof.[64]

---

63. Hughes v. Commissioners of Craven County, 107 N.C. 598, 12 S.E. 465 (1890).

64. United Taxpayers' Co. v. City & County of San Francisco, 259 P. 1101 (Cal. 1927).

The court's language indicates that the lien never attached to the property and that was why the creditor could not enforce it against a subsequent owner. The policy that underlies the basic rule barring liens against government property reinforces the California court's decision. That policy is to protect public assets against loss to a judgment creditor or other lienholder, and there is no reason to stop protecting against that loss simply because the assets are being converted to cash. If a lien could be enforced against a subsequent owner, the government's property would obviously be less valuable; the local government's assets would be directly affected.

C. Subdivision and Condominium Liens

The next section of this chapter explains that local governments may acquire property that is subject to restrictive covenants. Most modern residential or commercial developments are subject to covenants, and local governments occasionally acquire property in such a development. Similarly, office condominiums are a common form of office space, and some local governments have considered purchasing one or more units in an office condominium project. Residential or commercial development covenants usually establish a property owners' association and permit the association to levy assessments against property owners to finance maintenance of common areas and provision of services within the development. Similarly, condominium associations normally levy assessments against unit owners to finance maintenance of common elements within the condominium complex and perhaps provision of services as well. Both property owners' association and condominium association assessments are secured by liens against the assessed property. This section discusses whether those liens attach to property owned by a local government.

Statutory Liens. North Carolina has two condominium statutes, one applying to condominiums created before October 1, 1986, and the other to condominiums created on or after that date. Each of the statutes creates a lien in favor of the condominium association for unpaid assessments.[65] Neither statute specifically applies the lien to local government

---

65. The two statutes are G.S. 47A-22(a) for earlier condominiums and 47C-3-116(a) (Cum. Supp.) for later ones.

unit owners, and therefore under the principles discussed in this section, the statutory lien should not extend to any unit owned by a local government.[66]

Consensual Liens. A condominium unit owner is not only subject to a lien created by statute; the condominium declaration normally imposes a lien as well, one that a unit owner consents to by accepting a deed to the condominium unit. The lien on property in a residential or commercial development, securing property owners' association assessments, is entirely consensual, agreed to when accepting a deed to property in the development. But liens created by mortgages or deeds of trust are also consensual, and the courts have refused to enforce them without a statute authorizing a local government to give security interests in its property. Again, under the principles discussed in this section, these consensual liens also should not extend to property owned by a local government.

Association Remedies. Both condominium statutes make unit owners personally liable for assessments, over and above the liens just discussed,[67] as do condominium declarations and development covenants. There is no reason that this personal liability should not extend to local government owners. Therefore, associations are not without remedy against local governments that own condominium units or property within developments. The associations would just have to proceed directly against the local government, rather than the property.

---

66. The cases that have established the rules that bar application of statutory liens to governments have required an explicit extension of the lien to government property if such property is to be burdened by the lien. A 1986 supreme court decision, however, which was decided in a different context, could undercut the rigor of the earlier lien cases. A general principle of local government law prohibits imposing punitive damages on government tortfeasors unless a statute specifically permits doing so. In Jackson v. Housing Auth., 316 N.C. 259, 341 S.E.2d 523 (1986), the court affirmed the general rule on punitive damages but went on to hold that such damages could be imposed on a local government agency under the wrongful death statute. Although that statute did not specifically mention government tortfeasors, it did apply to "persons." The court relied on the general statement in G.S. 12-3 that statutory references to *persons* include municipal corporations. If a court were to take this same approach to statutory condominium liens, the assessment lien would apply to local governments owning condominium units.

67. G.S. 47A-22(b) and 47C-3-116(d) (Cum. Supp.).

§ 207. Particular Property Interests

Restrictive Covenants

In a few states, if a local government acquires property subject to restrictive covenants—for example, if a board of education purchases property for a school in a subdivision restricted to residential uses—the covenants do not apply to the governmental purchaser.[68] The North Carolina courts, however, have rejected that position; they have allied themselves with most courts and held that the covenants continue to apply, at least to the extent that if the local government violates the covenants, it must compensate those protected by them. In *City of Raleigh v. Edwards*,[69] the North Carolina Supreme Court held that restrictive covenants create property interests (not simply contractual rights) in each piece of property benefited by the covenants. Therefore, each owner of a benefited tract was entitled to compensation for the loss of that interest when the city condemned a tract for a use not permitted under the covenants.[70]

A subsidiary question arose in a court of appeals case decided a generation later.[71] A school board had purchased a subdivision lot subject to covenants and had begun construction of a use that violated the covenants. When neighboring owners sought to enjoin the construction, the court held that their only remedy was a suit in inverse condemnation for compensation for loss of the covenant. The court reasoned that because the school board could have condemned the lot for the use in question, it therefore could not be enjoined from making that use of the property.[72]

---

68. Friesen v. City of Glendale, 288 P. 1080 (Cal. 1930); Ryan v. Town of Manalapan, 414 So. 2d 193 (Fla. 1982); City of Riveroaks v. Moore, 272 S.W.2d 389 (Tex. Ct. Civ. App. 1954).

69. 235 N.C. 671, 71 S.E.2d 396 (1952).

70. Courts in a number of states have also held that if a local government acquires property in a subdivision and uses the property in a way that causes it to be no longer liable for homeowner assessments within the subdivision (for example, constructing a road), the homeowners' association is entitled to compensation for the resulting loss of the income stream for assessments on the lot. *See, e.g.*, Palm Beach County v. Cove Club Investors, Ltd., 734 So. 2d 379 (Fla. 1999).

71. Carolina Mills, Inc. v. Catawba County Bd. of Educ., 27 N.C. App. 524, 219 S.E.2d 509 (1975).

72. Not all state courts have reached the same conclusion. Two cases that permit injunctive relief until a condemnation is actually brought are Bales v. Michigan State Highway Comm'n, 249 N.W.2d 158 (Mich. Ct. App. 1976), and Meagher v. Appalachian Power Co., 77 S.E.2d 461 (Va. 1953).

The outcome is consistent with the related rule that a local government with condemnation power is not subject to ejectment when it wrongfully possesses or uses property; rather, the appropriate remedy there is also inverse condemnation.[73]

Although the court of appeals decision grows directly out of *Edwards* and in fact is clearly grounded in dicta in that earlier decision,[74] the rationale does raise an interesting possibility. Not all agencies or units of local government enjoy the power of eminent domain, nor do those with the power possess it for all purposes for which they may acquire property. For example, neither local ABC boards nor area mental health authorities may condemn property, nor may a county or city condemn property for community development purposes.[75] Given the rationale of the court of appeals decision, it may be that if such a unit or agency were to use property in violation of a restrictive covenant it would be subject to injunction.

§ 208. Particular Property Interests

Corporate Stock

Local governments sometimes wish to buy all the assets of a private corporation. In the most common example, a local government wishes to acquire a water or sewer system operated by a private corporation. Sometimes the corporation's owners prefer that the local government buy all of the corporation's stock rather than all of its assets. When the assets are private water or sewer systems, the local government cannot condemn them[76] and may have no choice but to purchase the stock. By doing so, the local government becomes owner of the assets through the corporation and might either liquidate the corporation and assume direct title to the assets or continue to use the assets through the

---

73. Costner v. City of Greensboro, 37 N.C. App. 563, 246 S.E.2d 552 (1978). *See infra* § 304-B.

74. In *Edwards* the court stated: "It is true that . . . other landowners may not enforce the restrictions [imposed by the covenants] against the condemnor." 235 N.C. at 677, 71 S.E.2d at 401.

75. For community development, *see* G.S. 153A-377 (counties) *and* 160A-457 (cities).

76. Under G.S. 40A-5(b), a local government may not condemn property held by a private condemnor unless the property "is not in actual public use or not necessary to the operation of the business of the owner." Corporations operating public water or sewer systems qualify as private condemnors. *Id.* § 40A-3(a)(1).

corporate structure. No North Carolina statute specifically authorizes a local government to acquire corporate stock in this way, and this section discusses whether such specific authority is necessary.

Although the matter is not free of doubt, specific authority is probably not necessary—a local government probably can acquire all of a corporation's stock under existing statutory authorizations, as long as the local government has statutory authority to engage in the activity for which the assets are wanted and to acquire property for that activity. For example, both counties and cities may "acquire" and "operate" public enterprises, including water and sewer systems.[77] Given that specific statutory authority, the general corporate power to "acquire and hold any property and rights of property, real and personal"[78] should be adequate authority to acquire a water or sewer system through purchase of a corporation's stock; stock itself is, after all, simply a form of intangible personal property.

No North Carolina cases discuss the need for specific statutory authority to acquire a corporation's stock, and no cases were found from elsewhere directly on point. A number of cases from other states, however, do offer strong indirect support of the conclusion outlined above. The strongest case is *Long v. Mayo*.[79] The State of Kentucky proposed to issue bonds and use the proceeds to buy the stock of a private bridge company. Its ultimate purpose was to acquire title to the corporation's bridge in order to stop the charging of tolls for use of the bridge. The court held that a 1928 act of the Kentucky legislature "gives specific authority for this transaction. . . . [The act] empowers the department of highways to purchase 'any bridge, real estate, or other property, real or personal, that in its opinion may be useful or helpful in ultimately doing away with toll bridges on the State Primary System of Highways.'"[80] The enabling act did not mention stock, but the court held it gave *specific* authority anyway. A second case is *State ex rel. Johnson v. Consumers Public Power District*.[81] *In Johnson* the district had acquired all the stock of a public utility corporation in order to acquire the utility's assets. The state attorney general then brought a quo warranto action challenging

---

77. G.S. 153A-275(a) (counties) and 160A-312(a) (cities).

78. G.S. 153A-11 (1991) (counties). G.S. 160A-11 (cities) reads almost the same, but does not include the phrase "rights of property." The omission is not meaningful.

79. 111 S.W.2d 633 (Ky. 1937).

80. *Id.* at 637.

81. 10 N.W.2d 784 (Neb. 1943).

the statutory and constitutional authority of the district to acquire the stock. The Nebraska Supreme Court noted that the district had statutory authority to acquire property and to acquire utility systems, and held that these statutes made quo warranto unavailable as a remedy. The attorney general could use quo warranto only to challenge actions beyond the district's legal authority and the acquisition of stock was not beyond that authority. These two cases support the position that the authority to acquire a corporation's property includes the authority to do so through acquisition of the corporation's stock.

Many state constitutions (although not North Carolina's) prohibit the state and its local governments from owning corporate stock.[82] Courts in several of those states have addressed the issue of whether governmental purchase of corporate stock in order to acquire corporate property violates the constitutional prohibition. By and large the courts have ruled it does not. For example, in *Cawood v. Coleman*,[83] the Kentucky Supreme Court held that the constitutional provision was inapplicable to such a stock purchase, because the "purchase of the [corporation's] stock will merely be the means of vesting the title to the [corporation's] properties."[84] Similarly, in *City of Springfield v. Monday*,[85] the Missouri Supreme Court held that state's constitutional provision inapplicable, because the city "has contracted with [the corporation] to buy all of its stock in order to become the owner of its physical utility properties and is purchasing the stock solely to acquire them."[86] These courts saw the reality of the transactions, rather than their surface manifestation, and it is likely a North Carolina court would do the same with the issue of statutory authority.

Federal Tax Consequences. Corporate owners usually ask local governments to acquire the corporation's stock rather than its assets because they expect to gain federal tax advantages from structuring the transaction in that way.[87] Before acquiring the stock, however, a local

---

82. *See, e.g.,* ALA. CONST. art. IV, § 94; *and* DEL. CONST. art. VIII, § 8.

83. 172 S.W.2d 548 (Ky. 1943).

84. *Id.* at 550.

85. 185 S.W.2d 788 (Mo. 1945).

86. *Id.* at 792. Other cases reaching the same conclusion are Long v. Mayo, 111 S.W.2d 633 (Ky. 1937); State *ex rel.* Johnson v. Consumers Public Power Dist., 10 N.W.2d 784 (Neb. 1943); and Brazos River Auth. v. Carr, 405 S.W.2d 689 (Tex. 1966).

87. "A sale of corporate assets followed by a liquidation of the selling corporation involves potential double taxation, that is, a tax at the corporate level upon

government should thoroughly investigate the federal tax consequences for itself arising from the transaction. The federal tax issues are quite complex, but both liquidating the private corporation and continuing to operate it but as part of the local government could result in tax recognition of a capital gain or loss, as if the corporation's assets had been conveyed. If there is a capital gain, it is the corporation's responsibility; as owner of the corporation the local government would be responsible for payment.[88]

§ 209. Consideration

A. Abuse of Discretion Standard

The consideration a local government pays for a parcel of or interest in real property is a matter of the government's discretion.[89] Unless an abuse of discretion can be shown—or a specific constitutional or statutory provision is violated—a court will not invalidate an acquisition because of the consideration paid.[90]

B. Nonmonetary Consideration

The usual consideration for property is cash, paid at closing. Sometimes, however, a seller prefers some other form of consideration, perhaps even nonmonetary consideration. Using the abuse of discretion standard, courts throughout the country have upheld several forms of nonmonetary consideration. Only if the consideration is well out of proportion to the value of the property being acquired have the courts intervened.

---

the sale of the assets, and a tax at the shareholder level upon the distribution of the proceeds of the sale in a complete liquidation by the selling corporation." THEODORE NESS & WILLIAM F. INDOE, TAX PLANNING FOR DISPOSITIONS OF BUSINESS INTERESTS § 2.01 (2d ed. 1990).

88. *See* Treas. Reg. § 1.337(d)-4 (1997).

89. Local governments buy most personal property by competitive bid, G.S. 143-129 and -131, and therefore the market sets the price. There is no bidding requirement, of course, for real property.

90. *See, e.g.,* Painter v. Wake County Bd. of Educ., 288 N.C. 165, 217 S.E.2d 650 (1975).

Exchanges or Construction of Facilities

The clearest set of national cases involve exchanges of one parcel of land for another, or government construction of facilities for the benefit of the grantor, or some combination of these. (G.S. 160A-271 specifically authorizes local governments to acquire and dispose of property by exchange.) Courts in other states have upheld the following:

1. A local government may purchase (or otherwise acquire) one parcel of property for the sole purpose of exchanging it for another parcel needed by the government.[91] If the property purchased and then exchanged is worth appreciably more than the property ultimately received, the parties should include cash to equalize consideration,[92] although there is some room for discretion here.[93]

2. A local government may construct private facilities for the grantor of property, either on property already owned by the grantor[94] or on property being conveyed to the grantor by exchange.[95] A local government may also, as consideration, agree to construct public facilities that benefit the grantor.[96]

---

91. Chitwood v. City & County of Denver, 201 P.2d 605 (Colo. 1948); Carter v. City of Greenville, 178 S.E. 508 (S.C. 1935). Under the Internal Revenue Code, if property is held for productive use in trade or business or for investment, no gain or loss is recognized when that property is exchanged for like property. I.R.C. § 1031 (West 1999).

92. Chitwood v. City & County of Denver, 201 P.2d 605 (Colo. 1948).

93. See Painter v. Wake County Bd. of Educ., 288 N.C. 165, 217 S.E.2d 650 (1975).

94. City of Fort Smith v. Bates, 544 S.W.2d 525 (Ark. 1976) (city may construct driveways on remaining property of grantor).

95. Herr v. City of St. Petersburg, 114 So. 2d 171 (Fla. 1959) (city will acquire land, construct a railroad terminal on land, and convey land and terminal to railroad in exchange for railroad's existing terminal).

96. Bancroft v. Mayor & Council of Wilmington, 123 A. 602 (Del. Ch. 1924) (city constructs public road in exchange for land needed for park); Whitaker v. City of Huntington, 107 S.E. 121 (W. Va. 1921) (city may agree to construct bridge and make park and road improvements in consideration of purchase of existing bridge). The North Carolina Attorney General's Office has issued an advisory letter to a local government, agreeing that the local government might acquire one tract of land for the consideration of clearing a separate tract of land belonging to the grantor. Letter to David A. Holec (Nov. 17, 1987) (on file with author). Another example of nonmonetary consideration known to the author arose when a North Carolina city that wished to acquire a lot containing a house agreed to move the house to another tract of city-owned land, which was then exchanged with the grantor for the lot that had held the house.

Three North Carolina cases indicate that this state's courts probably accept these general rules. In one case the North Carolina Supreme Court upheld a city's construction of facilities for a private grantor on lands retained by the grantor.[97] In a second case,[98] the state Highway Commission had purchased lands for a highway project, including the driveway providing the only access to M's property. In order to avoid having to pay M damages for loss of access, the Commission sought to condemn a small tract belonging to another private landowner, in order to construct a road providing access to M's lot. The supreme court upheld the condemnation, and the case lends strong support to a government's being able to acquire property solely for the purpose of exchange. In the third case, the state court of appeals held that a city could acquire property from an extraterritorial landowner and promise, as consideration, to thereafter provide fire protection to the landowner's remaining property.[99]

Forgiving Special Assessments or Fees

Another widely accepted form of nonmonetary consideration arises when a local government acquires a street right-of-way or utility easement. The cases uniformly uphold as proper consideration the government's promise not to levy special assessments (or the promise to pay the special assessments levied) on the remaining property of the grantor because of the street or utility project constructed within the right-of-way or easement.[100] (In North Carolina, all property is subject to special assessment unless specifically exempted,[101] and no statute specifically permits local governments to exempt property from assessment as part of the consideration for property acquisition. For that reason, rather than attempt an exemption a local government should levy the

---

97. Dudley v. City of Charlotte, 223 N.C. 638, 27 S.E.2d 732 (1943).

98. North Carolina State Highway Comm'n v. Asheville Sch., Inc., 276 N.C. 556, 173 S.E.2d 909 (1970).

99. Valevais v. City of New Bern, 10 N.C. App. 215, 178 S.E.2d 109 (1970).

100. *E.g.,* Coit v. City of Grand Rapids, 73 N.W. 811 (1898); Washington Water Power Co. v. City of Spokane, 154 P. 329 (Wash. 1916). In one case a city agreed to exempt the grantor's remaining property from *all* future special assessments, not just those related to the project for which the property was acquired. The court held that the consideration was excessive. City of Cleveland v. Edwards, 143 N.E. 181 (Ohio 1924).

101. G.S. 153A-188; 160A-220.

assessment but then pay it on behalf of the landowner.)[102] Comparable, and also upheld, are promises to exempt the grantor's remaining properties from fees levied for connection to the project.[103] If the promised consideration is considerably broader, however, or involves a clear loss of future discretion by the local government, the courts often find an abuse of discretion. For example, courts have invalidated promises of free sewer service in perpetuity,[104] or promises to permit the grantor of a formerly private sewer system to approve all future connections to the system.[105]

C. Prohibited Consideration: Property in Lieu of Taxes

Taxpayers sometimes suggest that instead of paying their property taxes in cash that they convey the taxed property to the taxing government. North Carolina law generally forbids such a transaction: G.S. 105-357(a) declares that deeds to real property may not be accepted in payment of taxes.[106]

D. Payment on Time

Occasionally an owner of property will, for tax reasons, ask that a local government purchasing the property from her spread its payment over time rather than make a single payment. If the owner takes a purchase money mortgage or deed of trust on the property to secure the unpaid portion of the purchase price, G.S. 160A-20 provides clear authority for the purchase by those local governments covered by the statute. Not all local governments are covered by the statute, however, and not all sellers want a purchase money mortgage or deed of trust, given the limitations associated with such instruments. Therefore the question arises of whether, if no mortgage or deed of trust is involved, a local government may agree to make payment for property over time.

---

102. Such an arrangement was suggested and approved in City of North Liberty v. Davis, 199 N.E. 451 (Ind. Ct. App. 1936).

103. Water Works & Sanitary Sewer Bd. v. Campbell, 103 So. 2d 165 (Ala. 1958); Morgan v. City of Rolla, 947 S.W.2d 837 (Mo. Ct. App. 1997).

104. Pittman v. City of Amarillo, 598 S.W.2d 941 (Tex. Civ. App. 1980).

105. G. Curtis Martin Investment Trust v. Clay, 266 S.E.2d 82 (S.C. 1980).

106. A few local governments have received local act authority to accept property in lieu of taxes. *E.g.*, Act of July 7, 1986, ch. 910, 1985 N.C. Sess. Laws (1986) (applicable to Farmville, Salisbury, Wilmington, and Durham County).

This question must be separated from the frequently associated question of whether a loan is involved, thus triggering the state constitutional provisions concerning debt.[107] If the government's payments are in fact debt service on a loan secured by its taxing power, the constitutional provisions require voter approval of the loan. Therefore it must be assumed that the transaction is simply payment spread over time and that there has been no loan from a third party.[108]

The cases relevant to the question, none of which are from North Carolina, are quite old; only one was decided later than 1908, and it dates from 1936, more than sixty years ago. Nevertheless the cases are uniform in their holdings: the authority to purchase includes the authority to pay over time.[109] Although a modern court might ignore these cases solely because of their antiquity, their result remains sound. If a selling owner seeks the tax advantages of payment over time and the buying government cannot agree to that arrangement, the owner is likely to insist on a higher cash price or even resist selling altogether. Either alternative would be more expensive than payment over time, and for that reason spreading payments over several years is a proper exercise of the government's discretion.

§ 210. Conflicts of Interest
A. The Prohibition on Self-dealing

G.S. 14-234 prohibits a public official from making a contract in his public capacity that benefits him in his private capacity. The basic prohibition is set out in the first sentence of the statute:

> If any person appointed or elected a commissioner or director to discharge any trust wherein the State or any county, city or town may be in any manner interested shall become an undertaker, or make any contract for his own benefit, under such authority, or be in any manner concerned or interested

---

107. N.C. Const. art. V, § 4.

108. Under the constitution a local government incurs debt when it *borrows money. Id.* at subsection (5). Paying a vendor in installments does not constitute borrowing money from that vendor.

109. *E.g.,* First Mun. of City of New Orleans v. McDonough, 2 Rob. 244 (La. 1842); City of Pontiac v. Ducharme, 270 N.W. 754 (Mich. 1936); Ketchum v. City of Buffalo, 14 N.Y. 356 (1856).

in making such contract, or in the profits thereof, either privately or openly, singly or jointly with another, he shall be
guilty of a misdemeanor.

Among the contracts covered by the prohibition are contracts for acquisition of property by a local government. This section first addresses the
question of which local officials are covered by the prohibition and then
discusses possible relief from the prohibition's rigor.

Which Officials Are Covered by the Statute?

The North Carolina Supreme Court has held that, for purposes of
G.S. 14-234, a member of a local government's governing board "makes"
all contracts entered into by the local government.[110] Consequently,
because the statute prohibits a public official from privately benefiting
from any contract that he makes in his public capacity, the statute effectively prohibits a board member from entering into any contract, in his
private capacity, with the unit with which he is an official. Although the
statute includes a number of exceptions, none apply to contracts under
which a local government acquires real property.[111] In other words, a
governing board member may not convey or contract to convey real
property to the unit for which he is a board member.

Application of the statute to officials beyond governing board members depends on the role these other officials play in making the contract
at issue. If an employee or appointed official takes an active role in the
process of acquiring the property in question, such as by recommending
a specific tract, negotiating on behalf of the unit, or advising the governing board on the issue, the person is helping to make the contract on

---

110. State v. Williams, 153 N.C. 595, 68 S.E. 900 (1910). *See* A. FLEMING BELL
II, ETHICS, CONFLICTS, AND OFFICES: A GUIDE FOR LOCAL OFFICIALS 52
(Institute of Government 1997), *and* FRAYDA S. BLUESTEIN, A LEGAL GUIDE TO
PURCHASING AND CONTRACTING FOR NORTH CAROLINA LOCAL GOVERN-
MENTS 90 (Institute of Government 1998). The North Carolina Attorney
General's Office has taken a somewhat narrower position—that G.S. 14-234 does
not apply to a governing board member when the board has no role in making or
approving the contract; *see* Advisory Opinion to Robert Oren Eades (Feb. 27,
1996) (copy on file with author). When a local government is acquiring fee
interests in real estate, however, the board is likely to have specifically appropriated the funds and many boards specifically approve each such acquisition.

111. The principal exception permits officials in smaller towns and counties
to sell up to $15,000 annually of *goods* or *services* to their unit. Real property is
neither a good nor a service.

behalf of the unit and cannot be the seller of the property. On the other hand, if a public official or employee plays no part in the acquisition process, the statute does not apply and the person may sell the property to the unit for which he or she works.

Avoiding the Statute

Personal property is often fungible, and a unit will therefore normally be able to purchase needed personal property even if the most convenient supplier is barred by G.S. 14-234. Real property, though, is unique, and sometimes the government requires a specific lot or tract—for a street, a reservoir, or a sewage treatment plant. If a board member or other involved official owns that lot or tract, can the property be acquired without violation of G.S. 14-234? Although no North Carolina court has addressed the question directly, the government can probably acquire the lot or tract through eminent domain.[112] Acquisition through eminent domain involves no contract; it is nonconsensual. Because G.S. 14-234 focuses on *contracts* with public agencies, the statute would not apply.[113] If condemnation is used to avoid the self-dealing prohibition, the official who owns the property should take no part in the deliberations or actions of the unit respecting the property.[114]

B. Other Possible Conflicts

The prohibitions of G.S. 14-234 are rigorous but narrow. The statute prohibits contracts from which a public official derives direct *personal* benefit. If the benefit of a contract runs instead to a close friend or even a relative of the public official, the statute does not apply.[115] Numerous

---

112. *See* Spadanuta v. Incorporated Village of Rockville Center, 239 N.Y.S.2d 598 (N.Y. Sup. Ct. 1963).

113. Because the statute does focus on contracts, it may be that it would be violated by a settlement or consent judgment entered in an eminent domain action.

114. Thompson v. Call, 699 P.2d 316 (Cal. 1985), illustrates an unsuccessful alternative to condemnation. In that case a council member sold land to a corporation, which then immediately sold the land to the city for which the original grantor was a council member. The California Supreme Court held that the corporation was a straw and that the transaction violated California's prohibition on self-dealing. The same result would be likely in this state.

115. In State v. Debnam, 196 N.C. 740, 146 S.E. 857 (1929), a board member's wife was interested in a contract with the board member's unit. The court held that fact, by itself, did not constitute an interest of the board member. (The court was applying G.S. 14-236, a statute related to G.S. 14-234.)

other situations present a potential conflict of interest but are covered by no statute. For example, public facility location decisions frequently affect the value of nearby properties, and sometimes nearby property is owned by officials of the agency making the location decision. Abuse of discretion is again the standard by which to test behavior in conflicts not covered by a statute. Unless there is proof that the potential conflict caused the affected official to exercise an improper or corrupt influence over others involved in the location or acquisition decision, thus indicating bad faith on the part of the agency itself, a court will not interfere with the property transaction.[116]

§ 211. Who May Challenge Property Acquisitions

The courts are usually generous in allowing taxpayers to challenge the validity of local government actions through litigation, in acknowledging that taxpayers have *standing* to bring such suits. This open access to court, however, does not include legal challenges to some property acquisitions—challenges that allege that a particular acquisition is *ultra vires*, or beyond the government's statutory powers. It is an accepted rule of private corporation law that only the state has standing to challenge the validity of a property acquisition by a business corporation,[117] and most courts have extended the same rule to property acquisitions by public corporations such as local governments.[118] Thus neither the stockholders of a private corporation nor the taxpayers of a public one may bring this sort of lawsuit. The North Carolina appellate courts have not addressed this question of standing in a case involving a local

---

116. Kistler v. Board of Educ., 233 N.C. 400, 64 S.E.2d 403 (1951) (allegation that one school board member owned land near site selected for purchase for high school was insufficient to support finding of bad faith by entire board).

117. *See* the cases cited in Mills v. Forest Preserve Dist. of Cook County, 178 N.E. 126 (Ill. 1931).

118. *E.g.,* Crystal Spring Finishing Co. v. Town of Freetown, 50 N.E.2d 34 (Mass. 1943); Campbell v. Board of Comm'rs, 30 P.2d 910 (Okla. 1934); Jones v. McConnell, 186 A.2d 915 (Pa. 1963). At least one state's courts also allow taxpayers to challenge acquisitions as *ultra vires.* Polanski v. Town of Eagle Point, 142 N.W.2d 281 (Wis. 1966); Schneider v. City of Menasha, 95 N.W. 94 (Wis. 1903).

government, but they have addressed and accepted the national rule on challenges to private corporate acquisitions.[119] Therefore extension of the rule to public corporations is likely.

The rule permitting only the state to challenge acquisitions arises most commonly when a grantor seeks to regain title to property she has conveyed to a government. In one Illinois case, for example, both the private grantor and the government grantee agreed that the government had no statutory authority to acquire the property. Yet the court rejected the grantor's suit to regain title, holding that only the state could challenge the completed conveyance.[120]

It must be stressed that this doctrine applies only to challenges alleging that the acquisition was *ultra vires*. It does not include challenges based on other grounds. Thus if the plaintiff agrees that the government was empowered to acquire the property in question but alleges that the government abused its discretion in doing so, the doctrine is inapplicable. Among the sorts of challenges that are included within the doctrine (that is, challenges that only the state can make) are the following:

1. The property was acquired for an unauthorized purpose—for example, a county acquiring land for a street.
2. The property is located beyond the unit's borders, and the unit is not authorized to make extraterritorial acquisitions for that purpose—for example, a city acquiring land for a street outside its borders.
3. The property interest is not one that the unit is authorized to acquire—for example, a council of governments purchasing a fee interest in property.

Finally, it should be stressed that this doctrine limits only challenges to property *acquisition*. The courts have been much freer in allowing plaintiffs to challenge *disposition* of government property.[121]

---

119. Cross v. Seaboard Air Line R.R. Co., 172 N.C. 119, 90 S.E. 14 (1916); Mallett v. Simpson, 94 N.C. 37 (1886).

120. Mills v. Forest Preserve Dist. of Cook County, 178 N.E. 126 (Ill. 1931).

121. *See infra* § 604-A.

III

Property Acquisition:
Methods and Procedures

§ 301. Methods

Introduction

Local governments may acquire property using the same methods as does a private person or entity: by purchase, gift, devise, bequest, or adverse possession. There is nothing special about governmental use of these common methods of acquisition and therefore no need to discuss them. (At one time—at the beginning of this century—two methods available to private persons and entities were denied to governments in some states. These outmoded limits are noted in a later section,[1] but they no longer carry any force.) One potential difference exists between government and private acquisition by adverse possession, and it is discussed below in Section 304.

Governments may also acquire property by methods not generally available to private persons or entities. Dedication is uniquely available to governments, and it is discussed in the next section. Eminent domain, although available to a few private entities,[2] is primarily a governmental

---

1. *See infra* § 305-A, -B.

2. Private condemnors, the most important of which are railroads and power companies, are listed in G.S. 40A-3(a) (Cum. Supp.). In addition, private property owners can sometimes condemn a way of access to a landlocked parcel of land through the cartway procedure found at *id.* §§ 136-68 and -69 (Cum. Supp.).

method of property acquisition. This book does not undertake a comprehensive review of the law of eminent domain,[3] but Section 303 includes a few selective points about this method.

§ 302. Methods

Dedication

A. Dedication Versus Grant

Dedication is a method by which a government agency acquires title to an interest in land without paying consideration; in other words, it is a form of gift. Strictly understood, however (and the courts are not always strict in their own understanding), a dedication differs in important ways from a gift of land made by grant.[4] First, a grant of land is made by deed; the government is the grantee. A dedication, on the other hand, is not made directly by deed. Frequently a dedication is inferred from the dedicator's actions, and if a deed is involved, some party other than the government is usually the grantee. In fact, in a dedication there is no named grantee. Rather, the dedication is to the "public" or to "public use." A second difference between grants and dedications is that a grant may convey a fee simple interest in the property. Normally, though, a dedication conveys only an easement for the appropriate public use or uses.[5] Third, a government normally enjoys greater discretion over the use of property held by grant than it does over property held through dedication.[6]

---

3. A book that does so is Ben F. Loeb, Jr., Eminent Domain Procedure for North Carolina Local Governments (Institute of Government, 2d ed. 1998).

4. The points made in this paragraph are drawn from 4 Herbert Thorndike Tiffany, The Law of Real Property § 1099 (3d ed. 1975) [hereinafter Tiffany], and Roger A. Cunningham & Saul Tischler, *Dedication of Land in New Jersey*, 15 Rutgers L. Rev. 372, 379–84 (1961).

5. Tiffany, *supra* note 4, at § 1112.

6. *See infra* §§ 405 *and* 503.

B. The Procedures for Dedication

Dedication requires an offer of dedication from the fee owner of the property and an acceptance of that offer by some appropriate public agency.[7] An offer of dedication may be express, presumptive, or implicit; in each case, the offer is said to reflect the intentions of the dedicator.

The most common form of an express offer of dedication is found on the modern subdivision plat, prepared pursuant to local subdivision regulations. The typical subdivision ordinance in North Carolina requires the subdivider to place on the face of the plat a signed certificate stating that the subdivider dedicates to public use the streets, easements, and other public spaces shown on the plat.[8]

The most common form of presumptive offer—and until subdivision ordinances became widespread the most common form of offer of any type—involves the sale of a subdivision lot by reference to a plat of that subdivision. When a subdivider makes the first sale of a lot, the law, in the absence of express contradictory evidence, conclusively presumes that the subdivider has offered to dedicate to public use all the streets and other public spaces shown on the plat.[9]

There is no single dominant form of an implicit offer of dedication; rather, implicit offers are matters of divining the intention of the putative offeror in a great many different circumstances. One common example, though, is a landowner's use of a putative street as a property boundary in a deed given to another party; the law implies that the landowner has thereby offered that street for dedication to public use.[10]

Acceptance also may take any of several forms. The most conclusive form occurs when the governing body of the appropriate local government or state agency adopts a motion or resolution formally accepting the offer of dedication. This formal step, however, is not the most common method. A local government or other public agency is more likely to indicate its acceptance indirectly, most often by beginning to

---

7. Dedication procedures, in the context of city streets, are discussed in detail in David M. Lawrence, Property Interests in North Carolina Streets §§ 1.02 through 1.16 (Institute of Government 1985).

8. For example, Hickory's subdivision ordinance requires that the approved subdivision plat include a statement from the subdivider that "I hereby . . . dedicate all streets, alleys, easements, walks, parks, and other sites to public or private use." Hickory, N.C., Subdivision Ordinance § 41.

9. *E.g.,* Wittson v. Dowling, 179 N.C. 542, 103 S.E. 18 (1920).

10. *See* Owens v. Elliott, 258 N.C. 314, 128 S.E.2d 583 (1962); Sugg v. Town of Greenville, 169 N.C. 606, 86 S.E. 695 (1915).

maintain the public space in question.[11] Another method of indirect acceptance occurs when a government assumes an authority over the space that is consistent only with acceptance of the dedication.[12]

The Effect of a Mortgage or Deed of Trust on a Dedication

A person cannot convey a greater interest in property than she owns, and this principle occasionally affects local government title to property that an owner has attempted to dedicate to the local government.[13] If the property in question is subject to a mortgage or deed of trust, the dedication may not adversely affect the interests of the creditor protected by the mortgage or deed of trust (the *mortgagee*) unless that creditor has in some manner consented to the dedication.[14] Fortunately for local governments, the courts have held that the mortgagee's consent may be implied and that the mortgagee (and its successors) can be estopped from denying that consent was given. The most common form of implied consent occurs when a mortgagee releases platted development lots from a mortgage or deed of trust as they are sold. By doing so, the mortgagee is held to ratify the plat, including dedication of any public spaces shown on the plat.[15] Because dedication most often occurs in conjunction with approval of a development plat or with the sale of lots pursuant to the plat, and because most commercial lenders release lots from the mortgage or deed of trust as they are sold, this kind of implied consent protects the great majority of dedications.

When it does not, however, a local government may have an imperfect title to the dedicated property. As a practical matter, the issue has most

---

11. Steadman v. Town of Pinetops, 251 N.C. 509, 112 S.E.2d 102 (1960) (maintenance of street for two or three years constitutes acceptance).

12. Haggard v. Mitchell, 180 N.C. 255, 104 S.E. 561 (1920) (town had hauled in fill and placed it on the land in issue, had formally adopted a plat of the town and shown the space as public, had placed a night light in the space, and had granted
utility companies the right to erect poles in the space). *See* Draper v. Connor, 187 N.C. 18, 121 S.E. 29 (1924) (exercise of "sanitary control"—which was not defined—over space could constitute acceptance).

13. A brief summary of the law on this issue and a listing of cases is found at L. S. Robers, Annotation, *Power of Mortgagor to Dedicate Land or Interest Therein*, 63 A.L.R. 1160 (1959).

14. *E.g.*, Hamilton v. Laesch, 184 So. 110 (Fla. 1938); Descheemaeker v. Anderson, 310 P.2d 587 (Mont. 1957).

15. *E.g.*, Weills v. City of Vero Beach, 119 So. 1160 (Fla. 1928); Fereday v. Mankedick, 34 A. 46 (Pa. 1896).

often arisen in three circumstances. First, if the mortgage or deed of trust is foreclosed, the mortgagee or a new owner of the property may claim that the foreclosure has extinguished the dedication. If a court finds there was no consent to the dedication by the mortgagee, the mortgagee or new owner will prevail.[16] Second, the local government may be attempting to widen a street or place utility lines in an existing right-of-way, and the owner of the fee claims that the government does not have title to the wider easement or a title that permits utility lines at all. If a court finds there was no consent to the dedication of the original street easement by the mortgagee, the fee owner will prevail.[17] Third, the local government may have installed public improvements in the alleged dedicated easement and may be attempting to levy special assessments for the improvements. If a court finds there was no consent to the dedication of the easement, the special assessment will not be allowed.[18]

All these issues arose in the recent case of *Tower Development Partners v. Zell*,[19] which illustrates the doctrine and the effect it might have on an attempted dedication. In *Zell* an owner offered to dedicate a street easement over property subject to a deed of trust; the city and state accepted the offer. Some time later the deed of trust was foreclosed, and the new owner argued that the foreclosure extinguished the dedication on the ground that the trustee under the deed of trust had never consented to the dedication. The court of appeals accepted the validity of this doctrinal argument but then held that the trustee had consented, in that the trustee

16. *E.g.,* Weills v. City of Vero Beach, 119 So. 1160 (Fla. 1928) (no consent found to dedications on one of three plats; court awards contested property to mortgagee); Descheemaeker v. Anderson, 310 P.2d 587 (Mont. 1957) (no consent found to dedication of road; court holds public has no title in road).

17. *E.g.,* City of Alton v. Fischback, 55 N.E. 150 (Ill. 1899) (city may not construct sidewalk because mortgagee did not consent to earlier dedication of easement within which sidewalk would be placed); Kiernan v. Mayor & Aldermen of Jersey City, 78 A. 228 (N.J. 1910) (city may not lay utility lines in bed of dedicated street because mortgagee did not consent to earlier dedication of street).

18. *E.g.,* Western Fertilizer & Cordage Co., Inc., v. BRG, Inc., 424 N.W.2d 588 (1988) (city's special assessment lien not entitled to statutory priority over mortgage lien because mortgagee had not consented to dedication and therefore improvement not made on public property).

19. 120 N.C. App. 136, 461 S.E.2d 17 (1995).

had released lots within the development from the deed of trust as they were sold. Thus the court also accepted the most common form of implied consent.[20]

C. Dedication by a Government Agency

North Carolina is one of a number of states in which the courts have held that a government agency may dedicate property to itself.[21] In announcing this doctrine, the North Carolina Supreme Court did not make clear just how such a dedication is completed,[22] but presumably it occurs when the agency places property in a particular use and maintains that use for some undefined period of time.[23] Courts in several other states have considered the question of offer and acceptance when a self-dedication is alleged, but the answers vary.

---

20. The court of appeals concluded this portion of its opinion by stating that because the dedication was enforceable against the mortgagee, the city and state were therefore owners of an interest in the property and entitled to notice in the foreclosure proceeding. Because they had not received notice, "[t]heir interest was therefore not extinguished by the foreclosure proceedings." *Id.* at 142, 461 S.E.2d at 21. This is an odd conclusion. If the mortgagee consented to the dedication, the effect was to release the public easements from the deed of trust. Therefore they would *not* be record owners of any interest in the property subject to the deed of trust; the foreclosure proceedings would be irrelevant to their interests. *See* Seashore Properties, Inc. v. East Fed. Sav. & Loan Ass'n of Kinston, 47 N.C. App. 675, 267 S.E.2d 693 (1980) (foreclosure statute, G.S. 45-21.16, requires notice to "record owner" of property subject to foreclosure; court holds a record owner is either the original mortgagor or a present owner who has purchased property *subject to the mortgage*).

21. Wishart v. City of Lumberton, 254 N.C. 94, 118 S.E.2d 35 (1961). "Self-dedication" of the kind involved in *Wishart* should not be confused with a local government's ability to dedicate nature preserves to the State under G.S. 113A-164.6. Under that statute one government offers to dedicate, and a separate government accepts the offer.

22. *Wishart* was before the court on an appeal from a preliminary injunction. The court concluded its opinion in *Wishart* by quoting a Kentucky case to the effect that a completed dedication would require "a clear and unequivocal intention" on the part of the city. Wishart v. City of Lumberton, 254 N.C. 94, 97, 118 S.E.2d at 37.

23. *Wishart's* quotation from the Kentucky court continued: "Perhaps, where a city has paid funds out of its treasury in making improvements for park purposes on lands owned by it to such an extent that it would be inequitable to abandon it or change its use, this might be construed as an establishment thereof." *Id.*

In each of two Pennsylvania cases, for example, a government agency adopted an ordinance that the court construed as an offer of dedication;[24] there had been no follow-up to the ordinance, however, and no maintenance of the property. In each case the court held that some form of acceptance, apart from the initial ordinance, was necessary. Two Wisconsin cases, on the other hand, hold that offer and acceptance depend on the same evidence and may be completed in a single transaction.[25] In one case the dedication was explicit, in the other, implied.[26]

Confusion over offer and acceptance is not surprising. The entire notion that a government can dedicate property to itself is unfortunate, a poorly considered extension of the law of dedication to a situation it does not fit. The courts developed the law of dedication to govern what were essentially gifts of private land to public use. Because no consideration passed to the dedicator, the courts were protective of her interests. They made it difficult for the accepting government to change the dedicated use of the property or to convey the property to someone else.[27] But if a government "dedicates" property to itself, there is no private dedicator to protect. Rather, the only effect is to limit judicially the discretion a local government otherwise enjoys to change the use or dispose of property it holds in fee.[28] Given the uncertainty about just what is

---

24. Appeal of Leech, 89 A.2d 351 (Pa. 1952); Board of Trustees v. Trustees of Univ. of Pa., 96 A. 126 (Pa. 1915).

25. State *ex rel.* La Follette v. Reuter, 153 N.W.2d 49 (Wis. 1967); Knox v. Roeht, 140 N.W. 1121 (Wis. 1913).

26. For whatever it's worth, it might be noted that the city opposed the "dedication" in the two Pennsylvania cases and favored it in the two Wisconsin cases; that is, the city won in each of the four cases. (Of course, the city lost in the North Carolina case.)

27. TIFFANY, *supra* note 4, at § 1103. *See infra* §§ 405 *and* 503.

28. Wishart v. City of Lumberton, 254 N.C. 94, 118 S.E.2d 35 (1961) (city wished to construct parking lot on portion of city park). By enactment of G.S. 160A-265, the General Assembly may have given local governments caught up in this doctrine the necessary legislative authority to change the use of or dispose of any property alleged to be self-dedicated. That statute permits local governments to "change the use . . . or sell . . . property, without regard to the method or purpose of its acquisition or to its intended or actual governmental or other prior use." *See infra* §§ 405 *and* 503.

necessary to complete a government's dedication to itself, the entire doctrine is little more than a device by which a court can second-guess the legislative and managerial decisions of a local government.[29]

§ 303. Methods

Eminent Domain

As was noted in Section 301, this book does not discuss either the substantive or the general procedural law of eminent domain. This section looks only at the need for express authority to exercise the power of eminent domain and at several special limitations that condition the eminent domain power of selected local agencies.

A. The Need for Statutory Authority

Local governments do not automatically possess the power of eminent domain. The General Assembly must give it to them expressly, and the basic corporate power to acquire and own property is not express enough.[30] The statutes must make *specific* mention of eminent domain or condemnation. Consequently not all local governments hold the power of eminent domain. Among the agencies authorized to acquire and own real property but without power to do so by condemnation are local ABC boards,[31] area mental health authorities,[32] soil and water conservation districts,[33] regional sports authorities,[34] and historic preservation

---

29. Not all courts accept self-dedication of property held in fee by a local government. *E.g.*, Carlson v. City of Fremont, 142 N.W.2d 157 (Neb. 1966) (city paid for parkland with general funds and may change use of property to fire station).

30. Commissioners of Beaufort County v. Bonner, 153 N.C. 66, 68 S.E. 970 (1910).

31. A local ABC board is authorized to "buy and lease" property and "receive property bequeathed or given." G.S. 18B-701(10).

32. With the permission of the board or boards of county commissioners of the county or counties that comprise an area authority, the authority may "acquire" real property. *Id.* § 122C-147(c).

33. A soil and water conservation district may acquire property by "purchase, exchange, lease, gift, grant, bequest, devise, or otherwise." *Id.* § 139-8(4).

34. A regional sports authority's charter may not confer the power of eminent domain on an authority, *Id.* § 160A-479.7(b)(3).

commissions.[35] Even if a local government does possess eminent domain authority, that authority may not extend to all the purposes for which the government may acquire property. For example, the legislature has authorized counties and cities to acquire real property for open space[36] and for community development projects,[37] but it has not allowed use of condemnation for either purpose.

B. State or Other Agency Approval

Normally a county, city, or other local government exercises its power of eminent domain subject only to judicial control; no other governmental agency must approve. In three instances, however, the statutes impose an additional control—the requirement of initial approval by a state agency or, in one case, one or more boards of county commissioners. Hospital authorities and housing authorities must receive a certificate of public convenience and necessity from the state Utilities Commission before they may begin condemnation proceedings.[38] And a regional natural gas district may not condemn property unless the board of county commissioners of the county in which the property is located has consented to the taking.[39]

---

35. A historic preservation commission may "acquire by any lawful means the fee or any lesser included interest." *Id.* § 160A-400.8(3). If the owner of historic property intends to demolish it, however, a city or county (rather than a historic preservation commission) may acquire the property by condemnation. G.S. 40A-3(b)(8) (Cum. Supp.).

36. *Id.* § 160A-403. Providing open space is not among the purposes for which G.S. 40A-3(b) permits counties and cities to condemn property.

37. *Id.* §§ 153A-377 (counties) and 160A-457 (cities). Each statute specifically authorizes acquisition by "voluntary purchase."

38. *Id.* §§ 131E-24(c) (hospital authority) *and* 157-28 (housing authority).

39. G.S. 160A-674(b) (Cum. Supp.).

§ 304. Methods

Adverse Possession and Prescription

A. Availability of Adverse Possession and Prescription

Local governments, like private parties, may acquire property by adverse possession.[40] They may also acquire easements by the comparable method of prescription.[41] Acquisition through adverse possession or prescription is not a taking for which compensation must be paid. Because the original owner has lost her interest by action of law, she retains nothing for which she must be compensated.[42]

B. Statute of Limitations

The period of possession required to acquire title through adverse possession is twenty years.[43] (If the possession is under color of title, the period is seven years.)[44] Similarly, the period of use required to acquire a prescriptive easement is twenty years.[45] But if a government is the

---

40. Williams v. North Carolina Bd. of Educ., 266 N.C. 761, 147 S.E.2d 381 (1966) (state); City of Raleigh v. Durfey, 163 N.C. 154, 79 S.E. 434 (1913) (city). In *Durfey* the court stated: "One of the methods of acquiring title to land is by adverse possession. We know of no reason or authority by which a municipality is excluded from that rule and rendered incompetent to acquire title by that method." 163 N.C. at 160, 79 S.E. at 436.

41. Hemphill v. Board of Aldermen, 212 N.C. 185, 193 S.E. 153 (1937). Prescription shares several of the elements of adverse possession. Nevertheless, because prescription is a means of acquiring title to easements, which are nonpossessory interests, prescription does not require actual and exclusive possession of the property at issue.

Prescription does, though, require that the adverse use be "open and notorious." This requirement makes it very difficult to gain prescriptive title to underground utility easements. *See* J. H. Crabb, Annotation, *Easement by Prescription in Artificial Drains, Pipes, or Sewers*, 55 A.L.R.2d 1144 § 9 (1957). A recent example of a city's successful gain of prescriptive title to a sewer easement, though, is Katz v. Metropolitan Sewer Dist., 690 N.E.2d 1357 (Ohio Ct. App. 1997).

42. *E.g.,* Board of County Comm'rs v. Flickinger, 687 P.2d 975 (Colo. 1984); State *ex rel.* A.A.A. Invs. v. City of Columbus, 478 N.E.2d 773 (Ohio 1985). *See also* A. M. Vann, Annotation, *Acquisition of Title to Land by Adverse Possession by State or Other Governmental Unit or Agency*, 18 A.L.R.3d 678 (1968).

43. G.S. 1-40.

44. *Id.* § 1-38 (1996).

45. *See* Hemphill v. Board of Aldermen, 212 N.C. 185, 193 S.E. 153 (1937).

adverse possessor or prescriptive user, the record owner must assert his rights within two years after the possession or use begins or apparently lose the right to do so.

The normal method by which a record owner interrupts possession by an adverse possessor is by bringing a legal action of ejectment, which turns the adverse holder out of the property.[46] Ejectment, however, appears to be unavailable against a government holding as an adverse possessor or prescriptive user, at least if that government holds the power of eminent domain.[47] Rather, the record owner's only remedy against the governmental possessor or user is an action in inverse condemnation, in which the recovery will be the value of the property interest involved.[48] The statute of limitations for inverse condemnation, however, is two years.[49] If the action is not brought within that short period, it cannot be brought at all.[50]

---

46. *See* TIFFANY, *supra* note 4, at § 1161.

47. Costner v. City of Greensboro, 37 N.C. App. 563, 246 S.E.2d 552 (1978). In *Costner* the court relied on two early supreme court decisions, Beasley v. Aberdeen & Rockfish R.R. Co., 147 N.C. 362, 61 S.E. 453 (1908) and Rhodes v. City of Durham, 165 N.C. 679, 81 S.E. 983 (1914). Both of these early cases, however, held only that a plaintiff may be required to seek permanent damages against a governmental possessor rather than bringing a series of actions for temporary trespass. Neither holds that permanent damages rather than ejectment must be sought; indeed, an even earlier case implied that a plaintiff could choose between permanent damages and ejectment. McDowell v. City of Asheville, 112 N.C. 747, 17 S.E. 537 (1893). Despite this misreading of precedent, the court of appeals' decision does mirror the case law elsewhere. *See* M. C. Dransfield, Injunction Against Exercise of Power of Eminent Domain, Annotation, 133 A.L.R. 11, 104 (1941).

48. Costner v. City of Greensboro, 37 N.C. App. 563, 246 S.E.2d 552 (1978). The holding in *Costner* is premised on the governmental possessor holding the power of eminent domain. That is, because the government could always condemn the property interest at issue, it makes no sense to eject the government from that interest. If the premise is unfounded because the governmental possessor does not have eminent domain power (*see supra* § 303-A) ejectment presumably is available and inverse condemnation not the only remedy.

49. G.S. 40A-51.

50. The result—an effective transfer of title after two years—is comparable to the result under the doctrine of "statutory presumption" that the North Carolina courts developed for railroads. Many early railroad charters provided that if, in the absence of a written contract for the railroad's acquisition of right-of-way, the fee holder did not sue for compensation within two years after the railroad began to use the right-of-way, the fee holder was conclusively presumed to have granted the easement to the railroad. The leading case upholding such a provision is

There is no question that this short statute of limitations is valid. The North Carolina Supreme Court upheld a comparable limitation on inverse condemnation actions against the State in *Wilcox v. North Carolina State Highway Commission*,[51] and the United States Supreme Court has accepted a six-year statute of limitations on inverse condemnation actions against the federal government.[52] Although the record owner loses her remedy after two years, title does not actually pass until the conclusion of the full statutory period. If the government's possession or use should be interrupted before the statutory period has run, the adverse possession or prescription fails, and the record owner may reassert her rights.[53]

§ 305. Methods
Some Obsolete Limitations
A. Tax and Execution Sales

In the nineteenth and early twentieth centuries, several state courts held that, absent legislative authority, a local government could not, as a way of protecting its tax levy, bid on property being sold for nonpayment of taxes.[54] The courts' rationale was that such a bid amounted to speculation in tax titles, and speculation by a government was unseemly. (None of these courts, however, denied that a local government could acquire property at a tax sale when the property was needed for a public use.)[55]

Barker v. Railroad, 137 N.C. 214, 49 S.E. 115 (1904). The doctrine was upheld most recently in Carolina & N.W.R.R. v. Piedmont Wagon Mfg. Co., 229 N.C. 695, 51 S.E.2d 301 (1949). A comparable city charter provision, applying to lands possessed by the city, was upheld and applied in Woods v. Durham, 200 N.C. 608, 158 S.E. 97 (1931).

51. 279 N.C. 185, 181 S.E.2d 435 (1971). The limitation in G.S. 40A-51 itself was applied by the court of appeals in Smith v. City of Charlotte, 79 N.C. App. 517, 339 S.E.2d 844 (1986) and in Robertson v. City of High Point, 129 N.C. App. 88, 497 S.E.2d 300 (1998).

52. *See* United States v. Dickinson, 331 U.S. 745 (1947).

53. Rogers v. City of Knoxville, 289 S.W.2d 868 (Tenn. Ct. App. 1955). The city had adversely held a utility easement for 14 years and then abandoned it. Although the fee owner did not initially seek damages within the one-year period of limitations established by Tennessee law, the court held that he could now reenter and reestablish his rights, because the easement had been abandoned before the 20-year adverse period had run.

54. Many early cases are cited in Young v. Mayor & City Council, 185 A. 450 (Md. 1936).

55. City of North Muskegon v. Rodgers, 154 N.W. 71 (Mich. 1915).

A few courts extended this rule to execution sales, refusing to allow local governments to bid at such sales when the government was the judgment creditor.[56] These early cases were duly reported in the municipal corporation treatises being written at the time, such as McQuillin's, and modern editions of these works continue to cite the cases as good law.[57]

These early cases make very little sense, and later courts have generally ignored them.[58] The more recent cases suggest that the power to bid and purchase at tax or execution sales is essential to the government's ability to protect its interest in the underlying taxes or judgment. The power is implicit in the authority to levy and collect taxes and the authority to sue and be sued.

In North Carolina the question has been settled by statute. G.S. 105-376 permits a local government to bid at a tax sale occasioned by taxes owed to that local government. And G.S. 153A-163 permits a local government to purchase real property at "a judicial sale, an execution sale, or a sale made pursuant to a power of sale, to secure a debt due" the local government. (Presumably a local government could not buy at such a sale simply to speculate in land. It must be either protecting a debt owed to it or buying the property for some public use.)

B. Devises

The English Statute of Wills expressly prohibited devises to government corporations.[59] Some early American decisions, relying on this English rule, held that local governments could not accept devises of land without express statutory authority.[60] This older rule was soon forgotten, however, and the modern rule clearly permits acquisition of property in this manner.[61]

---

56. Several cases are cited in Evans v. Power Co., 1 P.2d 614 (Idaho 1931).

57. 10 EUGENE McQUILLIN, LAW OF MUNICIPAL CORPORATIONS § 28.04 (3d ed. rev. vol. 1999) concludes that these cases state the "prevailing rule."

58. *E.g.,* McDowell v. State, 8 So. 2d 569 (Ala. 1942) (execution sale); Young v. Mayor & City Council, 185 A. 450 (1936) (tax sale).

59. Statute of Wills (1542), 34 Hen. 8, c. 5.

60. *See* McIntosh v. City of Charleston, 23 S.E. 943 (S.C. 1896).

61. *E.g.,* Korner v. Borck, 100 So. 2d 398 (Fla. 1958); Vestal v. Pickering, 267 P. 821 (Or. 1928). The old rule's existence, however, probably explains why some current statutes specifically authorize certain kinds of government agencies to acquire property by devise or bequest. *E.g.,* G.S. 153A-11 (counties), 157-9 (Cum.

§ 306. Procedures

Authorization and Acceptance

Although acquisition of tangible personal property is closely regulated by the purchasing statutes, for the most part the North Carolina statutes do not mandate any particular procedures for acquisition of real property by local governments. (The few specific procedural requirements are discussed in the following section.) Therefore each local government and local agency is free to develop is own procedures—normally by tradition rather than specification—and thus a variety of procedures are in fact followed.

A. Governing Board Authorization

The one constant is that the governing board, at some point in the process, must authorize the acquisition. (In a few local governments a local act from the General Assembly permits the manager to authorize land acquisitions below a specified dollar amount.[62] Even in such units, however, the governing board must still appropriate the necessary funds.) There is substantial variety in the form and timing of the governing board's authorization. Some of the more common variations are as follows:

1. The governing board appropriates the money necessary for property acquisition, either in the annual budget ordinance or in a project ordinance. The unit's staff considers the appropriation sufficient authority to acquire the property necessary for the project, up to the amount of the appropriation, and therefore the board has no further involvement, even if condemnation becomes necessary.
2. The governing board adopts a separate motion or resolution specifically delegating to one or more administrative officials (such as the manager and attorney) the authority to acquire property for a

---

Supp.) (housing authorities), 160A-11 (cities), and 160A-512(6) (redevelopment commissions).

62. *See, e.g.,* Charlotte City Charter § 4.25(1), permitting the city manager to acquire real property valued up to $10,000.

specific project. The administrative officials might or might not consider it necessary to return to the board if condemnation proves necessary, depending on the unit's customs.[63]

3. Administrative staff negotiate with the property owner, reaching a tentative agreement. (The board may be asked for advice if difficulties arise during negotiations.) The unit acquires an option to purchase the property, or signs a contract of purchase conditioned on board approval; and the option or contract is taken to the board for its approval. If condemnation is necessary, the board gives formal authorization to proceed.

4. The board itself, or an individual member or a committee of the board, negotiates the acquisition, and the full board approves it.

In the absence of statutorily required procedures, there is room in law for each of the above methods, and for modified versions as well.

B. Acceptance

North Carolina in general follows the widespread rule that an actual and formal acceptance of a deed, by the grantee, is unnecessary.[64] Rather, acceptance can be presumed from the actions of the grantee.[65] This general rule also applies to local governments.

The common rule nationally is that it is not necessary that the governing board formally accept a deed to a local government or even that there be a formal presentation to the board.[66] The acts that will support a presumption of acceptance include directing payment for the

---

63. Under I.R.C. § 1033 (West 1999), if a person conveys her property through condemnation, *or under threat of condemnation*, she can in certain circumstances postpone recognition of any capital gain on the property conveyed. For that reason, some local governments routinely authorize condemnation so that such a threat can be said to have been made.

64. PATRICK K. HETRICK & JAMES B. MCLAUGHLIN, JR., WEBSTER'S REAL ESTATE LAW IN NORTH CAROLINA § 10-58 (4th ed. 1994) [hereinafter WEBSTER].

65. *Id.*

66. Wood v. City of Montpelier, 82 A. 671 (Vt. 1912).

property;[67] recording the deed;[68] including the deed among the unit's land records;[69] using the property for the unit's purposes;[70] and no longer levying taxes on the property.[71]

§ 307. Procedures

Some Special Rules

A. Local School Units

Acquiring School Sites

The School Budget and Fiscal Control Act directs that "no contract for the purchase of a site shall be executed [by a school administrative unit] nor any funds expended therefor unless the board of county commissioners has approved the amount to be spent on the site."[72] Although the direction uses the single word *site*, it is in a subsection that earlier refers to *school sites*, differentiating them from land acquired for other purposes, such as for playing fields, administrative buildings, and garages. The requirement of county commissioner approval probably refers back to that earlier phrase and for that reason applies only when a school administrative unit is acquiring land for a school as opposed to for other purposes. If the commissioners refuse to give their approval, the two boards are to arbitrate the dispute in the same manner as budget disputes are arbitrated.[73]

Although the statute uses absolute language—"no contract," "any funds"—a supreme court decision creates one exception to its reach and suggests others. In addition, the logic of the provision suggests at least one other exception. To begin with the court decision, in 1975 the North Carolina Supreme Court considered an earlier version of this statute but one that used the same language as the present law.[74] In that case the

---

67. *Id.*

68. Bartlett v. City of Boston, 65 N.E. 827 (Mass. 1903); Wood v. City of Montpelier, 82 A. 671 (Vt. 1912). *See also* WEBSTER, *supra* note 64, at § 10.58.

69. Bartlett v. City of Boston, 65 N.E. 827 (Mass. 1903).

70. *Id.*; Wood v. City of Montpelier, 82 A. 671 (Vt. 1912).

71. Wood v. City of Montpelier, 82 A. 671 (Vt. 1912).

72. G.S. 115C-426(f).

73. The arbitration procedure is found in *id.* § 115C-431.

74. Painter v. Wake County Bd. of Educ., 288 N.C. 165, 217 S.E.2d 650 (1975).

court held that commissioner approval was unnecessary when the school board acquired property through an exchange for property it already owned. Therefore exchanges are excluded from the statute's reach.

The court went on to observe that the statute required commissioner approval only when a site was to be "purchased by [a board] of education with money furnished by county commissioners for the current budget year."[75] Although the quoted statement was dicta (after all, the case involved an exchange, not a purchase), it suggests two additional exceptions to the statute's requirement. First, if the money used by the school administrative unit comes from some source other than the county, such as from the State or a gift, commissioner approval is unnecessary. Second, the court's mention of money furnished by the county "for the current budget year" suggests that if property is acquired with money held by a school unit in fund balance—money, that is, furnished by the county in an earlier budget year—commissioner approval is again unnecessary. Such an outcome is consistent with the facts in the case itself: in both instances the school unit would be using assets that are now generally beyond county commissioner control for its acquisition—property that the school unit owns, used in an exchange, and money in fund balance.

The court's willingness to find exceptions to the statutory requirement of commissioner approval also supports recognizing an exception when property is acquired by eminent domain. In such a case, the judicial process has determined the value of the property being acquired, and there is no point in the county commissioners' reviewing that decision. Of course, if a condemnation case is settled rather than carried to trial, that logic no longer applies, and the requirement probably extends to such an agreed-upon amount.

Finally, the statute on its face does not appear to apply if the school administrative unit has only acquired an option to purchase the property. Before the school unit may exercise the option, however, the county commissioners must approve the amount the school unit will pay for the property.

---

75. *Id.* at 182–83, 217 S.E.2d at 661.

Leasing School Buildings and Facilities

G.S. 115C-530 permits school administrative units to enter into operational leases of real or personal property.[76] Many such leases are not subject to any outside approval, but some might need county commissioner approval and a few of those might also require approval of the state Local Government Commission.

If an operational lease extends for three years or more, it must be approved by the board of county commissioners. By giving their approval, the commissioners become bound to appropriate to the school unit the funds necessary for lease payments for each year the lease continues. If an operational lease extends for five years or more and the school unit's total payment obligation under the lease is $500,000 or more, G.S. 115C-530 requires that the lease also be approved by the Local Government Commission.

B. Community and Technical Colleges

Under G.S. 115D-5, the State Board of Community Colleges must approve all sites for community and technical college facilities, regardless of the source of funding. Therefore, before a college may acquire any real property, even donated property, it must receive state-level approval.

C. Economic Development Property

G.S. 158-7.1(b) permits counties and cities (but not other local governments) to acquire and develop land for an industrial park for industrial or commercial use, to acquire separate parcels of property for industrial or commercial use, to acquire options to purchase such property, and to construct or acquire shell buildings. Before the county or city may appropriate or expend money for any of these purposes, however, subsection (c) of the statute requires that the governing body hold a public hearing on the project, having given at least ten days' published notice of the hearing. (This means that for a meeting on, say, the twenty-second of

---

76. Under an operational lease, the school unit is not seeking eventual ownership of the leased asset. When ownership is the goal, the lease is a capital lease.

the month, the notice must be published no later than the twelfth of the month.)[77] When the proposal involves acquiring an interest in real property, the statute requires that the notice describe

- the interest to be acquired,
- the proposed cost of the interest,
- the governing board's intention to acquire the interest,
- the source of moneys to fund the acquisition, and
- any other information needed to reasonably describe the acquisition.

Preliminary Costs of Land Acquisition

The statute requires that the public hearing be held before any expenditures are made on the project. What if the local government makes expenditures before actual acquisition, as part of the process of deciding whether to acquire the site? At least two sorts of preliminary expenditures are frequently made. First, the government might pay for surveys or environmental or other testing on the site, to determine if the site is suitable for industrial uses. Second, the government might acquire an option on the site, paying the owner for the option. If the ultimate authority to acquire a site is G.S. 158-7.1, any preliminary expenditures related to that site are also pursuant to the statute, and the hearing should be held before the preliminary expenditures are made. Thus both of the examples listed above trigger the requirement of a public hearing under this reading of the statute (and the government would not need to hold a further hearing when it was actually ready to acquire the property).

Once the hearing has been held, the governing board may authorize the local government to expend funds for the property.

D. Local Libraries

Most local libraries are agencies of county or city government, and normally the county or city itself acquires any real property necessary for library facilities. If a county or city has appointed a library board of trustees, however, G.S. 153A-263(3) requires the county or city to seek the recommendations of the trustees before acquiring property for the library by purchase, lease, or eminent domain.

---

77. *See infra* § 604-G for a discussion of how days are counted for notice requirements.

E. Uniform Relocation Act

If a local government acquires real property and pays for the property, in whole or part, with federal moneys, the transaction normally is subject to the Uniform Relocation Assistance and Real Property Acquisition Policies Act of 1970, usually called the Uniform Relocation Act.[78] This act mandates procedures governing the negotiations to purchase the property and requires financial assistance, in addition to just compensation for real property, to persons and businesses displaced by federally financed projects. The additional financial assistance includes payment of moving expenses and payments for replacement housing. The Uniform Relocation Act and its implementing regulations are detailed, and they will not be summarized or discussed in this book. Rather, local governments receiving grant funds that subject them to the act should work with the grantor agency to ensure that the act's requirements are met.[79]

§ 308. Procedures

The Open Meetings Law

The North Carolina open meetings law[80] contains two provisions that allow closed sessions to discuss certain matters related to acquiring real property. This section discusses those provisions and mentions now-repealed provisions of the law that once allowed closed sessions for other property-related discussions.[81]

A. Acquisition of Real Property

The most important of these provisions permits a public body to hold a closed session to "establish, or to instruct the public body's staff or negotiating agents concerning the position to be taken by or on behalf of the public body in negotiating the price and other material terms of a contract or proposed contract for the acquisition of real property by purchase, option, exchange, or lease [143-318.11(a)(5)]." The statutory

---

78. 42 U.S.C. §§ 4601 through 4638 (1995).

79. North Carolina law implements the Uniform Relocation Act in G.S. 133-5 through -18.

80. G.S. 143-318.9 through -318.18.

81. The open meetings law, including the provisions summarized in this section, is fully discussed in DAVID M. LAWRENCE, OPEN MEETINGS AND LOCAL GOVERNMENTS IN NORTH CAROLINA: SOME QUESTIONS AND ANSWERS (Institute of Government, 5th ed. 1998).

language includes two important limitations on the use of this closed-session authorization. First, it only applies to acquiring *real* property; no provision of the open meetings law permits closed sessions to discuss acquiring *personal* property. Second, it only applies to acquisitions by purchase, option, exchange, or lease. If someone offers to donate property to a local government, the provision does not permit a closed session to discuss the terms of the donation. (It does not apply to acquisition by eminent domain either, but another provision of the open meetings law, discussed next, allows discussions of condemnation actions in closed session.)

Site Selection. An earlier version of this provision in the open meetings law also explicitly permitted closed sessions at which a public body could discuss which parcels of property it wished to acquire. That language was removed from the statute in 1994 and public bodies may, in general, no longer hold closed sessions to consider site selection. Of course, if site selection itself is a matter to be negotiated with the property owner (for example, one owner has two or three potential sites), that is a material term of the contract of purchase, and the statute allows a closed session to discuss any material term.[82]

B. Eminent Domain Actions

Another important provision permits a closed session to "consider and give instructions to an attorney concerning the handling or settlement of a claim, judicial action, mediation, arbitration, or administrative procedure [143-318.11(a)(3)]." This provision supports closed sessions to authorize eminent domain actions and to discuss those actions once they have been brought.

C. Repealed Provisions

Before 1994 the open meetings law also permitted closed sessions (1) to consider and authorize gifts or bequests of personal property and (2) to consider and authorize acquisition of paintings, sculptures, manuscripts, and other works suitable for a museum, library, or archive. Both provisions were repealed in 1994, and the open meetings law no longer permits closed sessions for those purposes.

---

82. The state Attorney General's Office agreed with this interpretation of the law in a letter to John L. Holshouser, Jr., Feb. 13, 1995, copy on file with author.

§ 309. Procedures

Payment of Taxes

When a public agency acquires property from a private party, the property is normally subject to a property tax lien; it may also be subject to a lien for special assessments. For example, if property is acquired in May, a property tax lien for the *succeeding* fiscal year (starting the next July 1) attached to the property on the preceding January 1.[83] When a local government buys property subject to a property tax lien, G.S. 105-385(c) requires the government to deduct from the purchase price the amount of any taxes constituting a lien and the amount of any special assessments or installments then due. The purchaser then pays these amounts to the proper taxing or assessing unit or units. If the purchasing local government fails to make this deduction and payment, the statute makes it liable to the taxing and assessing unit or units for the amount of the tax or assessment. Presumably, the purchasing government also remains liable for any special assessment installments falling due in future years.

§ 310. Procedures

Federal Tax Information Returns

The Internal Revenue Code requires a local government, like others, to file tax information returns in certain situations in which the local government acquires property. This section describes the local government's obligations with respect to two such returns: Form 1099 returns when the local government acquires property in any way, and forms 8282 and 8283 when it receives gifts of property.

A. Form 1099

Section 6045(e) of the Internal Revenue Code requires the person in charge of the closing on many real estate transactions to file an information return with the Internal Revenue Service concerning each transaction.[84] In North Carolina the person in charge of the closing is normally the attorney representing the buyer or other transferee of the property.

---

83. G.S. 105-355.

84. The return is made on Form 1099S, Proceeds from Real Estate Transactions.

Although the tax regulations exempt from the reporting requirement transactions in which a government is *conveying* the property, they do not exempt transactions in which a government is *acquiring* the property.[85]

Subject to the exceptions noted below, this real estate information return must be filed whenever a local government acquires property through a "real estate transaction"—a sale or exchange supported by consideration of "money, indebtedness, property other than money, or services."[86] The two principal groups of exceptions concern the nature of the transfer and the nature of the transferor. First, the requirement does not apply to gifts, because the transferee (the acquiring government in our case) has not offered consideration in that situation. It does not apply to transfers of property "in full or partial satisfaction of any indebtedness secured by the property." And it does not apply when the total consideration given for the property is less than $600.[87] Second, the requirement does not apply when the transferor is a corporation, a government, or a developer who in the current year (or in either of the two previous years) expects to or will sell or exchange at least twenty-five separate parcels of property to at least twenty-five different buyers.[88]

Thus, given the exceptions, when a local government acquires property from one or more individuals, from a partnership, from a trust, or from any other entity that is not a corporation, a government, or a developer with a sufficient number of real estate transactions, the person in charge of the closing will usually have to comply with the real estate–reporting requirement. The requirement applies not only to voluntary acquisitions but also to acquisitions made through use of the power of eminent domain. There are three kinds of acquisitions, however, that governments make to which the requirement does not or might not apply.

First, it does not apply to easements received through dedication. The most common form of dedication, as noted earlier in Section 302-B, occurs when a subdivider includes an express offer of dedication on the face of the subdivision plat. Although the subdivider receives economic

---

85. This subject is discussed in greater detail in David M. Lawrence & William L. Christopher, *Informational Returns on Real Estate Transactions*, Loc. Gov't Law Bull. No. 45 (Institute of Government, Aug. 1992).

86. Treas. Reg. § 1.6045-4(b)(1) (1992).

87. This first group of exceptions is set out in *id.* § 1.6045-4(c).

88. This second group of exceptions is set out in *id.* § 1.6045-4(d).

benefit from making the offer of dedication—she receives subdivision plat approval—she does not receive money, indebtedness, property, or services from the government. Therefore this most common form of dedication does not meet the regulatory definition of a real estate transaction. Other, less common forms of dedication are even more in the nature of gifts, and so they too are not included within the transactions that must be reported.

Second, it appears that the information-reporting requirement does not apply to foreclosures resulting from unpaid property taxes or special assessments. As noted earlier, the regulations except transfers "in full or partial satisfaction of any indebtedness secured by the property so transferred including a foreclosure."[89] Property taxes and special assessments are debts owed to government, and North Carolina law creates a lien on the taxed or assessed property in favor of the government to secure payment of these debts. Therefore tax and assessment foreclosures fit within the exception.

Third, the requirement does not apply to many utility easement acquisitions, because the consideration paid by the local government is less than $600. If the government pays $600 or more, however, this "de minimis" exception does not apply and the information return must be prepared and filed.

B. Forms 8282 and 8283 (Gifts of Property)

If a federal taxpayer makes a gift to a local government, the taxpayer is entitled to a deduction from taxable income for a charitable contribution; one form of charitable contribution to a local government is a gift of property. The Internal Revenue Code denies a deduction for a charitable contribution of $250 or more "unless the taxpayer substantiates the contribution by a contemporaneous written acknowledgment of the contribution by the donee organization."[90] The donee organization's acknowledgment must include "a description (but not value) of any property other than cash contributed."[91] A letter from a local government that has received a donation of property will satisfy this acknowledgment requirement.

---

89. *Id.* § 1.6045-4(c)(ii).

90. I.R.C. § 170(f)(8)(A) (West 1999). The taxpayer escapes this requirement if the "donee organization files a return, on such form and in accordance with such regulations as the Secretary [of the Treasury] may prescribe." *Id.* § 170(f)(8)(D).

91. *Id.* § 170(f)(8)(B).

Taxpayers who contribute property worth more than $5,000 to a government (or other charity) face additional substantiation requirements, and these directly implicate the donee organization, including any donee local government. If the taxpayer values the property at $5,000 or more, the taxpayer must have the property appraised and then prepare an *appraisal summary* that is attached to the taxpayer's tax return. The appraisal summary is included on Form 8283, and tax regulations require that the form be signed by an official of the donee organization. By signing, the donee organization signals its understanding that if the property is sold or otherwise conveyed within the next two years, then the Internal Revenue Code imposes additional reporting requirements on the donee organization.[92] The regulations make clear, however, that the donee organization bears no responsibility for the value placed on the property; that is, between the taxpayer and the Internal Revenue Service.

If the donee organization sells, exchanges, or otherwise disposes of donated property worth more than $5,000 within two years after receiving the property, the Internal Revenue Code requires that the organization (including a local government) file an information return within 125 days after the disposition. The return, made on Form 8282, requires a description of the property and when it was donated, the amount received by the donee on disposition, and the date of disposition.[93] The donee organization must also send a copy of this return to the donor.

---

92. Treas. Reg. § 1.170A-13(c)(4)(iii) (1984). The pertinent language in the regulation reads as follows:

> In the case of a donee that is a governmental unit, the person who signs the appraisal summary for such donee shall be the official authorized by such donee to sign appraisal summaries. The signature of the donee on the appraisal summary does not represent concurrence in the appraised value of the contributed property. Rather, it represents acknowledgment of receipt of the property described in the appraisal summary, on the date specified in the appraisal summary and that the donee understands the information reporting requirements imposed by section 6050L and § 1.6050L-1.

93. I.R.C. § 6050L (West 1999). The 125-day deadline is established by Treas. Reg. § 1.6050L-1(f)(2)(i) (1988).

IV

Changing the Use of Property

§ 401. Introduction

When a local government acquires property, it usually intends a specific use for the property. Sometimes that specific use is reflected in the interest acquired. For example, a city may purchase an easement specifically limited to street or utility purposes. Or a county may be given a defeasible fee in land, conditioned on the property's use as a park. In addition, when property is acquired through dedication, the interest acquired is an easement, limited in its permitted uses. Oftentimes, of course, the local government acquires a fee simple absolute, and therefore the land records do not reveal the government's intended use of the property.

This chapter considers the real, and alleged, restrictions on a local government's ability to change the uses to which it puts its property. With certain classes of property a government may not change the use of the property without bringing an eminent domain action to acquire interests in the property held by others. In most cases, however, a government can make a change in use without difficulty.

It should be noted that much of what is said in this chapter about changes of use also applies when a local government decides to dispose of property it no longer needs.

§ 402. Change in Use

The Usual Case

When a local government holds title to property in fee simple absolute and none of the special limitations discussed later in this chapter apply (and they apply only rarely), the law permits changes in use. Whether to change the use of property and what the new use will be are matters within the discretion of the unit's governing body.[1] Furthermore, the person who originally conveyed the property to the local government retains no interest in the property and may not, upon a change in use, demand a reversion of the fee or a right to repurchase the property.[2] These rules were established by the courts and have been confirmed by G.S. 160A-265, which expressly permits those local governments subject to Article 12 of G.S. Chapter 160A to change the use of government-owned property.

§ 403. Property Held in Defeasible Fee

A. In General

Section 204 noted that a local government's statutory authority to acquire property normally includes authority to acquire title in fee simple defeasible. A frequent condition attached to a defeasible fee held by a local government is that the property be used for a specific purpose, such as a park,[3] a school,[4] a parking lot,[5] or a library.[6] If the government abandons or changes the required use, that action either terminates the government's title in the property (if the government holds a fee simple determinable) or activates the grantor's right of reentry (if the

---

1. School Dist. v. Kansas City, 382 S.W.2d 688 (Mo. 1964) (within city's discretion to permit school district to build library in city park); Carlson v. City of Fremont, 142 N.W.2d 157 (Neb. 1966) (within city's discretion to construct fire station in city park). In Haynes v. Faulkner County, 932 S.W.2d 328 (Ark. 1996), a county attempted to bind itself to a single use of property by entering into a 99-year "lease" of the property with a county department. The court held that the "lease" was invalid and that future county officials would retain the discretion to change the use of the property.

2. Turgeon v. City of Somersworth, 358 A.2d 672 (N.H. 1976).

3. See, e.g., East Chicago Co. v. City of East Chicago, 87 N.E. 17 (Ind. 1909).

4. See, e.g., Lackey v. Hamlet City Bd. of Educ., 258 N.C. 460, 128 S.E.2d 806 (1963); Duplin County Bd. of Educ. v. Carr, 15 N.C. App. 690, 190 S.E.2d 653 (1972).

5. See, e.g., City of Laurel v. Powers, 366 So. 2d 1079 (Miss. 1979).

6. See, e.g., City of Klamath Falls v. Bell, 490 P.2d 515 (Or. Ct. App. 1971).

Local governments also acquire fee simple defeasible titles subject to other conditions. For example, in Henry H. Stambaugh Auditorium Ass'n v. City of Youngstown, 55 N.E.2d 672 (Ohio Ct. App. 1943), the condition was that the city construct a road through donated land within ten years. When the city did not, the court allowed the grantor to reclaim the land.

government holds a fee simple subject to a condition subsequent). Thus without a waiver of the grantor's rights a local government holding property by defeasible fee may not change the use of the property and continue to hold title to it.

If a local government wishes to change the use of property it believes it holds in defeasible fee, the government should first examine the title documents closely. Defeasible fees are legal, but because they allow one generation to bind later generations in the use of land the courts have resisted their easy creation. Unless the grantor's intention to create a fee simple defeasible is unmistakable, a court is likely to hold the title to be a fee simple absolute.[7] This sort of judicial construction has helped North Carolina local governments in the past.[8] Therefore a government that holds a possible fee simple defeasible interest in land should consider whether the title documents can be construed as creating a fee simple absolute.

Ultimately, though, governments hold some property in fee simple defeasible, conditioned on a specific use of the property. The grantor's interest, whether a possibility of reverter or a right of reentry, is not subject to the Rule Against Perpetuities,[9] nor is it necessarily extinguished by the Marketable Title Act.[10] Therefore, even if the local government acquired title generations ago, a change of use (or attempted

---

7. PATRICK K. HETRICK & JAMES B. MCLAUGHLIN, JR., WEBSTER'S REAL ESTATE LAW IN NORTH CAROLINA § 4-13 (4th ed. 1994) (hereinafter WEBSTER).

8. E.g., Washington City Bd. of Educ. v. Edgerton, 244 N.C. 576, 94 S.E.2d 661 (1956) (property deeded to school unit "upon condition that the [property] shall be held and possessed by the [school unit] only so long as the said property shall be used for school purposes"; because the deed included no power of termination or right of reentry, the court held it conveyed a fee simple absolute); Station Assoc., Inc. v. Dare County, 350 N.C. 367, 513 S.E.2d 789 (1999) (property deeded to United States "for the purpose of carrying out the intentions of Congress in providing for the establishment of Life-Saving Stations" and to be held by the United States "for the purposes above named for the term of this covenant"; because the deed included no power of termination or right of reentry, the court held it conveyed a fee simple absolute and United States could later convey property to Dare County).

9. WEBSTER, supra note 7, § 4-14. The Rule Against Perpetuities is defined in the glossary.

10. Even when the local government has held title to the property for more than thirty years, it will usually be the initial grantee of the defeasible fee, and therefore its deed will disclose the possibility of reverter or right of reentry. Because of that, the Marketable Title Act does not apply. G.S. 47B-3(1) (Cum. Supp.). (The Marketable Title Act is defined in the glossary.)

sale) might still extinguish the government's interest in the property. Nor may the General Assembly permit the owning government to change the use; legislation to that end would constitute a taking of the grantor's interest. If a local government wishes to retain the property but change the use, its only choices are to negotiate with the grantor (or whoever now holds the grantor's interest) or to bring an action to condemn the grantor's interest and thereby vest a fee simple absolute in the government.[11]

B. Title to Buildings on Land Held by Defeasible Fee

If a local government has constructed buildings or other improvements on land it holds in fee simple defeasible, who holds title to the buildings if the local government breaches a condition attached to the fee and loses its title to the land? Normally, buildings and other improvements are fixtures and follow title to the land. Thus the usual expectation is that loss of the fee in the land also causes loss of any buildings on the land.

Loss of buildings has not, however, been the inevitable result when a public agency has been the owner of the defeasible fee. Although several state courts have held that public buildings revert along with the fee,[12] others have held they do not, thereby permitting the local government to move the building to another location.[13] Courts in this latter group have adopted one of two rationales for their decisions. Some of the courts argue that a reversion of any building is inconsistent with statutory

---

11. If the local government has statutory authority to condemn the grantor's interest, it is possible that a court could deny use of a right of reentry and instead require the grantor to seek damages under the inverse condemnation statute. *See* Martin v. City of Seattle, 728 P.2d 1091 (1986), in which the court refused to allow the grantor's heirs to exercise their right of reentry against the city but instead directed the city to compensate the heirs for taking their interest in the property. Damages in inverse condemnation was also the relief granted in City of Laurel v. Powers, 366 So. 2d 1079 (Miss. 1979).

12. Williams v. Kirby Sch. Dist. No. 32, 181 S.W.2d 488 (Ark. 1944) (school building); New Hebron Consol. Sch. Dist. v. Sutton, 118 So. 303 (Miss. 1928) (school building); North Hampton Sch. Dist. v. North Hampton Congregational Soc'y, 84 A.2d 833 (N.H. 1951) (school building).

13. *E.g.,* Low v. Blakeney, 85 N.E.2d 741 (Ill. 1949) (school building); Rose v. Board of Directors, 179 P.2d 181 (Kan. 1947) (school building); Dickenson v. Board of Trustees, 204 S.W.2d 418 (Tex. Civ. App. 1947) (school building).

requirements that public buildings be sold by competitive procedures.[14] This argument, however, assumes the point in issue—that there is a title to the buildings separate from that in the land. Otherwise, the requirement for competitive sale would also block reversion of the land itself, and no court has suggested that outcome.

The second rationale characterizes the buildings as trade fixtures, which generally are exceptions to the rule that fixtures become part of the real estate.[15] Although no North Carolina case is directly on point, one early decision suggests that the North Carolina courts might accept this rationale. In *Western N.C. Railroad v. Deal*,[16] a railroad had abandoned an easement on which it had built a station house. When the fee holder asserted title to the building, the court held that it was a trade fixture, built solely for the railroad's business and not to aid in the enjoyment of the freehold. Consequently the court permitted the railroad to remove the building. Thus North Carolina law recognizes that buildings can be trade fixtures, opening the possibility that this state's courts might accept this second rationale.

§ 404. Property Held Under a Right of Repurchase

Much of what was just said about changing the use of property held in fee simple defeasible also applies to property held subject to an option to repurchase. A frequent condition triggering the option right is a change in use of the property. If that is the condition, and the local government owner changes the use it makes of the property, the original grantor can require the government to resell the property to her.

There is one important difference between an option to repurchase and a defeasible fee. As the last section noted, the grantor's future interest under a defeasible fee is not subject to the Rule Against Perpetuities. An option to repurchase, however, is, and for that reason some options

---

14. *E.g.,* Independent School Dist. No. 7 v. Barnes, 228 P.2d 939 (Id. 1951); Rose v. Board of Directors, 179 P.2d 181 (Kan. 1947); Schwing v. McClure, 166 N.E. 230 (Ohio 1929).

15. Dickerman v. Town of Pittsford, 80 A.2d 529 (Vt. 1951).

16. 90 N.C. 110 (1884).

are unenforceable.[17] If the Rule has invalidated the option right, the owning government may change the use it makes of the property without endangering its title.

§ 405. Property Acquired Through Dedication

No North Carolina case deals directly with a local government's authority to change the use of (or convey) property acquired by dedication from a private dedicator. The text writers, though, are unanimous on the issue: property acquired through dedication may not be put to a use inconsistent with the dedication (nor conveyed for an inconsistent use) unless, at the least, the dedicator has relinquished or conveyed to the government her rights in the property.[18]

This result conforms to the theory of dedication. Under that theory, dedication conveys to the public an easement for one or more public uses; the dedicator retains the fee.[19] This is true whether the dedication is of a street right-of-way, a use normally conveyed by easement, or of a park or other activity that we usually associate with fee ownership by the government.[20] An easement, of course, is a limited interest, and with a dedication the easement is limited to the use or uses permitted by the dedication. Any other use, even a public one, constitutes an additional burden on the fee interest for which the fee holder is entitled to compensation.[21]

---

17. Peele v. Wilson County Bd. of Educ., 56 N.C. App. 555, 289 S.E.2d 890 (1982).

18. 1 SANDRA M. STEVENSON, ANTIEAU ON LOCAL GOVERNMENT LAW § 24.12(2) (2d ed. 1999); 11A EUGENE MCQUILLIN, THE LAW OF MUNICIPAL CORPORATIONS §§ 33.74, 33.77 (3d ed. rev. vol. 1991) (hereinafter McQuillin); 4 HERBERT THORNDIKE TIFFANY, THE LAW OF REAL PROPERTY § 1113 (3d ed. 1975) [hereinafter TIFFANY].

19. White v. Northwestern N.C.R.R. Co., 113 N.C. 611, 18 S.E. 330 (1893); MCQUILLIN, *supra* note 18, § 33.68.

In many subdivision street dedications, the subdivider conveys the fee in the street to the abutting lot owners; in such a case, what is said in the section about the fee interest of the dedicator applies instead to these abutters.

20. TIFFANY *supra* note 18, at § 1112.

21. *E.g.,* Rouse v. City of Kinston, 188 N.C. 1, 123 S.E. 482 (1924) (water lines in street additional burden on fee).

Issues sometimes arise as to whether or not a new use of a dedicated easement is within the terms of the dedication. *See, e.g.,* City of Scottsdale v. Thomas, 753 P.2d 1207 (Ariz. Ct. App. 1988) (easement for flood protection

Furthermore, with some dedicated property, persons besides the dedicator or her heirs or assigns have rights in the property, and a change in use might constitute a taking of these other rights. When a developer sells a lot in a subdivision by reference to a plat, that sale not only constitutes an offer of dedication to the public of all the public spaces shown on the plat; it also conveys a private easement in those spaces to each person owning a lot in the subdivision.[22] When the offer of public dedication is accepted, the private rights merge with the public rights, but a change in use probably separates the two sets of rights again, raising a possible need to compensate those lot owners as well as the fee holder.[23]

The General Assembly can no more authorize a local government to change the use of (or convey for an inconsistent use) dedicated property, without compensation to the owners of these private interests, than it can authorize a government to take, without compensation, any other private estate or interest in land.[24]

---

and roadway allows use as an equestrian trail); Lawson v. State, 730 P.2d 1308 (Wash. 1986) (railroad easement, transferred to local government, does not include use as hiking trail).

22. *E.g.*, Brooks v. Muirhead, 223 N.C. 227, 25 S.E.2d 889 (1943); Conrad v. W. End Hotel & Land Co., 126 N.C. 776, 36 S.E. 282 (1900).

23. *See* Town of Blowing Rock v. Gregorie, 243 N.C. 364, 90 S.E.2d 898 (1956) (city may not vacate subdivision street without consent of lot owners). *See also* the discussion in DAVID M. LAWRENCE, PROPERTY INTERESTS IN NORTH CAROLINA CITY STREETS § 4.03 (Institute of Government 1985).

24. In the case of Wishart v. City of Lumberton, 254 N.C. 94, 118 S.E.2d 35 (1961), the North Carolina Supreme Court might be understood to have suggested that such legislative authority was possible. (This case was discussed in § 302-C, *supra*.) In *Wishart* the court stated:

> Where, however, property is purchased for the declared purpose of use as a public park or *dedicated by gift for that purpose*, or if acquired without any specific intent as to its use, has thereafter been definitely set aside for the sole and specific use as a public park, the governing authorities of a municipality may not, *without legislative authority*, dispose of the property or put it to an entirely different and inconsistent use. *Id.* at 96, 118 S.E.2d at 36 (emphasis added).

But it must be remembered that *Wishart* involved only a quasi-dedication, in which the dedicator was the government itself. In such an instance the fee holder is either the local government itself or the public for which it acts. If the latter, the General Assembly should be able to act on that public's behalf to release its rights in the property. If the fee holder rights are held by identifiable private

§ 406. Property Held in Trust

If a local government holds property in trust and the trust requires a specific use of the property, and if circumstances suggest that the property's use should be changed, the local government may be able to accomplish the change through the *cy-pres* doctrine. Nevertheless, if the change is desired because of the government's needs, rather than because conditions have caused a failure of the trust, the doctrine may not be applied. In that instance, it may be necessary to condemn the interest in the trust properties held by the settlor or his heirs.

§ 407. Property Acquired Through Condemnation

Property acquired through the power of eminent domain is, by force of the procedure, acquired for a specific use. If circumstances thereafter change, and the property is not needed for that use, the former owners of the property have sometimes sought either an outright return of the property or a right to repurchase. The courts, including North Carolina's, have uniformly rejected these attempts.[25] They point out that the government acquired a fee simple absolute, and while the intended use justified the condemnation, it did not limit the estate conveyed to the government. (Of course, if the government acquired only an easement, it may not change the use to one not encompassed within the easement.)

This judicial result has been reinforced in North Carolina by statute. G.S. 40A-10 provides that when condemned property "is no longer needed for the purpose for which it was condemned, it may be used for any other public purpose."[26]

---

parties, however, not even legislative consent would avoid the need for compensation for taking the fee holder's interest.

25. Torrence v. City of Charlotte, 163 N.C. 562, 80 S.E. 53 (1913) (no reversion to original owner when use for which property condemned is changed); *cf.* Town of Morganton v. Hutton & Bourbonnais Co., 251 N.C. 531, 112 S.E.2d 111 (1960) (original owner retains no rights in property condemned in fee simple). Some of the more recent cases from other states are Mainer v. Canal Auth., 461 So. 2d 989 (Fla. 1985); Galloway v. Board of Comm'rs, 271 S.E.2d 784 (Ga. 1980); Bottillo v. State, 386 N.Y.S.2d 475 (N.Y. App. Div. 1976); and Gilbert v. Franklin County Water Dist., 520 S.W.2d 503 (Tex. Civ. App. 1975).

26. G.S. 40A-70 (Cum. Supp.) permits, but does not require, a public condemnor to reconvey back to the condemnee any property taken by condemnation and no longer needed for the purpose for which it was condemned. This authorization is described in § 608-K4, *infra*.

§ 408. Property Acquired with Earmarked Moneys

A. Bond Proceeds

1. State Law

Two modern cases have considered whether a local government may change the use of or dispose of a general-obligation bond–financed facility. In 1982 the Georgia Supreme Court held that a local government could change the use of a bond-financed facility, as long as the change was not an abuse of discretion.[27] Four years later the Nebraska Supreme Court held that in some circumstances a local government could not dispose of property financed with voter-approved bonds, at least not without legislative authority.[28] The Nebraska court did not support its holding with any reasoning, however, and the Georgia court's conclusion seems preferable. If circumstances change so that it is to the local government's advantage to shift the use of or sell land or a facility, it is wasteful to prohibit the change or sale simply because acquisition or construction of the property was financed—perhaps decades earlier—by borrowed funds. If the governing board is practicing a fraud on the voters, the abuse of discretion standard fully protects the voters' interest.

There is no North Carolina case law directly on point, but a 1961 North Carolina Supreme Court decision[29] can be read to suggest that a North Carolina local government *may not* change the use of or sell property purchased or constructed with bond proceeds without either voter or legislative approval. On closer analysis, however, this interpretation is a misreading of the decision.

In the case, Reidsville had contracted to sell its former airport property and had sued to force the other party to carry out the contract. The trial court ruled for the city, but the Supreme Court vacated that decision and remanded the case to the trial court on the ground that the evidence was insufficient to support the lower court's findings and conclusions. Among the questions the court said should have been answered

---

27. Wheeler v. Dekalb County, 292 S.E.2d 855 (Ga. 1982). In 1904 the Missouri Court of Appeals stated that property purchased with bond proceeds could not be diverted to other purposes. Pickett v. Town of Mercer, 80 S.W. 285 (Mo. Ct. App. 1904). That was more a passing comment, however, than a direct holding, and the case was decided in an era that did not accord governing boards the discretion regarding governmental property that is standard today.

28. Abboud v. Lakeview, Inc., 391 N.W.2d 575 (Neb. 1986).

29. City of Reidsville v. Citizens Dev. Corp., 255 N.C. 274, 120 S.E.2d 730 (1961).

at the trial level was whether the property had been acquired by bond proceeds and whether any of the bonds remained outstanding.[30] The majority did not state why these questions needed answers, but a one-judge concurrence argued that the case presented this question: "May a municipal corporation which has with the approval of the electorate, incurred a debt to provide airport service, by order of the city council cease to furnish such service, sell the property, and use the proceeds in such manner as the city council may desire?"[31] The concurring opinion went on to make clear that its author, at least, thought the answer was no.[32]

To read the opinions in the Reidsville case, however, as suggesting a limit on changing the use of or selling property because it was originally financed with bond proceeds reads too much into the decision. A careful reading makes clear that the concurring judge was disturbed not about the bond-financed character of the property but about the possibility that the city was getting out of the airport business altogether. The other questions asked by the majority opinion make sense only if that was the concern of those judges as well.[33] For those reasons, the North Carolina case does not contradict the decision of the Georgia Supreme Court with which this section began.[34]

---

30. The court stated: "It does not appear from the record whether the 155.52 acres known as the Airport was acquired by the City of Reidsville from funds realized from [a] bond issue . . . or by other means, [and] whether there are presently any outstanding airport bonds . . . ." Id. at 276–77, 120 S.E.2d at 731.

31. Id. at 277, 120 S.E.2d at 732. Four judges joined the majority opinion, one judge concurred, and two judges dissented without opinion.

32. The concurring judge wrote: "If the city fathers would sell the property and thereby disable the community from rendering the service as directed by the electorate, special legislative authority must be obtained." Id. at 279, 120 S.E.2d at 733.

33. Those questions were:

[W]hether the [airport property] is the entire tract originally acquired for airport purposes, whether an airport is now being operated on a portion of the original tract with the 155.52 acres being surplus property not needed in that connection, whether an airport is being operated on other and separate property and this tract is no longer necessary for airport purposes, whether Reidsville has even constructed, maintained, and operated an airport, or whether an airport was formerly operated and was before [the sale] abandoned.

Id. at 277, 120 S.E.2d at 731–32.

34. Even if a court were to read the Reidsville case as limiting a local government's discretion in conveying bond-financed property and as requiring legislative authority for such a conveyance, it may be that G.S. 160A-265 is broad

2. Internal Revenue Code

If the bonds that financed the property are still outstanding and if the interest on those bonds was exempt from federal income tax, the Internal Revenue Code places limits on a local government's ability to change the use of bond-financed property. Basically, the new use cannot be one that, had it been the original use of the property, would have caused the bonds to lose their tax exemption. This issue is more likely to arise if a local government sells bond-financed property (rather than changes its use by the government itself), and so it is treated in detail in the next chapter, in Section 505-A.

B. Federal Funds

If a local government owns property acquired in whole or in part with federal funds, that funding source can affect the government's decision to change the use of or sell the property. This federal effect may arise either from the particular federal grant program that supplied the funds or from the general rules applicable to all grant-in-aid programs. Because of this possibility, a local government should check with the granting agency to ascertain any federal requirements before changing the use of or conveying property purchased with funds from that agency.

The possible effect of a particular grant program can be illustrated by the Community Development Block Grant (CDBG) program. This program imposes limitations on a government that has acquired real property with CDBG funds if that government wishes to change the use of the property, either for its own use or by conveying the property to someone else who will put it to a different use.[35] First, the government must give any affected citizens notice of the proposed change and an opportunity to comment on it. Second, the new use must be one that qualifies as meeting one of the national objectives of the CDBG program or, if it does not, the local government must reimburse its own CDBG program for the current fair market value of the property. These requirements apply until five years after an entitlement government stops participating in the CDBG program or until five years after the closeout of the specific CDBG grant that financed the property.

---

enough to provide the necessary legislative authority. That section specifically permits the local governments subject to Article 12 of G.S. Chapter 160A to change the use of property "without regard to the method or purpose of its acquisition or to its intended or actual governmental or other prior use."

35. These requirements are set out in 24 C.F.R. § 570.505 (1988).

In addition to statutory requirements affecting individual federal programs, all federal agencies that make grants to state and local governments have adopted a *Common Rule* that, among other topics, addresses the change of use or conveyance of property bought or constructed with federal grant moneys. Section ___.31[36] of the Common Rule deals with changes of use and disposition of real property, while Section ___ .32 deals with the use and disposition of equipment. Section ___ .31 requires that when federally financed real property is no longer needed by the grantee government, the government must seek disposition instructions from the federal agency that made the original grant. The agency can instruct the local government to retain the property for a different use, to sell the property, or to transfer it to the agency or to a third party. In the first two options, the local government must compensate the federal agency for the property. Section ___ .32 requires that if grant-funded equipment is no longer needed for the grant-funded purpose, it should either be retained and used in another program that is eligible for federal support or sold. (Sale requirements are set out below in Section 505-B.) Various actions with respect to such equipment may require approval from the granting agency. The Common Rule does not specify for how long property is subject to these requirements.

§ 409. Older Cemeteries

G.S. 160A-343 authorizes cities to change the use of city-owned properties no longer actively used as cemeteries. If no interment has occurred in the cemetery for at least ten years, the city may abandon the property for cemetery purposes, transfer all monuments and graves to other cemeteries, and either change the use of or sell the property.

---

36. Each agency has placed the Common Rule in that volume of the Code of Federal Regulations applicable to the agency. For example, the property change and disposition provisions for the Department of Housing and Urban Development are found at 24 C.F.R. §§ 85.31 and 85.32 (1988).

V

Disposing of Property:
Substantive Limitations

§ 501. Introduction

A. Ability to Dispose

Local governments typically possess, as a basic corporate power, general statutory authority to dispose of property.[1] The statutes also typically set out one or more detailed procedures by which a government may do so.[2] It would be natural to infer from this combination of statutes that a local government may sell or otherwise dispose of any property held by it, as long as it followed the appropriate statutory procedures. But that inference would be wrong.

Beginning in the nineteenth century, the courts—both nationally and in North Carolina—established limits on the apparent authority summarized above. They refused to allow disposal of certain categories of property, either because of the government's use of the property, or because of how the government acquired the property, or because of what moneys the government used to acquire the property. This chapter discusses those judicial limitations (as well as some limitations suggested by litigants but not adopted by the courts) and identifies those that have been overridden by legislative action. The chapter also discusses property interests that local governments may not convey without specific legislative authority;

---

1. For example, G.S. 160A-11 states that all North Carolina cities are municipal corporations and, among other corporate powers, may acquire and hold property and "from time to time may hold, invest, sell, or dispose of the same."

2. *See, e.g.,* G.S. Chapter 160A, Art. 12, discussed at length in Chapter VI, *infra*.

the susceptibility of local government property to adverse possession; the kinds and amount of consideration that a government may accept for its property; potential conflicts of interest when a government disposes of property; and a variety of rules concerning leases of local government property.

B. Whether to Dispose

Assuming that a local government possesses sufficient statutory authority to dispose of a parcel of property, whether it will do so is generally a matter of the government's discretion. In *Moore v. Wykle*[3] a group of citizens brought suit to (among other things) challenge the decision of a local school board to sell an old school it had been using for administrative offices. The trial court held that the challenge failed to state a claim for relief and the court of appeals affirmed. The appellate court noted that the decision as to whether a particular parcel is no longer needed and should be sold is "within the sound discretion of a board of education and cannot be restrained by the courts absent a manifest abuse of discretion or a disregard of law."[4]

§ 502. Limitations on Disposition

Property in Governmental Use

A. Introduction

At an early date the courts in North Carolina and elsewhere ruled that, absent legislative authority, a local government may not dispose of property currently held in governmental use.[5] Furthermore, the courts held

---

3. 107 N.C. App. 120, 419 S.E.2d 164 (1992).

4. *Id.* at 138, 419 S.E.2d at 175.

5. The earliest statement of this limitation in North Carolina is found in City of Southport v. Stanly, 125 N.C. 464, 34 S.E. 641 (1899) (town may not convey town common). *See also, e.g.,* Turner v. Commissioners of Hillsboro, 127 N.C. 153, 37 S.E. 191 (1900) (because town had specific authority to sell streets, adverse possession could run against the streets); Carstarphen v. Town of Plymouth, 180 N.C. 26, 103 S.E. 899 (1920) (town may not convey town hall); and Cline v. City of Hickory, 207 N.C. 125, 176 S.E. 250 (1934) (city may lease auditorium in city hall because city had never made use of it for city purposes).

National acceptance of the limitation is documented in 1 SANDRA M. STEVENSON, ANTIEAU ON LOCAL GOVERNMENT LAW § 24.12[5] (2d ed. 1999), and 10 EUGENE MCQUILLIN, LAW OF MUNICIPAL CORPORATIONS §§ 28.37, 28.38 (3d ed. rev. vol. 1999) [hereinafter MCQUILLIN].

that a general statutory authority to dispose of property was not sufficiently specific to authorize conveyance of *governmental* property. Rather,
the general authority extended only to property held in the government's
private capacity. The General Assembly appears to have attempted to
grant the specific statutory authority necessary to override this limitation through enactment of G.S. 160A-265, but the statute is not as plain
as it might be and does not apply to all kinds of local governments.
Therefore, the limitation might still be relevant.

Although the North Carolina Supreme Court mentioned the limitation as recently as 1966,[6] the last case in which the court actually invalidated a sale because of the limitation was decided in 1920.[7] That the
most recent judicial use of the limitation occurred eighty years ago raises
the question of whether it remains good law or is just the residue of an
outdated judicial assertiveness toward local government property transactions. The only policy justification offered by the North Carolina
Supreme Court for the limitation appears in the first case to announce
it. In *City of Southport v. Stanly*,[8] the court suggested that if a city could
sell one parcel of property currently in governmental use, it could sell
every parcel and thereby effectively abolish itself—a slippery slope
indeed.[9] Should actions that bizarre actually be threatened, the abuse of
discretion standard discussed in Section 101 would protect the public's
interest; for that reason the rigid limitation may be unnecessary. Nevertheless, absent further judicial decision, local governments should consider the limitation still in force; indeed, it remains alive in other states.[10]
If the limitation does remain valid, it affects a government's ability to
convey property still being actively used for governmental purposes; as a

---

6. In Bagwell v. Town of Brevard, 267 N.C. 604, 148 S.E.2d 635 (1966), the
court summarized the facts and holding of *Carstarphen, supra* note 5.

7. Carstarphen v. Town of Plymouth, 180 N.C. 26, 103 S.E. 899 (1920).

8. 125 N.C. 464, 34 S.E. 641 (1899).

9. "If the commissioners or aldermen could . . . sell one public square or
park, or building used for government purpose, why they could logically sell
every building owned by the town, and every public square, and by that means
destroy the means of properly governing the municipality." *Id.* at 467, 34 S.E. at
642.

10. Recent cases upholding the limitation include McRobie v. Mayor &
Comm'rs, 272 A.2d 655 (Md. 1971) (parking lot) and Valley View Tenant's Ass'n
v. Doorley, 312 A.2d 209 (R.I. 1973) (public housing).

practical matter it is most likely to be raised if a local government seeks to sell some or all of an existing park or to sell property at the margin of a large facility, such as a school or hospital campus.

B. Governmental Versus Private Use

The North Carolina courts have not defined *governmental* in the context of this doctrine, but the word appears to carry a much broader meaning here than it does in the familiar tort law distinction between governmental and proprietary activities. Courts of other states, applying the limitation in their states, have interpreted the word expansively. For example, they have characterized as governmental properties that were used for public utilities, for airports, for wharves, and for parking lots, all uses that are usually considered proprietary in the tort law context.[11] These courts essentially equate *governmental use* with public use. If the property is being used by the government for a public function, the limitation on sale applies.

For these courts, therefore, little property is held in *private* use. As a practical matter, property in private use usually falls into one of three categories. The first is property acquired through tax foreclosure or to protect other debts owed the government.[12] This kind of property is never intended for public use and usually is held only so long as is necessary to find a buyer. It is the quintessential example of property held in the government's private capacity. The second category is property acquired for a public use but for some reason never needed for the intended use.[13] And the third is property that was once put to a public use but that has been taken out of that use and now lies idle.[14] These second and third categories can be jointly characterized as *surplus* property.

Although, as noted above, no North Carolina case has specifically defined governmental and private uses, a number of decisions include statements consistent with the national understanding of those terms. In *City of Southport v. Stanly*, the court stated that a general authority to

---

11. See the cases cited in 2A Chester Antieau, Municipal Corporation Law § 20.32 (1984). (The newest edition of this work no longer includes a listing of cases organized by use of the property.)

12. *See* McSweeney v. Bazinct, 55 N.Y.S.2d 558 (N.Y. App. Div. 1945).

13. Carpenter v. City of Buffalo, 244 N.Y.S. 224 (N.Y. Sup. Ct. 1930), *aff'd*, 249 N.Y.S. 929 (N.Y. App. Div. 1931).

14. *E.g.*, Carter v. City of Greenville, 178 S.E. 508 (S.C. 1935).

sell city property did not extend to "any real estate with or without the building on it which is devoted to the purposes of government, including town or city hall, market houses, houses used for fire departments or for water supply, or for public squares or parks."[15] In *Cline v. City of Hickory*, the court noted that the city hall auditorium at issue in that case had never been used by the city in *any* of its activities and therefore had not been placed in a governmental use.[16]

C. Legislative Authority to Dispose of Property Held in Governmental Use

A general statutory authority to sell local government property is insufficient as authority to sell such property held in governmental use. What sort of additional authority is necessary? The earliest North Carolina case announcing the limitation implied that the General Assembly must specifically authorize each sale of such property,[17] but the state supreme court soon decided that a general authority to sell specific property or categories of property sufficed.[18] Furthermore, in 1919 the court held that the statute requiring voter approval before an electric distribution

---

15. 125 N.C. 464, 467, 34 S.E. 641, 642 (1899). *See also* Allen v. Town of Reidsville, 178 N.C. 513, 101 S.E. 267 (1919), in which the court quoted from the *Stanly* decision and then commented:

> The effect of [the *Stanly*] decision is that property of the city or town, such as parks, markets, city halls, waterworks, lighting plants, etc., held for the use of the public, are not within the provisions [of the statute generally authorizing sales of government property], and cannot be sold thereunder, and that, if sold at all, additional authority must be conferred by the General Assembly. 178 N.C. 513, 524, 101 S.E. at 272.

16. 207 N.C. 125, 176 S.E. 250 (1934).

17. In *Stanly* the court concluded its opinion by stating that "to enable the town or city authorities to sell such of the real estate of the towns or cities as is [in governmental use], there must be a special act of the General Assembly authorizing such sale or lease." *Id.* at 467–68, 34 S.E. at 642.

18. In Turner v. Commissioners of Hillsboro, 127 N.C. 153, 37 S.E. 191 (1900), the court upheld a sale of town commons pursuant to charter authority "to sell or dispose of from time to time . . . all or any part of the commons of said town." In Church v. Dula, 148 N.C. 262, 61 S.E. 639 (1908), the court upheld a sale of a street bed under charter authority to sell "all the land laid off as streets in the map of said town which is not now used as streets."

system could be sold constituted the necessary specific authority to sell that governmental operation;[19] that holding presumably extends to the modern counterpart of the 1919 statute.[20]

In 1982 the General Assembly enacted G.S. 160A-265, which appears to attempt to give blanket authorization to dispose of property held in governmental use. The statute authorizes any local government subject to Article 12 of G.S. Chapter 160A to "sell or dispose of real and personal property, without regard . . . to its intended or actual governmental or other prior use." The statute contains the magic word *governmental*; the difficulty arises from the concluding phrase "or other prior use" and specifically from inclusion of the word *other*. Grammatically, "other" must refer to an earlier word, and the natural choice is the word "governmental." If that is so, then the meaning of the statute is that property can be sold, without regard to its "actual [prior] governmental" use or "other prior use." That is, the reference is to property once but no longer in governmental use. Such a reading, though, reduces this portion of the statute to an authorization to dispose of surplus property. Because local governments already had authority to dispose of surplus property, a court might give a generous reading to the language in order to find meaning in it at all, and hold that it permits disposition of property *currently* in governmental use.[21] It would be preferable, though, to clarify the statute.[22]

---

19. Allen v. Town of Reidsville, 178 N.C. 513, 101 S.E. 267 (1919).

20. G.S. 160A-321.

21. This appears to have been done in Watts v. Town of Valdese, 65 N.C. App. 822, 310 S.E.2d 152 (1984). In that case the court upheld a sale of town property on the authority of G.S. 160A-265. Although the court did not identify the nature of the property involved or discuss how the statute resolved the dispute, the record reveals that the property was a city park and that the plaintiff alleged that the property had been declared surplus in order to sell it. (Record at 2–3, 5). The defendant city denied the allegation of subterfuge, and the trial court awarded summary judgment to the city, apparently believing that whether the property was in fact surplus was immaterial. The court of appeals affirmed.

22. Section 604-B discusses whether it is necessary for a local government's governing board to make a specific determination that property is surplus before beginning proceedings to convey the property.

§ 503. Limitations on Disposition

Property Acquired Through Dedication

Section 405 discusses in detail the barriers to changing the use made of property acquired through dedication. That discussion notes that the same barriers generally prevent the sale or other disposition of dedicated property, and the reader should refer to that section for details. In summary, a completed dedication conveys to the government only an easement for one or more public uses, and a sale (or a change in use) is likely to intrude on the dedicator's (or another's) retained interest in the fee. If that occurs, not even legislative authority obviates the need to compensate the fee holder for the loss of her interest.

Two exceptions exist to this general rule prohibiting disposition of dedicated property. First, if the property has been dedicated by the government to itself, then the General Assembly, as noted in Section 405, may permit a change in use or a conveyance of the property. The legislature has given the necessary permission through enactment of G.S. 160A-265.[23]

Second, a local government holding dedicated property should be able to convey that property to some other public agency or, indeed, private entity, that will continue to put the property to the dedicated use. As noted in Section 302-A, an offer of dedication is to the public generally, and the government accepts on behalf of the public. Changing the government that controls the property changes neither the use nor the public's right to the property and so has no effect on the retained rights of the dedicator. The same is true of a transfer to a private entity that will continue the dedicated use, such as transfer of utility easements to a privately owned utility that assumes responsibility for utility service within a community. Although no North Carolina case addresses this particular exception, administrative practice within North Carolina clearly recognizes it. The Department of Transportation controls many rural residential streets that it has acquired by dedication; when the streets are annexed by a city, the state routinely turns title to and control of the streets over to the city. Similarly, agreements between cities and counties sometimes provide that county-owned utility lines are automatically transferred to the city upon annexation, and those lines often

---

23. In appropriate part, G.S. 160A-265 permits a local government to "sell or dispose of real and personal property, without regard to the method . . . of its acquisition."

include dedicated utility easements. Although it is not clear whether special legislative authority is necessary for a local government to transfer dedicated property to another entity, if special authority is necessary G.S. 160A-265 is sufficient.

§ 504. Limitations on Disposition

Property Acquired Through Eminent Domain

Section 407 notes that persons whose property has been acquired by eminent domain sometimes seek return of the property if the condemning government changes the property's use from the purpose for which it was condemned. The same effort is sometimes made if the government decides to dispose of the condemned property. As was true with changes of use, the courts have uniformly rejected these attempts to interfere with disposition of the property.[24]

G.S. 40A-70 does permit a local government that no longer needs condemned property to convey it back to the original owner by private sale, but the statute does not mandate such a conveyance.[25] Rather, G.S. 40A-10 more generally permits a local government that no longer needs property for the purpose for which it was condemned to sell or otherwise dispose of the property "in the manner prescribed by law for the sale and disposition of surplus property."

§ 505. Limitations on Disposition

Property Acquired with Earmarked Moneys

A. Bond Proceeds

State Law

Section 408-A discusses the possibility of limitations under state law on either changing the use of or disposing of property acquired with bond proceeds; the reader should refer to that section.

---

24. *E.g.*, Neurlios v. City of Mobile, 57 So. 2d 819 (Ala. 1952); Torrence v. City of Charlotte, 163 N.C. 562, 80 S.E. 53 (1913).

25. This statute is described more fully in § 608-K4, *infra*.

Internal Revenue Code

In general the Internal Revenue Code (the Code) excludes from federal taxation the interest on local government bonds and other local government debt obligations.[26] (These bonds and other obligations are usually referred to collectively as *municipal bonds*.) Not all municipal bonds, however, are tax-exempt under federal law. Federal tax policy attempts to restrict the use of tax-exempt bonds by local governments to those projects that build or buy assets that are used by the government itself or by the public generally, so-called traditional governmental projects. If the proceeds of a municipal bond issue are used to finance the activities of private persons or entities, the Internal Revenue Code directs that, in many cases, the interest paid on that bond issue be included in taxable income.

Under federal law, if a private person or company participates in the ownership or operation of a bond-financed project or otherwise benefits from the project, the bond issue may be characterized as a *private activity* bond issue.[27] Although the Code makes some exceptions (for *qualified* private activity bonds), in general the interest paid on a private activity bond issue is not exempt from federal income tax.[28] Normally, a municipal bond issue is recognized as a private activity bond issue at the time the bonds are issued. But if the issuing government at a later date takes a "deliberate action" that causes the Code's private activity bond tests to be met at that later date (a private person or entity now owns the project or receives significant benefits from the project), the issue can at that time become a private activity bond issue.[29] If that happens, unless the issue becomes a qualified private activity issue the remaining interest payments on the bond issue will no longer be exempt from federal income tax. (Once bonds have been fully retired, the Internal Revenue Code is no longer interested in the bond project.) Among the kinds of actions that can cause a bond issue to become a private activity issue are changing the use of the bond-financed project, conveying the project to someone else, or leasing the project to someone else. (If the conveyance is to another government, or the change of use is to another governmental purpose, the

---

26. I.R.C. § 103 (West 1999).

27. *Id.* § 141.

28. *Id.* § 103.

29. A *deliberate action* is any action taken by the bond issuer that is within its control. Thus, the tax consequences of the action may well be inadvertent. Treas. Reg. § 1.141-2(d)(3) (1997).

Code rules do not apply.) The remaining paragraphs of this subsection summarize the rules about changes of use or conveyances of bond-financed projects. Before a local government changes the use of or disposes of any property financed with bonds that are still outstanding, however, the government should consult with its bond counsel about whether the planned change of use or sale will cause the remaining bonds to become taxable and how the government might avoid that outcome.

Sales in the ordinary course of business. If a local government borrows money to purchase personal property, such as automobiles; has a regular program of disposing of the property when it is no longer suitable for governmental purposes, such as auctioning off surplus automobiles; and places sales proceeds into a regular governmental fund so that they will be expended within six months; then sales pursuant to such a policy do not cause the borrowing to become a private activity bond issue.[30] This is true even if a particular sale takes place sooner than the policy normally provides for.[31]

Other sales or changes of use. For other conveyances or changes of use that might cause a bond issue to become a private activity bond issue and thus cause the remaining interest payments on the issue to become taxable, the local government can avoid that consequence by taking one of the remedial actions set out in the federal tax regulations. There are three possible remedial actions. First, the government can use the sale proceeds to pay off the remaining bonds in the bond issue (or to set up an escrow account for that purpose if the bonds cannot yet be paid off).[32] Second, the government can take the sale proceeds in cash and use that cash as if it were bond proceeds, for a use that does not qualify as a private activity bond.[33] For example, if a local government sells a bond-financed hospital, an appropriate remedial action would be to use the sale proceeds to construct a water treatment plant. Third, the government

---

30. *Id.* § 1.141-2(d)(4)(i) (1997).

31. The regulations give as an example the following: A city borrows to purchase police cars and has a policy of selling used police cars after five years to a local taxicab company. At that time, the city reasonably expects that the cars are worth no more than 25 percent of their original cost. If cars are sold pursuant to the policy, the sales have no effect on the taxability of the bond issue; even if the cars are sold after three years, the bonds remain tax-exempt if the city puts the sale proceeds into the general fund and reasonably expects to spend the proceeds within six months. *Id.* § 1.141-2(g) (example 4) (1997).

32. *Id.* § 1.141-2(d) (1997).

33. *Id.* § 1.141-2(e) (1997).

can assure that the new user of the property is a person or entity such that, if she or it had been the original user, the bonds would have been *qualified* private activity bonds.[34] As noted above, interest on qualified private activity bonds is still exempt from federal income tax.

B. Federal Grant Funds

Section 408-B discusses the limitations on changing the use or disposing of property acquired with federal assistance and notes that such limitations can arise both from the specific federal grant program involved and from the general requirements of the Common Rule adopted by all federal granting agencies (see Chapter 4, n. 36). Section ___.31 of the Common Rule directs that a local government that wishes to dispose of real property acquired with federal grant funds seek disposition instructions from the granting federal agency. Section ___.32, which applies to equipment acquired with federal grant funds and having a value at disposition of more than $5,000, gives the granting agency a right to reimbursement for the fair market value of the equipment at the time of disposition. (If the equipment is valued at $5,000 or less at the time of disposition, the local government has no obligation to the granting federal agency.) Therefore before a local government begins proceedings to dispose of federal grant-financed real property of any value or personal property worth more than $5,000, it should contact the granting agency for any special limitations or instructions.

C. Special Assessments

The courts of other states have occasionally been presented with the question of whether a local government may dispose of improvements financed in whole or in part with special assessments. The consistent answer has been yes, that the method of financing does not impose any special limitations on disposition.[35] Therefore North Carolina local governments may reasonably assume the answer would be the same in this state should the question be litigated here.

---

34. Treas. Reg. § 1.141-2(f) (1997).

35. *E.g.,* Ross v. City of Dearborn, 216 N.W.2d 419 (Mich. 1974) (citing other cases); Fisher v. Becker, 302 N.Y.S.2d 470 (N.Y. App. Div. 1969). Both these cases involved parking lots financed with special assessments.

§ 506. Limitations on Disposition

Particular Interests

In general the statutory authority to sell or otherwise dispose of property includes the authority to dispose of the fee or any lesser interest.[36] Nevertheless, the courts in North Carolina and elsewhere have established a few exceptions to that broad statement, and this section discusses those exceptions.

A. Security Interests

The authority to convey property does not, in and of itself, include authority to mortgage or otherwise create a security interest in property. This exception is fully discussed in Section 206, and the reader is referred to that section.

B. Options

Courts in a few states—although not all that have addressed the issue—have held that a local government's authority to convey property does not include authority to grant an option to purchase that property.[37] These courts typically argue that local government officials have fiduciary obligations similar to those of a trustee and then rely on the general rule that a trustee under a general power of sale may not give an option.[38] The rationale of these cases—both private trust and local government—is that the trustee's or government official's responsibility to determine whether a sale is appropriate must be exercised at the time of sale, not some months or even years before, when the option is granted.

---

36. *E.g.,* Huron-Clinton Metropolitan Auth. v. Attorney General, 379 N.W.2d 474 (Mich. Ct. App. 1985) (authority to sell includes authority to lease, citing cases from Arkansas, Kentucky, Ohio, and South Carolina); City of Idaho Springs v. Golden Sav. & Loan Ass'n, 480 P.2d 847 (Colo. Ct. App. 1970) (authority to sell includes authority to convey fee simple determinable). *But see* County Bd. v. Brown, 329 S.E.2d 468 (Va. 1985) (authority to sell permits conveyance of fee simple only and not leasehold).

37. *E.g.,* City of Tuskegee v. Sharpe, 288 So. 2d 122 (Ala. 1973); Rogers v. City of South Charleston, 256 S.E.2d 557 (W. Va. 1979). It should be noted that both these cases are fairly recent; this is not a doctrine that is suspect because of age.

38. *E.g.,* Adler v. Adler, 118 S.E.2d 456 (Ga. 1961); RESTATEMENT (SECOND) OF TRUSTS § 190(k); 3 AUSTIN WAKEMAN SCOTT & WILLIAM FRANKLIN FRATCHER, THE LAW OF TRUSTS § 190.8 (4th ed. 1988).

The North Carolina courts do not appear to have addressed this question, either for trusts or for local governments.[39] One hopes that the North Carolina courts would, should the issue arise, follow those states that do not require special legislative authority for options.[40] The cases denying the power to option make very little sense. If it is important that local government officials be able to exercise their discretion when they convey government property, why is that discretion less properly exercised at the time an option is given than when title is actually transferred? That officials made a poor deal is normally not grounds for invalidating a transaction, and it should not be so here. Until the North Carolina courts or the General Assembly address the question, however, some small doubt will linger about the ability of this state's local governments to grant options.

C. Street Easements

G.S. 160A-299 sets out a procedure under which a city may vacate a city street or alley.[41] Upon vacation, the city's property interest in the street or alley ends, and fee simple title is vested in the abutting owners.[42] Occasionally questions arise about whether a city must use this statute when it wishes to end its property interest in a street or whether it may use alternative methods. First, may a city *sell* its interest, perhaps to only one of the abutters, without using the vacation statute at all? Second, if a city does use the vacation statute, may it impose a charge on the abutters as a condition of closing the street? The charge would amount to compensation for the city's interest in the property.

The answer to the first question is in most cases no, although it may be yes if the city owns the fee simple interest in the street. The answer to the second question is always no. These conclusions are based on the following policy and legal considerations.

---

39. Some North Carolina appellate cases have involved options granted by local governments, but the litigants apparently did not question their validity. *E.g.*, Watts v. Town of Valdese, 65 N.C. App. 822, 310 S.E.2d 152 (1984).

40. *E.g.*, Siler v. City of Rossville, 315 S.E.2d 898 (Ga. 1984); Dahl v. City of Grafton, 286 N.W.2d 774 (N.D. 1980).

41. Counties have similar authority under G.S. 153A-241. Counties, however, have no ownership interests in the streets involved, and therefore the questions raised in this section are irrelevant to them.

42. *Id.* §160A-299(c). This statutory procedure is examined in detail in DAVID LAWRENCE, PROPERTY INTERESTS IN NORTH CAROLINA CITY STREETS §§ 4.01 through 4.06 (Institute of Government 1985).

1. In most cases the city holds only an easement in the street. An easement is the interest acquired when the city's title arises either from dedication or prescription.[43] Even when they acquire the street by purchase or eminent domain, many cities still acquire only an easement. If all the city holds is an easement for a public street, that is all it has to convey. Therefore once the city decides that no street is necessary, the city has nothing of value to sell.

2. Even if the city holds the fee to the street, abutting property owners also have an easement of sorts in the street, entitling them to access to their property from the street system.[44] If a street provides the only access to the property, this private right of access survives vacation of the street,[45] further reducing what the city has to sell.

3. If these private rights of access do not survive, however (because alternative access exists), and if the city does hold fee simple title to the street, the city may have the choice of following the vacation procedure and thereby abandoning all title to the street or of ignoring the vacation procedure and treating the street as normal surplus property. Courts in other states have allowed cities holding fee title to streets to convey the streets as surplus property.[46]

4. The vacation statute includes no provision for payment for the vacated streets. In such a circumstance, case law from other states holds that a city may not condition use of the statute on payment, any more than other police power actions may be conditioned upon payments from benefited citizens.[47] The North Carolina courts would probably agree.

Even though courts in some states support a city's right to sell a street it holds in fee, a city considering such a sale may still wish to obtain specific legislative authority to do so. The question is sufficiently unclear that the absence of legislation may create uncertainties about the title.

---

43. White v. Northwestern N.C. R.R. Co., 113 N.C. 611, 18 S.E. 330 (1893).
44. Department of Transp. v. Harkey, 308 N.C. 148, 301 S.E.2d 64 (1983).
45. Mosteller v. Southern Ry., 220 N.C. 275, 17 S.E.2d 133 (1941).
46. *E.g.,* Hoogenboom v. City of Beaufort, 433 S.E. 2d 875 (S.C. Ct. App. 1992). *But see* Walker v. Coleman, 540 So. 2d 983 (La. Ct. App. 1989), in which the court held that a city that no longer wants a street right-of-way must proceed through the vacation procedure rather than the general authority to sell surplus property.
47. Overton v. Scott Co., 356 So. 2d 134 (Ala. 1978).

The General Assembly can clearly enact such authority,[48] and it can enact authority permitting a city to require some payment from abutters before vacating the right-of-way.[49]

D. City Cemeteries

G.S. 160A-342 authorizes a city to convey a city cemetery, but only upon certain conditions. The sale must be to a religious organization or a cemetery licensed by the state. The grantee must agree to continue to use the property as a cemetery, must agree to maintain the cemetery, and must agree to use any perpetual care funds included in the conveyance only for cemetery maintenance. Apparently a city may not convey property used as a cemetery unless these conditions are met.

§ 507. Adverse Possession Against Local Government Property

Although inconsistent cases and incomplete statutes leave some residual doubt, North Carolina local government property, except for public streets and squares, apparently is vulnerable to adverse possession.[50] This state of the law is contrary to the general rule nationally, which excludes most government property from the normal doctrine of adverse possession.[51]

Two statutes are relevant to the question, although neither is decisive. G.S. 1-35 permits an assertion of title against the *state*, upon thirty years' adverse possession (or twenty-one years under color of title). Because the usual common law rule nationally is that there can be no adverse possession against a state,[52] one might infer that this statute was

---

48. In Church v. Dula, 148 N.C. 262, 61 S.E. 639 (1908), the North Carolina Supreme Court upheld statutory authority to sell city streets, granted in a local act of the General Assembly.

49. *Cf.* Parks v. Watson, 716 F.2d 646 (9th Cir. 1980) (city's charter procedure requires just compensation from abutter; the court holds that the city is asking too much in this case but does not question the city's basic entitlement to compensation).

50. The elements of adverse possession are listed in the glossary, *infra*.

51. The general rule nationally is summarized in R. P. Davis, *Annotation, Acquisition by Adverse Possession or Use of Public Property Held by Municipal Corporation or Other Governmental Unit Otherwise Than for Streets, Alleys, Parks, or Common*, 55 A.L.R.2d 554 (1957).

52. *Id.* § 13.

enacted to overcome the common law rule; absent the statute, state property would not be subject to adverse possession. Because the common law nationally also excludes most local government property from adverse possession[53] and because there is no comparable North Carolina statute that overturns that rule for local government property, the consequent implication is that there can be no adverse possession against local government property in this state. It would be an odd state of affairs, however, for the General Assembly to permit adverse possession against state property but not against the property of the state's political subdivisions.

The second statute, G.S. 1-45, specifically denies the possibility of adverse possession against "any part of a public road, street, lane, alley, square or public way." One might argue that this exception demonstrates that adverse possession is possible against local government property; otherwise there would be no need for special protection for streets and squares. This argument, however, forgets that the *state* also may have title to streets and squares, and in the absence of G.S. 1-45 these state properties would be susceptible to adverse possession under G.S. 1-35. Therefore the statutes are inconclusive.

The North Carolina cases, unfortunately, flatly contradict each other, but the more recent ones permit adverse possession against local government property. Five cases are relevant. The first is *State v. Long*,[54] decided in 1886, which held that twenty years' adverse possession of a portion of the public square in Rockingham was sufficient to vest title in the possessor. Just three years later, however, and without reference to *Long*, the court in *Moose v. Carson* stated flatly that no one could acquire city streets by adverse possession.[55] (The statute that is now G.S. 1-45 was not enacted until two years after this second case.) A decade later, in *Turner v. Commissioners of Hillsboro*, the court took yet another position, permitting adverse possession against property that the town had specific legislative authority to convey.[56] (*Moose* was distinguished in that there was no statutory power to convey a street, which was held in "trust for the public use.")[57]

---

53. *Id.* §§ 34, 46.
54. 94 N.C. 896 (1886).
55. 104 N.C. 431, 10 S.E. 689 (1889).
56. 127 N.C. 153, 37 S.E. 191 (1900).
57. *Id.* at 155, 37 S.E.2d at 192–93.

In 1916 the supreme court decided the fourth case and questioned the authority of both *Moose* and *Turner,* noting that those decisions seemed to "have overlooked the decision of the court in *State v. Long.*"[58] Finally (but still more than seventy years ago), the court simply permitted adverse possession to operate against town property, without mention of the earlier cases and without suggestion that there could be any doubt on the matter. In that final case, *Tadlock v. Mizell,*[59] the claimant had had thirty-five years' adverse possession of a street in Windsor by 1891, when the statutory bar on adverse possession of public streets was first enacted. Therefore, the court stated, the jury finding that the possession was in fact adverse "is determinative of the controversy."[60]

Thus the two most recent statements by the court permit adverse possession against local government property, except as limited by G.S. 1-45. This result is consistent with the express legislative policy that permits adverse possession against state-owned property and therefore should be assumed to be the law today.[61]

§ 508. Consideration

A. Introduction

There is a constitutional element to the question of whether a local government has received adequate consideration for property it conveys to another. Article I, Section 32, of the North Carolina Constitution provides that "[no] person or set of persons is entitled to exclusive or separate emoluments or privileges from the community but in consideration of public services." This Privileges and Emoluments Clause prohibits the state or any local government from making a gift of money or other public assets, and the North Carolina Supreme Court has indicated that giving away public property or selling it at well below its market value

---

58. Threadgill v. Wadesboro, 170 N.C. 641, 643, 87 S.E. 521 (1916) (court allows adverse possession against town street because possessor had occupied land under color of title for 43 years before enactment of G.S. 1-45).

59. 195 N.C. 473, 142 S.E. 713 (1928).

60. *Id.* at 476, 142 S.E. at 714.

61. Although the statutorily required period for adverse possession against state property is 30 years, none of the cases suggests that any period longer than the standard 20 years, *see* G.S. 1-40 (or seven years under color of title, *id.* § 1-38), is necessary for adverse possession against local government property.

falls within the prohibition.[62] Most of the procedures by which a local government is permitted to sell or otherwise dispose of property are competitive, and the court has indicated that the price resulting from an open and competitive procedure will be accepted as the fair market value of the property.[63] If a sale is privately negotiated, often factors besides price are part of the local government's calculation of whether to sell and to whom. Because of these additional factors, the consideration received will probably be considered constitutionally adequate unless strong evidence indicates that any nonmonetary consideration received is constitutionally inappropriate[64] or that the price received is so significantly below market value as to show an abuse of discretion.[65]

B. Nonmonetary Consideration

Although a government may not give away its property, the consideration it receives need not in all cases be monetary. The courts of North Carolina and elsewhere have accepted various forms of nonmonetary consideration, and this section discusses a few principles drawn from the cases.

1. Continued Public Use

It is well established that if a government conveys property to another party who will put the property to some public use, the promise to continue the property in public use constitutes sufficient consideration for the

---

62. *See* Redevelopment Comm'n v. Security Nat'l Bank, 252 N.C. 595, 114 S.E.2d 688 (1960).

63. *Id.*

64. *E.g.,* in Annunziato v. New Haven Bd. of Aldermen, 555 F. Supp. 427 (D. Conn. 1982), the city conveyed an abandoned school to a church-affiliated day school for one dollar. The court held the nonmonetary consideration was the continued operation of the day school; because it was church-affiliated, the subsidy to the school breached the constitutional wall between church and state.

65. Painter v. Wake County Bd. of Educ., 288 N.C. 165, 217 S.E.2d 650 (1975). *See* L'Esperance v. Town of Charlotte, 704 A.2d 760 (Vt. 1997), in which the court upheld, against the town, renewal clauses in leases of town property. The leases called for rental payments at a multiple of town tax rates, and changes in assessment practices had significantly lowered town tax rates since the leases were first entered into. Consequently, the town was receiving far less from the leases than it had originally anticipated. The court acknowledged the general point that rentals might be so low as to violate constitutional prohibitions on gifts of public property, but it held that the reasonableness of the leases was to be judged as of the time the leases were entered into and not later.

conveyance. The leading North Carolina case, *Brumley v. Baxter*,[66] illustrates the principle. The city of Charlotte conveyed surplus city property worth at least $52,500 to the Charlotte Veterans' Recreation Authority, without monetary consideration. Because the authority planned to put the property to a public use—recreation for veterans—the North Carolina Supreme Court held that the transaction did not violate the Privileges and Emoluments Clause of the constitution.[67] This principle offers constitutional context for G.S. 160A-279, which permits cities and counties to convey property by private sale to a nonprofit entity, if that nonprofit entity is carrying out a public purpose. Although the statute says nothing about consideration, the principle articulated in *Brumley* allows a conveyance to be made without monetary consideration. The recipient's use of the property to carry out a public purpose provides constitutionally adequate consideration.[68]

The rationale of the cases that uphold a government's ability to accept the continued public use of the property as adequate consideration for conveyance of property is that the property will continue to benefit the public for whose ultimate benefit it was originally acquired. In *Brumley*, for example, the property was conveyed by the city of Charlotte to the Charlotte Veterans' Recreation Authority; both grantor and grantee served the people of Charlotte. Likewise, the cases from other states involve conveyances to entities that serve the same public as the government making the conveyance. When the conveyance is of real property, this rationale will almost certainly hold true, inasmuch as real property cannot be moved. But personal property is moveable, and if the grantor

---

66. 225 N.C. 691, 36 S.E.2d 281 (1945).

67. Other states accept this principle. *E.g.*, Ulrich v. Board of Comm'rs, 676 P.2d 127 (Kan. 1984) (county may transfer hospital to nonprofit corporation that will provide hospital facilities; continued operation of hospital constitutes sufficient consideration); Brown v. Wildwood Volunteer Fire Co. 1, 550 A.2d 520 (N.J. Super. Ct. Ch. Div. (1988)) (city may lease space on boardwalk, for nominal consideration, to volunteer fire department, which uses space for fund-raising; provision of fire protection by department constitutes sufficient consideration); Rath v. Two Rivers Community Hosp., Inc., 467 N.W.2d 150 (Wis. Ct. App. 1991) (city may transfer hospital to nonprofit corporation that will provide hospital facilities; continued operation of hospital constitutes sufficient consideration).

68. The principle also offers more direct constitutional support for G.S. 160A-277, which explicitly permits a local government to convey real property without monetary consideration to a volunteer fire department or rescue squad. The recipient's use of the property to provide fire department or rescue squad facilities constitutes constitutionally adequate consideration.

and grantee of personal property serve quite different publics, the rationale no longer holds. In that case a court might find that the principle is inapplicable as well. That is, if a government conveys personal property to another local government or some private organization, and the grantee government or organization is located at some remove from the conveying government and uses the property to serve a public significantly different from that of the conveying government, the conveying government may not be able constitutionally to accept continued public use as consideration for the property.[69]

When the continued public use of the property is the consideration that supports a conveyance, the conveying government should ensure that the consideration does not fail because the recipient soon stops using the property for the intended public use.[70] One means of doing so is to convey only a defeasible fee, providing for a reversion of the property if the recipient ends its public use.[71]

2. Economic Development as Consideration

G.S. 158-7.1(d) permits counties and cities to convey property to private companies for industrial or commercial use. The subsection requires that the county or city receive as consideration the fair market value of the property, but subsection (d2) of that section permits the local government to count as consideration the "prospective tax revenues from improvements to be constructed on the property, prospective sales tax revenues to be generated in the area, as well as any other prospective tax revenue or income coming to the county or city over the next 10 years

---

69. In Rock County v. Spire, 455 N.W.2d 763 (Neb. 1990), the state took over administration of categorical social services from counties and, as part of the change, took title to all county personal property used in social services. A few years later, the state closed its Rock County office and moved operations to a second county; it intended to serve both counties from the new location. The Nebraska court held that the state could take the personal property from the Rock County office to the new office, because the property would continue to be used for the benefit of Rock County citizens. The implication is that if the Rock County citizens received no benefit from the new use of the property, transferring title to the property might have been improper.

70. G.S. 160A-279, discussed in the text, requires the county or city conveying the property to "attach to any such conveyance covenants or conditions which assure that the property will be put to a public use by the recipient entity."

71. In Brumley v. Baxter, 225 N.C. 691, 36 S.E.2d 281 (1945), the court required the city's deed to the recreation authority to provide for such a reversion.

as a result of the conveyance." Because these tax and other revenues would come to the county or city in any event whenever it conveys property for industrial or commercial use, the statute in effect authorizes a county or city to give the property to the private company. The real consideration for the conveyance is the company's promise to construct industrial or commercial facilities on the property and use the property in such a way as to create permanent jobs. In *Maready v. City of Winston-Salem*,[72] the North Carolina Supreme Court held that it served a public purpose for a local government to give cash and other things of value to a private company in order to generate economic development; consequently the authorizations for property conveyance in G.S. 158-7.1(d) and (d2) are constitutional. In a sense, the company will put the property to the public use of economic development, and conveyances for this purpose are in effect a subgroup of those for which continued public use is the consideration given for the conveyance of government-owned property.

3. Transfer of School Property

Although in general governments may convey property to each other without monetary consideration when the recipient will put the property to a public use, if the conveying government is a school administrative unit (or a community or technical college),[73] the North Carolina Constitution imposes a special restriction. Article IX, Section 7, of the constitution provides that "[a]ll moneys, stocks, bonds, and other property belonging to a county school fund . . . shall belong to and remain in the several counties, and shall be faithfully appropriated and used exclusively for maintaining free public schools." The North Carolina Supreme Court has held that this provision prohibits a conveyance of school property without monetary consideration, even to a governmental agency that will put the property to a public (but nonschool) use.[74] Thus while it is constitutionally permissible for a city to give surplus property to a school

---

72. 342 N.C. 708, 467 S.E.2d 615 (1996).

73. *See* Benvenue Parent-Teacher Ass'n v. Nash County Bd. of Educ., 4 N.C. App. 617, 167 S.E.2d 538 (1969).

74. Boney v. Board of Trustees, 229 N.C. 136, 48 S.E.2d 56 (1948). In Benvenue Parent-Teacher Ass'n v. Nash County Bd. of Educ., 4 N.C. App. 617, 167 S.E.2d 538 (1969), the court of appeals held that a technical institute was such a part of the county's school system that a school unit could transfer its property to the institute, for its use, without monetary consideration.

administrative unit for use as a school site, the school unit may not give the site of a former school to a city for use as a fire station.[75] The city must pay market value.[76]

C. Payment on Time

The final question concerning consideration is whether a government may accept payment over time, taking back a purchase-money security interest in the property it sells, or whether it must receive full consideration at the time of conveyance. The North Carolina statutes are silent on this point, and the matter has not come before the state's appellate courts. Indeed, there appear to be only two recent decisions nationally on this question, and they reach opposing conclusions. The more recent is *Dudley v. Little River County*,[77] in which the Arkansas Supreme Court held that when a county attempted to sell gravel on credit, the sale violated that state's constitutional ban on a local government lending its credit. This interpretation of a constitutional loan of credit provision conflicts with earlier cases elsewhere and seems incorrect: the government was extending credit, not loaning it; and the government's own credit was not at risk.[78] The more persuasive recent case is *Singer Architectural Services Company v. Doyle*,[79] in which the Michigan Court of Appeals upheld against both statutory and constitutional attack a school board's sale of real property by land contract. (A land contract is essentially an installment sale of land, with legal title passing upon final payment.[80] The analysis would be no different if the transaction had followed

---

75. Of course the city and school unit could *exchange* properties pursuant to G.S. 160A-271.

76. G.S. 115C-238.29E(e) permits a local board of education to lease unneeded school property to a charter school "free of charge." This authorization is consistent with the constitutional requirements, because the charter school will be putting the property to an educational use.

77. 805 S.W.2d 645 (Ark. 1991).

78. City of Clovis v. Southwestern Public Service Co., 161 P.2d 878 (N.M. 1945) (city sale of utility system with payment on time no loan of credit; transaction does not involve city's credit at all but rather buyer's credit); Vitacolonna v. City of Philadelphia, 115 A.2d 178 (Pa. 1955) (city gives customers three years to pay for city installation of water meters; transaction not a loan of city's credit but rather arrangement for payment and collection of money owed to the city).

79. 254 N.W.2d 587 (Mich. Ct. App. 1977).

80. A land contract is rare but not unknown in North Carolina. *See* James W. Narron, *Installment Land Contracts in North Carolina*, 3 CAMP. L. REV. 29 (1981).

the form more common in North Carolina—immediate conveyance of legal title, with the seller taking a purchase money security interest.) The Michigan court held, first, that the transaction was permitted under a general statutory authority to sell and, second, that it in no way loaned the seller school board's credit to the buyer of the property. Obviously these cases do not settle the question in North Carolina, but the Michigan court's opinion is careful and persuasive and offers useful support for a local government's sale of property on time.[81]

§ 509. Conflicts of Interest

A. The Prohibition on Self-dealing

Section 210 of this book discusses the applicability of G.S. 14-234, the self-dealing statute, to property acquisitions. The statute also applies to disposing of property and therefore bars some local government officials from acquiring property from local government. The statute prohibits officials from benefiting from a contract, regardless of how the contract came into being, and consequently applies to competitive as well as negotiated sales of property. The prohibition includes board members, as well as any other officials or employees actively involved in the decision-making process for the sale or other disposition. The prohibition does not include employees who have no part in the transaction, and therefore they may purchase property from the government. (Some governments have adopted policies that prohibit employees from acquiring property from the government even though the statute does not prohibit such transactions.)

The statute, in subsection (d1), makes one exception to its basic prohibition that does allow smaller local governments to contract with elected officials. The exception extends to elected officials in cities or towns of 7,500 or less and to elected officials in counties that have no incorporated cities or towns of more than 7,500. In a covered city or county, and with the specific approval of the governing body, an elected official may contract with the city or town for as much as $15,000 in

---

81. A minor amendment in 1980 to G.S. 160A-269, the upset bid procedure statute, offers some support to the availability of time payments for local government land in North Carolina. From its enactment in 1971 until 1980, the statute required that the sale be made to the ultimate highest bidder "for cash." In 1980 the quoted words were deleted. Act of June 25, 1980, ch. 1247, § 25, 1979 N.C. Sess. Laws 168 (2d Sess. 1980).

"goods" in any twelve-month period. This appears to allow the government to convey personal property, up to the $15,000 annual limit, to elected officials, inasmuch as personal property constitutes goods. Because of the need for specific approval of each transaction by the governing body, this exception is more usable if the property is being conveyed to the elected official by private sale (although such a sale may create political difficulties); it could be made to fit an auction or other competitive sale, however, if the governing body wished it to. Any local government wishing to use this exception from G.S. 14-234 in order to convey personal property to an elected official should consult with its attorney to be sure all the statutory steps have been taken.

B. Other Possible Conflicts

In situations that present conflicts of interest not included within the prohibitions of G.S. 14-234, the standard of behavior presumably is abuse of discretion.[82] Unless there is proof that the potential conflict caused the affected official to exercise an improper or corrupt influence over others involved in the disposition decision, thereby indicating bad faith on the part of the government itself, a court probably will not interfere with the property transaction.

§ 510. Leases

If a local government has no current need for a parcel of real property but is not willing to dispose of the property entirely, it may decide to lease the property for a term of years. This section discusses a number of legal issues regarding leases of local government property.

A. Leases Compared with Other Property Transactions

It is sometimes difficult to determine whether a particular property-related transaction creates a leasehold in the property or some other interest.[83] Identification of the interest may be important for

---

82. "Presumably," because there is almost no case law, anywhere, on this subject.

83. Miller v. City of New York, 203 N.E.2d 478 (N.Y. 1964), illustrates the difficulty. The city's parks commissioner granted a private corporation the right to construct and operate a golf driving range on a 30-acre tract in a city park. The parties labeled the agreement, which extended for 20 years, a license. A taxpayer challenged the grant on the grounds that it was a lease, not a license,

determining the procedure the local government owner must follow in the transaction and may also have implications for such tangential issues as the property's taxability[84] or susceptibility to liens.[85] The interests that are sometimes confused with leases are licenses, contracts (including concessions), and easements.

1. Licenses

Licenses are a miscellaneous group of privileges to use real property, which lack the elements of an easement or lease.[86] In the absence of the license, the licensee would be a trespasser. No formalities need attend creation of a license nor must the license be in writing.[87] The courts and commentators generally hold that a license is revocable at the will of the licensor.[88]

---

and void because the city had not followed the statutory procedure for entering into leases. In a 4-3 decision the New York Court of Appeals agreed with the taxpayer.

The majority, in holding that the agreement was a lease, emphasized that the tract was a specifically bounded 30-acre site; that the agreement extended 20 years; that the payment to the city was based on a percentage of gross receipts; and that the grantee was responsible for construction and repair of his own buildings. The dissent, in arguing that the agreement was a license, emphasized that the parties labeled it a license, that the parks commissioner could terminate the agreement at any time on five days' notice when, in his sole judgment, the premises were needed for parks purposes; that the city gained or retained title to all buildings; and that the city exercised strict control over the grantee's prices, time of operation, and choice of employees.

84. A considerable amount of the litigation over whether a particular transaction creates a lease arises in states in which leaseholds of government-owned property are subject to property tax while other interests, such as licenses, are not. *E.g.*, Richmond County Bd. of Tax Assessors v. Richmond Bonded Warehouse Corp., 325 S.E.2d 891 (Ga. 1985); Jackson Park Yacht Club v. Illinois Dep't of Local Gov't Affairs, 417 N.E.2d 1039 (Ill. Ct. App. 1981); Port of Coos Bay v. Dep't of Revenue, 691 P.2d 100 (Or. 1984).

85. Although local government property generally is immune from liens, liens may be attached to leasehold interests in such property. *See supra* § 206-A3.

86. JON W. BRUCE & JAMES W. ELY, JR., THE LAW OF EASEMENTS AND LICENSES IN LAND § 11.01 (rev. ed. 1995) [hereinafter BRUCE & ELY]. The authors note that inadequate attempts to create an easement may result in a license.

87. *Id.*

88. *Id.* § 11.06. The authors note that in some circumstances some courts have held licenses to be irrevocable, at least for a term of years, and 3 HERBERT THORNDIKE TIFFANY, LAW OF REAL PROPERTY, § 834 (3d ed., Jones, 1939) agrees. TIFFANY lists North Carolina, however, among those states not recognizing irrevocable licenses, citing Richmond & Danville Railroad v. Durham & North-

A number of examples illustrate the possible use of licenses by local governments:

1. A city permits patrons to use a city-operated swimming pool.
2. A county permits a farmer to plant hay in the approach zones to the county airport in return for the farmer's agreement to keep the hay cut.
3. A city permits a driver to park at a city parking facility.

North Carolina statutes create no special procedures that a local government must follow in granting a license, perhaps because a license is revocable at the will of the licensor and creates no interest in real property.

2. Contracts

Many cases that declare that a transaction created a license do so only by default. The parties are litigating whether the transaction created something else—for example a lease—and once the court determines that no lease was created, the case is over. Although the court may label the resulting interest a license, that labeling does not reflect serious consideration of the issue.

The problem such an approach creates lies in the revocability of licenses. Just because an interest is not a lease or has not been created in the manner required for easements should not therefore mean that it is revocable at the will of the grantor.[89] Governments also enter into contracts, with fixed terms, under which the other party may make use of the government's property.[90] These contracts are not licenses because

---

ern Railway Co., 104 N.C. 658, 10 S.E. 659 (1889), and the case does support the citation.

89. This point is forcefully made in Alfred F. Conrad, *An Analysis of Licenses in Land*, 42 COLUM. L. REV. 809 (1942).

90. *See* Richmond County Bd. of Tax Assessors v. Richmond Bonded Warehouse Corp., 325 S.E.2d 891 (Ga. 1985), in which the court characterized a 50-year agreement under which the warehouse corporation could use land and buildings owned by the state ports authority as a "usufruct" rather than a lease. Georgia statutes defined a usufruct as a right to possess and enjoy land either for a fixed term or at the will of the grantor, without creating an estate in the grantee.

they are not revocable at the grantor's will, nor are they leases because the local government has not yielded complete control of the property to the other party. Again, some examples illustrate the use of contracts:

1. A city that owns three parking lots in the downtown area engages a private company to operate the lots subject to the city's supervision of rates and operating policies. The agreement extends for five years.
2. A city permits a local gardener to maintain a stall at the city market, under a contract that runs from March until November.
3. A county contracts for a nonprofit organization to operate a daycare center on county-owned property for the children of county employees. The contract runs three years.[91]

North Carolina statutes do not create any special requirements for entering into service contracts such as those listed above.

Concessions. One type of contract involving real property is the concession. *Concession* is a term frequently used in some local government activities, particularly airports, parks, stadiums, and convention centers. Although no fully accepted definition of the term exists, it usually involves an arrangement under which the concessionaire provides some sort of service for the public at a publicly owned facility. Concessions are frequently for a term of years and thus cannot be characterized as licenses.[92] They are in fact a form of contract but are worth special listing because of their frequently complex nature and because they often give the concession holder an exclusive entitlement to occupy space in the public facility. Oftentimes, too, the local government exercises a large degree of control over the operations of the concessionaire. The

---

91. For other examples *see, e.g., In re* Fasi, 634 P.2d 98 (Haw. 1981) (agreement to operate state-owned airport parking facilities is "service agreement" rather than lease); Chemical Petroleum Exch., Inc. v. Metropolitan Sanitary Dist., 401 N.E.2d 1203 (Ill. Ct. App. 1980) (arrangement under which party permitted to store petroleum products on unspecified land was "agreement" rather than lease).

92. Concessions also bear some resemblance to franchises. Franchises, however, usually involve a nonexclusive use of public streets, while a concessionaire frequently holds an exclusive right to specific space in a public facility.

large amount of retained government control over operations distinguishes the concession from the lease.[93] Examples of concessions include the following:

1. A city contracts with a company to construct and operate a miniature train ride in a city park.
2. A county contracts with a food service operator to operate a restaurant at the county's airport.
3. A city contracts with a golf professional for operation of the pro shop at the city's public golf course.

North Carolina statutes do not set out any special requirements or procedures for entering into concession contracts.[94]

3. Easements and Profits

In theory easements (and profits)[95] are distinguished from leases by whether there is exclusive possession by the holder of the interest. A lease is a possessory interest, and a tenant is entitled to exclusive possession even against the landlord. An easement (or profit) is nonpossessory. This difference, however, almost disappears in close cases, as a New Jersey case illustrates.[96] A landfill operator held the land under a lease that prohibited subleases. In settlement of a lawsuit, the operator permitted a city to dispose of wastes in the landfill, in areas designated by the operator. The agreement was for a term of years. The fee holder sued the landfill

---

93. I AMER. LAW OF PROPERTY § 3.3 (1952) comments that the more narrowly an agreement limits the uses that the possessor under the agreement may make of the property, the less likely it is that the agreement will be characterized as a lease. Under concessions, the possessor is typically limited to a single use or a group of closely related uses. The differences between a concession and a lease are discussed in County of Kent v. City of Grand Rapids, 167 N.W.2d 287 (Mich. 1969).

94. In Metropolitan Park Dist. of Tacoma v. Griffith, 723 P.2d 1093 (Wash. 1986), the Washington Supreme Court upheld a concession agreement that had a possible term of 30 years. Although the public entity wanted out of the agreement, the court held the term was permissible and that the district had bargained for the various provisions in the agreement.

95. A *profit à prendre* (or profit) is the right to sever and remove materials from another's land, such as minerals, sand and gravel, or timber. BRUCE & ELY, *supra* note 86, at § 1.04. The authors note that profits are governed by the same legal principles as easements; the distinguishing character of the profit is that its holder may "remove a portion of the burdened property." *Id.*

96. Town of Kearny v. Municipal Sanitary Landfill Auth., 363 A.2d 390 (N.J. Super. Ct. Law Div. 1976).

operator, arguing that the lawsuit settlement created a sublease to the city, thereby breaking the primary lease of the property. The court disagreed, holding that because the city did not have exclusive possession under the settlement agreement, the agreement created an easement rather than a lease.

The next chapter, in Section 610, discusses the procedures (or lack thereof) under which a local government may convey an easement or profit in its property.

B. Lease Terms a Matter of Discretion

The terms of a lease of local government property are within the discretion of the governing board, challengeable only upon a showing that the board has abused its discretion. A few examples illustrate this point.

1. *Length of Lease.* The term of a lease is a matter of government discretion. Absent a showing of abuse of discretion courts have upheld leases as long as fifty and even ninety-nine years.[97] Readers of G.S. 160A-272 sometimes conclude that the statute prohibits local governments from leasing their property for longer than ten years. The pertinent language reads: "Any property owned by a city may be leased or rented for such terms and upon such conditions as the council may determine, *but not for longer than 10 years (except as otherwise provided herein). . . ."* The first part of the italicized phrase does seem to limit the length of leases, but the parenthetical language indicates that there are exceptions to the statement. If one reads on to the last sentence of the statute, it is clear that leases may be entered into for longer than ten years. That sentence reads: "Leases for terms of more than 10 years shall be treated as a sale of property and may be executed by following any of the procedures authorized for sale of real property."

---

97. City of Phoenix v. Landrum & Mills Realty Co., 227 P.2d 1011 (Ariz. 1951) (50 years not so "improvident" as to amount to an abuse of discretion); Lindburg v. Bennett, 219 N.W. 851 (Neb. 1928) (99 years acceptable as long as consideration is adequate and there is no fraud). The length of a lease in North Carolina affects the procedure that the local government will have to follow in entering into it; *see infra* § 610-A.

2. *Lessor Expenditures.* It is clearly open to a local government lessor to continue to make expenditures on the property during the term of the lease, such as for insurance or to make improvements.[98] After all, the government continues to hold an interest in the property and may act to protect that interest.

3. *Consideration.* The general comments made above in Section 508 about consideration apply as much to leases as to sales of property.

4. *The Use Made of the Property.* In general, a local government may lease property to a private party who will devote the property to a private use.[99] For example, a city may have constructed a city hall with more space than it currently needs; the excess may be leased to private users. The North Carolina Court of Appeals has suggested one limit to this general practice. It held that a city could not lease property to another with the lease specifying a particular use, when the use in question is not permitted by the city's zoning ordinance.[100] The court's reasoning was that such a lease seemed to oblige the city to rezone the property, and a city may not contract away its discretion over exercise of the police power in that fashion.

C. Taxation, Mortgages, and Other Charges on the Lessee's Interest

1. *Taxation.* The Machinery Act defines intangible personal property to include leasehold interests in real property that is exempt from property tax.[101] G.S. 105-275(31) classifies and excludes from the tax base all intangible property except leasehold interests in exempted real property, and therefore privately held leaseholds of local government property are subject to tax. In addition, if the lessee holds title to any improvements

98. Hansen v. Kootenai County Bd. of County Comm'rs, 471 P.2d 42 (Idaho 1970) (county may pay for fire insurance on leasehold improvements constructed by lessee because they will become county property upon termination of the lease).

99. *E.g.,* Cline v. City of Hickory, 207 N.C. 125, 176 S.E. 250 (1934) (upholding lease of city hall auditorium to private party intending to operate a movie theater).

100. Lewis v. City of Washington, 63 N.C. App. 552, 305 S.E.2d 752 (1983), *modified,* 309 N.C. 818, 310 S.E.2d 610 (1983). The supreme court's modification of the court of appeals decision did not involve the holding set out in the text.

101. G.S. 105-273(8) (Cum. Supp.).

on leased land,[102] the improvements also are subject to tax. In the absence of a contractual agreement to the contrary, the lessee is responsible for paying any tax levied against a leasehold.[103]

2. *Mortgages.* The discussion in Section 206-A3 notes that the general presumption against local governments conveying or creating security interests in their property does not prohibit a private lessee of government property from mortgaging the leasehold interest. Of course, only the leasehold would be subject to foreclosure under such a security interest. Presumably, a private leasehold is also subject to common law and statutory liens.

3. *Subordinated Ground Leases.* In recent years local governments have joined private parties in joint economic development projects, and often part of the government's responsibility has been to lease to the private developer the land necessary for the project. The question has then sometimes arisen as to whether the government's interest in the property may be subordinated to the interest of the private developer's creditors. That is, may the government's fee interest be pledged as security for development loans to the developer? Clearly such a subordination amounts to a mortgage of the government's interest in the property, and therefore subordination is not possible in the absence of specific legislative authority. If that authority is given, though, there is no constitutional bar to the transaction. The legislature may authorize local governments to give security interests in their land,[104] and a properly authorized subordinated ground lease should be treated no differently. After all, an agreement to subordinate would normally be reflected in the consideration and other terms of the lease; for example, the government might expect a higher rental payment and a shorter term.[105]

---

102. *Id.* § 105-302(b)(11), which sets out the responsibilities for listing real property for property taxes, recognizes the possibility that title to the land may be in one party and title to the improvements in another.

103. The operation of these rules is illustrated in Bragg Investment Co., Inc. v. Cumberland County, 245 N.C. 492, 96 S.E.2d 341 (1957). The investment company had leased 120 acres in Fort Bragg from the federal government in order to construct and operate housing. The lease was for 75 years and during that term title to the improvements was in the lessee. The county valued the improvements and fixtures at $1,435,754, and the leasehold at $1,196; the court upheld the valuations.

104. *See supra* § 206-A1.

105. Steve A. Borell, *The Subordinated Ground Lease*, 23 Prac. Law, Sept. 1, 1977, at 41.

§ 511. The Proceeds of Sale

Except as described in the following paragraphs of this section, no statutory directions govern use of the proceeds from the sale or other disposition of property. The proceeds are simply a miscellaneous revenue of the local government. Under generally accepted accounting principles, the proceeds of sale of general fixed assets should be placed in the unit's general fund, while the proceeds from sale of assets of a proprietary fund, such as a water and sewer fund, should be credited to that fund.

A. Local Educational Property

G.S. 115C-518(a) directs that the proceeds from the sale of any property owned by a school administrative unit or from any lease of such property extending longer than one year be used for one of two purposes: (1) debt service on county-bonded indebtedness incurred for facilities of that school unit or (2) that school unit's capital outlay purposes. Presumably the choice between purposes is made by the school unit rather than the county.

With one exception, G.S. 115D-15 directs that the proceeds from the sale of property owned by a community or technical college or from any lease of such property of longer than one year be used for the college's capital outlay purposes. The exception applies to property that has been donated to a college for a specific educational purpose. The proceeds from sale of that property may be used pursuant to the terms of the donation.

B. Sales of Seized or Abandoned Property

Article 2 of G.S. Chapter 15 sets out a procedure for registering and disposing of personal property that is confiscated, seized, or found by local law enforcement agencies.[106] If the items of property are not, within statutory periods, claimed by their owners, the law enforcement agency is to sell them by public auction. G.S. 15-15 directs that the net proceeds of the sale are to be turned over to the "treasurer of the county board of education," for use for school purposes.[107]

---

106. This procedure is discussed in § 612-B, *infra*.

107. This statutory direction seems intended to implement the constitutional requirement that the clear proceeds of all fines, penalties, and forfeitures be placed in the county school fund. N.C. CONST., art. IX, § 7. To the extent that is true, in a county with two or more school administrative units it would be

C. Sales of Abandoned or Junked Motor Vehicles

Counties, under G.S. 153A-132 and -132.2, and cities, under G.S. 160A-303 and -303.2, may adopt ordinances calling for removal and disposal of junked or abandoned motor vehicles. The ordinances permit a sale of the vehicle, under G.S. Chapter 44A or under a locally established procedure that is similar to the Chapter 44A procedure. Under G.S. 44A-5, the proceeds from the sale of a junked or abandoned motor vehicle go first to pay the expenses of sale, second to pay the tower of the vehicle, and third (if any proceeds remain) to the vehicle's owner. Any local procedures must provide for a comparable use of the proceeds.

D. Sales of Property Acquired Through Tax or Special Assessment Foreclosures

When property has been foreclosed for nonpayment of taxes or special assessments, the owner of the property is entitled to any surplus proceeds of sales, after payment of the taxes or assessments, sale expenses, and other permitted costs.[108] Most frequently, of course, there is no surplus, and thus the owner gets nothing. If the taxing or assessing unit purchases the property at the foreclosure sale, it frequently holds the property for some time before selling it, and occasionally it will show an apparent profit on that later sale, receiving more for the property than it paid. In recent years the previous owners of such property in other states have made a number of attempts to claim the eventual profit made by the taxing or assessing unit upon resale. The courts have generally rejected these claims,[109] and the North Carolina statutes conform to the weight of judicial authority. Under G.S. 105-376(b) any such profit belongs to the government.

---

improper to turn the entire amount over to the *county* board of education. The one or more city units would also be entitled to a share of the proceeds.

108. G.S. 105-374(q)(6). G.S. 153A-200(c) and 160A-233(c) provide that special assessment liens may be foreclosed in the same manner as property tax liens.

109. Cases rejecting the owner's claim include City of Auburn v. Mandarelli, 320 A.2d 22 (Me. 1974); Kelly v. City of Boston, 204 N.E.2d 123 (Mass. 1965); Spurgias v. Morrissette, 249 A.2d 685 (N.H. 1969); and Oosterwyk v. County of Milwaukee, 143 N.W.2d 497 (Wis. 1966). An exception to the national trend is Boger v. Town of Barnet, 270 A.2d 898 (Vt. 1970).

E. Sales of Property Financed with Bonds that Are Still Outstanding

Section 505-A discussed the limitations that the Internal Revenue Code places upon a local government when it conveys property financed by bonds that are still outstanding. The applicable Treasury regulations do not mandate the use of the proceeds from any such sale, but ignoring the regulations will cause the interest on the remaining bonds in the bond issue to be taxable. Therefore, as a practical matter, a local government must comply with the regulations. To quickly reiterate the regulations, the proceeds from the sale of personal property should be placed in the government's general fund (or appropriate proprietary fund) and expended within six months. The proceeds from the sale of real property should either be used to retire the remaining bonds in the bond issue (or placed in an escrow account for that purpose) or should be used for a capital purpose that qualifies for tax-exempt financing.

F. Sales of Property Financed with Federal Grant Funds

If a local government sells real or personal property that was financed or purchased with federal grant funds, various federal regulations may require that the proceeds be turned over to the federal granting agency. See the discussion in Section 505-B.

VI

Disposing of Property: Procedures

§601. Introduction

The primary set of procedures by which local governments dispose of property are those found in G.S. Chapter 160A, Article 12. These procedures were originally enacted to govern property disposition by cities and have since been extended to counties and several other kinds of local governments. In addition, the procedures are often used by local governments not required to do so. Because of the pervasiveness of the Article 12 procedures, a substantial part of this chapter is devoted to them. But other procedures apply as well. Most of the local governments that are subject to Article 12 may dispose of some kinds of property under other procedures, and a variety of specialized local governments are not subject to Article 12 at all, instead being subject either to separate statutory procedures or to no procedural requirements at all. This chapter also discusses those other procedures and other governments.

§602. The Coverage of Article 12

Governments

A. Governments Covered

Article 12 is part of G.S. Chapter 160A, the General Statutes chapter regulating city government, and therefore it obviously applies to cities. Since its enactment in 1971, the Article has been extended to a number of other kinds of local governments. The list below sets out those other local governments subject to Article 12, together with the statute extending the Article to each kind of government.

> *Counties* (G.S. 153A-176)
> *Sanitary districts* (G.S. 130A-55(20))
> *School administrative units* (G.S. 115C-518(a))
> *Community and technical colleges* (G.S. 115D-15)
> *Local ABC boards* (G.S. 18B-701(12))
> *Regional solid waste management authorities* (G.S. 153A-427(b))

B. Governments Not Covered

Disposition of two varieties of local government property—redevelopment property and hospital facilities—is governed by special procedures that apply uniformly to all the types of local governments that hold such property. These special procedures are discussed in Section 614. In addition, a number of special-purpose local governments are either specifically permitted to dispose of all property by private sale, with no special procedural requirements, or are simply authorized to dispose of property without mention of any statutory procedure at all. The list below sets out those local governments *not* subject to Article 12.

> *Housing authorities* (G.S. 157-9)
> *Historic preservation commissions* (G.S. 160A-400.8(3))
> *Water and sewer authorities* (G.S. 162A-6(10))
> *Metropolitan water districts* (G.S. 162A-36(10))
> *Metropolitan sewerage districts* (G.S. 162A-69(10))
> *County water and sewer districts* (G.S. 162A-88)
> *Drainage districts* (G.S. 156-138.1)
> *Soil and water conservation districts* (G.S. 139-8(4))
> *Area mental health, developmental disabilities, and substance abuse authorities* (G.S. 122C-147)
> *Regional public transportation authorities* (G.S. 160A-610(7))
> *Regional transportation authorities* (G.S. 160A-639(7))
> *Parking authorities* (G.S. 160A-557(e))
> *Regional sports authorities* (G.S. 160A-479.7(a)(11))
> *Facility authorities* (G.S. 160A-480.4(11))
> *Cemetery trustees* (G.S. 160A-349.13)

Disposition of property by these local governments is discussed more specifically in Section 614-C.

C. Nonprofit Organizations

Local governments frequently appropriate money to and otherwise use nonprofit organizations to undertake activities on the local governments' behalf. A county might appropriate money to several volunteer fire departments, to a nonprofit corporation operating a county-owned hospital, or to an economic development organization. A city might appropriate money to a downtown economic development corporation, to a community group that operates youth recreation leagues, or to a nonprofit corporation that operates a local museum. Sometimes the nonprofit organization uses the city or county money to acquire real or personal property. This section examines whether these nonprofit organizations must follow the same procedures as counties or cities when they dispose of property acquired with county or city appropriations.[1]

Dependent Nonprofit Corporations

Facially, nonprofit organizations are private entities; if they are corporations, they are set up under a statute, G.S. Chapter 55A, that is intended to authorize private corporations rather than government agencies. Sometimes, however, a local government is actively involved in the creation or operation of a nonprofit corporation. By using the nonprofit organization, the government seeks freedom from some of the constraints that apply to governments but not to the private sector; but the government doesn't want the nonprofit corporation to operate fully free of governmental control. Thus the local government retains some formal control over the nonprofit—appointing or approving some or all members of the board of directors, approving the corporation's annual budget, placing public employees on the board of directors, and so on. In addition, a government may provide assistance to the corporation through appropriations, loaned employees, or office space. At some point the government's formal controls over and other relationships with the nonprofit organization become so significant that the courts treat the organization as if it were a governmental agency and not a private organization. For example, in *News &*

---

1. Frayda S. Bluestein, A Legal Guide to Purchasing and Contracting for North Carolina Local Governments 18–19 (Institute of Government 1998), discusses the applicability of the state's local government purchasing statutes to nonprofit corporations.

Observer Publishing Co. v. Wake County Hospital System, Inc.,[2] the newspaper sought records held by the hospital corporation. The newspaper was proceeding pursuant to the state public records law, and the hospital claimed that, because it was organized as a private nonprofit corporation, the records statute did not apply. The court agreed with the newspaper. It noted that the county commissioners approved appointments to the hospital corporation's board of directors, the commissioners approved the corporation's annual budget, the county was entitled to audit the corporation's books, the corporation operated the county's hospital under a one-dollar-a-year lease, the hospital's revenues were pledged to payment of county hospital bonds, and the corporation could not change its articles of incorporation without county approval. In total, these connections gave the county sufficient control over the corporation that the latter was characterized as a county agency.[3]

No appellate case has examined whether a nonprofit organization subject to this level of control by a county or city is subject to the county and city property disposition statutes, but there is a strong possibility that it would be.[4]

Independent Nonprofit Organizations

If a nonprofit organization is not subject to the kinds of controls outlined above, it is simply a governmental contractor. If it uses moneys paid to it by a local government to acquire property, that property

---

2. 55 N.C. App. 1, 284 S.E.2d 542 (1981).

3. *See also* Coats v. Sampson County Memorial Hospital, Inc., 264 N.C. 332, 141 S.E.2d 490 (1965). In that case the plaintiff sued the hospital in a county other than the one in which the hospital was located. A venue statute required that local government agencies be sued in the county in which they were located, and the hospital argued that the statute applied to it. Although the hospital was organized as a private nonprofit corporation, the county commissioners appointed its board of directors and it occupied a county-owned hospital. Without much discussion, the supreme court held that the hospital was a county agency and the venue statute applied.

4. A 1999 amendment to G.S. 160A-20 supports the possibility that dependent nonprofit organizations are subject to the property disposition rules that apply to local governments. That amendment included in the list of entities subject to G.S. 160A-20 any "nonprofit corporation or association operating or leasing a public hospital." S.L. 1999-386 (H 1120). Thus these corporations or associations may borrow money and pledge property as security for the loan, as permitted by G.S. 160A-20. This statutory change is unnecessary unless these sorts of nonprofit entities are subject to the same rules on borrowing and pledging their property as are counties and cities.

belongs to the organization, and it may dispose of the property in whatever way it wishes, unless its contract with the funding government imposes limitations.

§603. The Coverage of Article 12

Transactions Excluded Because of the Local Government's Title or Because They Are Not Dispositions

A number of transactions by which a local government transfers title to property are not subject to Article 12, nor to any procedural alternative to Article 12, because the property interest held by the local government, or conditions on that interest, makes the standard disposition procedures impossible or inappropriate to use. This section details the most common of those interests. It also notes one kind of transaction—demolition of a structure—that is not subject to Article 12 because it is not a disposition of property.

A. Property Held in a Defeasible Fee

Section 204 noted that local governments, by virtue of their capacity to acquire property, have authority to acquire title in fee simple defeasible. If the condition on which such a title depends is broken, the fee either reverts to the grantor (or her heirs or assigns) or is subject to a right of reentry. In either case normal disposition procedures are irrelevant.[5]

Occasionally a local government that expects to breach the condition on property it holds by fee simple subject to a condition subsequent is able to negotiate with the holder of the right of reentry. The government will agree to convey the property to the holder of the right and will receive valuable consideration in return. When a government makes such a conveyance in good-faith anticipation of its own breach of the condition, which could cause loss of the property for no consideration at all, the courts have held that the conveyance need not comply with normal procedural requirements.[6]

---

5. Those North Carolina cases involving local government property held in defeasible fee have simply noted the return of the property to the grantor without remarking on the inapplicability of normal disposition procedures. *E.g.,* Lackey v. Hamlet City Bd. of Educ., 258 N.C. 460, 128 S.E.2d 806 (1963); Duplin County Bd. of Educ. v. Carr, 15 N.C. App. 690, 190 S.E.2d 653 (1972).

6. East Chicago Co. v. City of East Chicago, 87 N.E. 17 (Ind. 1909); Grant v. Koenig, 333 N.Y.S.2d 591 (N.Y. App. Div. 1972).

B. Property Held Subject to a Right of Repurchase

Section 204 also noted that local governments sometimes acquire property subject to the grantor's right (or option) to repurchase the property. Exercise of a right of repurchase obviously is inconsistent with a competitive sale of the property, and the North Carolina courts would probably recognize the inconsistency and permit repurchase without compliance with competitive procedural requirements.[7]

C. Property Held Subject to Preemptive Rights

Although the question is not settled, at least some property held subject to a preemptive right (or a right of first refusal) is partially exempt from competitive sale requirements.[8] If the preemptive price was required to match the highest offer received, a local government could still follow competitive sale procedures but the holder of the preemptive right would be entitled to match the highest price received under the procedures. This result would deprive the high bidder of her own right of purchase, and the existence of the preemptive right might therefore be thought to

---

7. In Peele v. Wilson County Bd. of Educ., 56 N.C. App. 555, 289 S.E.2d 890 (1982), the plaintiffs held a right to repurchase school property at the original purchase price. When they sought to exercise the right, the court held that it was invalid because it violated the Rule Against Perpetuities. All parties seemed to believe that if the right had not been invalid, the holder could have exercised it without regard for statutory sales procedures.

In Byars v. Cherokee County, 118 S.E.2d 324 (S.C. 1961), the court held that a right of repurchase was not subject to the normal limitations on property disposition. *Cf.* Amick v. Richland County, 255 S.E.2d 855 (S.C. 1979), in which the court discussed a right of repurchase with no suggestion of invalidity.

The two South Carolina cases involved rights of repurchase presumably created at the initiative of the original *grantor* of the property. An Arizona case holds that it does violate rules for competitive sale of local government property for a local government *grantee* to insist on an *obligation* of repurchase when it buys equipment. McGinnis Equipment Co. v. Riggs, 422 P.2d 187 (Ariz. Ct. App. 1967) (city advertising for bids for motor graders, with one requirement of bid being a guarantee of repurchase of the equipment by the seller after four years).

8. The author found no case dealing directly with the potential conflict between preemptive rights given when property was acquired and property sale procedures. In Berger v. Johnson, 151 P.2d 586 (Mont. 1944), the court raised the question but did not have to resolve it. In Atchinson v. City of Englewood, 568 P.2d 13 (Colo. 1977), the court upheld a preemptive right that the defendant city was trying mightily to defeat. The issue of inconsistency with sale procedures was not raised, however, perhaps because the city appears to have been authorized to dispose of property by private sale.

deter bidders or depress the size of their bids. But if the preemptive right was created when the local government acquired the property, it presumably affected the consideration, if any, the government paid.[9] Thus any reduction the right might cause in sales price might simply match a reduced purchase price.[10]

The outcome may differ if the government grants the preemptive right at a time other than when it acquires the property. When the right is given to the seller of the property, it may have been a necessary condition to closing the deal. But in other circumstances the city has more control over the situation and less need to grant a preemptive right. That was the situation in a recent Iowa case. In *Riley v. City of Hartley*,[11] the city leased a lot it owned and in addition gave the lessee a preemptive right to purchase the lot should the city ever decide to sell it. When the lease was ending, the city did receive an offer for the lot, and it preferred selling to the new offeror (who stated he would construct a building on the site) rather than the holder of the preemptive right (who would keep it vacant). The Iowa Supreme Court held that the preemptive right was not enforceable, because the city did not follow the statutory procedures for disposing of real estate when the right was included in the lease.

D. Partition of Property Held in Common

When a local government holds property as a tenant in common and there is a partition of the land, the partition is not considered a conveyance.[12]

E. Property Held in Trust

In the unusual circumstance in which a local government holds property as trustee under a charitable trust, courts have suggested that the property should be conveyed under the rules applicable to trusts rather than

---

9. Atchinson v. City of Englewood, 568 P.2d 13 (Colo. 1977).

10. Of course the preemptive right must be valid in order to override the property sale procedures. As Pinehurst discovered in Village of Pinehurst v. Regional Investments of Moore, 330 N.C. 725, 412 S.E.2d 645 (1992), preemptive rights are subject to the Rule Against Perpetuities.

11. 565 N.W.2d 344 (Iowa 1997).

12. Craven County v. First Citizens Bank & Trust Co., 237 N.C. 502, 75 S.E.2d 620 (1953).

under those applicable to the general run of local government property.[13] Although no North Carolina cases address this point, an attorney general's opinion on a related topic suggests agreement with those other courts.[14]

F. No Interest Held at All

Occasionally a local government holds a faint yet colorable claim to real property, the chief effect of which is to cloud the fee holder's title. If the governing board makes a good-faith determination that the local government's claim to the property is without substance, it may authorize giving the fee holder a deed quitclaiming all government interest in the property. Because the government in fact denies having any interest in the property, it need not follow property sale procedures in giving the deed.[15]

G. Demolition of Structures

When a local government demolishes a structure on land it owns, it is not conveying the structure (to the demolition company, one supposes) or otherwise disposing of it. Rather, it is entering into a service contract, one without any statutory regulation.[16] Although the demolition company may remove and retain the ruins of the demolished structure, that is incidental to its contractual service of demolishing the building. (Of course, if the local government dismantles the building before final demolition, sale of the dismantled parts is subject to the property disposition statutes.)

---

13. *E.g., In re* Clayton's Estate, 259 P.2d 617 (Colo. 1953); Kapiolani Park Preservation Soc'y v. City and County of Honolulu, 751 P.2d 1022 (Haw. 1988).

14. The Attorney General argued that individual patient funds held in trust by state institutions are not subject to investment pursuant to the law regulating investment of state funds. Rather, the opinion looked to principles of trust law and argued that investment by the trustee depended on the terms of the trust. 56 Op. N.C. Att'y Gen. 10 (1986).

15. An example of such a transaction is found in Covington County v. Page, 456 So. 2d 739 (Miss. 1984).

16. Demolition is neither construction nor repair, and so the contracting procedures set out in G.S. 143-129 do not apply to demolition contracts. FRAYDA S. BLUESTEIN, A LEGAL GUIDE TO PURCHASING AND CONTRACTING FOR NORTH CAROLINA LOCAL GOVERNMENTS 29 (Institute of Government 1998) [hereinafter BLUESTEIN].

§604. Procedures

General Comments

A. Procedures Must Be Carefully Followed

The North Carolina Supreme Court has made clear that statutory procedures for disposing of property must be followed exactly or the transaction risks invalidation.[17] A 1966 case illustrates the point.[18] At that time cities could sell property only upon thirty days' published notice. Because of an error in its first advertisement, the city gave only twenty-six days' notice of its sale. Although this notice was published four times, and there was no evidence that anyone was kept from the sale by the failure to give the full thirty days' notice, the court invalidated the sale. It did so at the instance of the city, even though the city was responsible for the mistake. Thus both governmental grantors and their grantees must be certain that no procedural missteps are made.

In this regard it should be noted that the rules on standing to challenge government property *dispositions* are much broader than those on standing to challenge government property *acquisitions*.[19] Without comment the North Carolina Supreme Court has permitted attacks on property dispositions by taxpayers,[20] by the buyer,[21] by unsuccessful buyers,[22] and by the local government itself.[23]

This need for exactitude probably extends to those unusual situations in which a North Carolina local government conveys property located in some other state, usually property that has been given to it. The courts of other states agree with North Carolina's courts that property disposition procedures must be followed exactly to insure validity.[24] Therefore, if a

---

17. Bagwell v. Town of Brevard, 267 N.C. 604, 148 S.E.2d 635 (1966) (inadequate notice); City of Asheville v. Herbert, 190 N.C. 732, 130 S.E. 861 (1925) (private sale when general law required auction); Carstarphen v. Town of Plymouth, 180 N.C. 26, 103 S.E. 899 (1920) (inadequate notice).

18. Bagwell v. Town of Brevard, 267 N.C. 604, 148 S.E.2d 635.

19. *See supra* § 211.

20. *E.g.,* Campbell v. First Baptist Church, 298 N.C. 476, 259 S.E.2d 558 (1979); Mullen v. Town of Louisburg, 225 N.C. 53, 33 S.E.2d 484 (1945).

21. Craven County v. First Citizens Bank & Trust Co., 237 N.C. 502, 75 S.E.2d 620 (1953); City of Asheville v. Herbert, 190 N.C. 732, 130 S.E. 861 (1925).

22. Bowles v. Fayetteville Graded Sch., 211 N.C. 36, 188 S.E. 615 (1936).

23. Bagwell v. Town of Brevard, 267 N.C. 604, 148 S.E.2d 635 (1966); City of Southport v. Stanly, 125 N.C. 464, 34 S.E. 641 (1899).

24. *E.g.,* Harter v. City of Colome, 310 N.W.2d 165 (S.D. 1981) (notice gave wrong location of property).

local government is disposing of its property that is located in another state, it should still comply with the statutes applicable to North Carolina local governments.

B. Determination that Property Is Surplus

Section 502 discussed the long-standing rule that general sale procedures, such as those included in Article 12, apply only to property that is not in governmental use, particularly surplus property. A local government may convey property still in governmental use only with specific legislative authority. Section 502 noted the likelihood that G.S. 160A-265 constitutes the necessary legislative authority, but the section also pointed out some difficulties with that statute. Because of those difficulties, it remains possible that Article 12 procedures are available only for surplus property. In that circumstance, is it necessary that the local government's governing board formally declare that the property being sold is surplus before beginning the procedure?

Many local governments make such a declaration as a matter of course, and doing so does no harm and may do some good. If a dispute arises over whether the property is in fact surplus, the board's declaration to that effect should, at the least, be entitled to the benefit of the doubt. If the matter were litigated, the proper question would be not whether the property was surplus but whether the board abused its discretion in declaring it to be so. A court might not agree with the board's determination, but it could still find that the board was not unreasonable in making that determination and therefore uphold the determination. Without an express determination by the board, the court might be more likely to deal directly with the basic question of whether the property is in fact surplus.

For most local governments, the preceding paragraph sets out tactics rather than legal necessity. If the Article 12 procedures are available only for surplus property, then by beginning the procedures the board has determined by implication that the property is surplus. A formal action changes the form of the determination, but the determination has been made in any case. Therefore, the board's declaration that property is surplus is probably not a necessary condition to selling the property.[25]

---

25. G.S. 160A-272, which governs leases, perhaps adds support to the conclusion reached in this paragraph. That statute specifically requires a board finding that the property to be leased is surplus. The need to specify that finding in this section of Article 12 implies that it is not generally required for other

School administrative units and community and technical colleges are exceptions to what has been said in this discussion. G.S. 115C-518(a) permits a school unit to dispose of real and personal property only after the local school board has determined that use of the property is "unnecessary or undesirable for public school purposes," and G.S. 115D-15 requires a comparable determination by college boards of trustees before a college may dispose of its property. These determinations amount to determinations that the property is surplus.

C. Preparing Property for Disposition

Although there is no North Carolina case law on point and very little elsewhere,[26] it is likely that a local government may expend money to improve property in order to enhance the market for disposing of that property. If the expenditure will be recouped by a higher sales price, or if sale would be unlikely without the expenditure, such an expenditure is well within the government's discretion. (Of course, if the expenditure is *not* reflected in the sales price, it might look like an unconstitutional gift to the buyer.) In addition to expenditures that improve the property, a local government can probably subdivide its property and sell it in lots and tracts rather than as a single tract. Again, the prospect of a higher total price brings such a step within the government's discretion.[27]

D. Commissioners' Right of First Refusal on School and College Property

G.S. 115C-518 requires that before a school administrative unit may dispose of real property, it give the county an opportunity to purchase the property. The price is to be either the "fair market value" as

---

dispositions pursuant to that Article. *See also id.* § 90-112(d)(4). Under that section, before a law enforcement agency may sell vehicles that it has seized for violations of the controlled substances law, the agency's director must determine that the vehicles are surplus.

26. In Walrath v. City of Salamanca, 6 N.Y.S.2d 513 (N.Y. App. Div. 1938), the court upheld the use of public moneys to renovate a building, acquired through tax foreclosure, to the point that it could be leased.

27. In Puett v. Gaston County, 19 N.C. App. 231, 198 S.E.2d 440 (1973), discussed below in subsection F of this section, the county had subdivided a 21-acre tract into 17 lots. The court invalidated a planned sale because the restrictions that the county placed on the lots allegedly drove down the prices that might be offered for them. But if subdividing a tract of land enhances the tract's value, the rationale of *Puett* clearly supports doing so.

established by the school board or a price negotiated by the school unit and the county. Only if the county chooses not to purchase the property may the school unit commence other sale procedures. G.S. 115D-15 provides that community and technical colleges are to sell property pursuant to the same procedures as school administrative units, and consequently the county commissioners enjoy a right of first refusal for college property as well. It should be noted that the commissioner's right extends only to the interest in the property that the school board or college proposes to sell. If the school unit or college proposes to lease the property or grant an easement over the property, it is only a lease or an easement that the county has any right to purchase.

There is one probable exception to the commissioners' right of first refusal—leases of school property to a charter school. G.S. 115C-238.29E(e) provides that if a charter school requests that the local board of education lease school property to it, the school board "shall lease any available building or land to the charter school unless the board demonstrates that the lease is not economically or practically feasible or that the local board does not have adequate classroom space to meet its enrollment needs." Thus, once the school board decides that the property requested by the charter school is available, the statute mandates that it lease the property to the charter school. Giving the county commissioners the right to lease the property instead is flatly inconsistent with this statutory direction.

A separate question arises when a school unit intends to *exchange* its property for other property. On its face, G.S. 115C-518 applies to any disposition of property, but the case of *Painter v. Wake County Board of Education*[28] may suggest that exchanges are not covered. In that case the North Carolina Supreme Court held that the requirement that county commissioners approve the price a school unit proposed to pay to acquire property[29] did not apply to property acquired through an exchange. A court might consequently conclude that this other involvement of county commissioners in school property transactions does not apply to exchanges either. Such a conclusion seems unwarranted. The county commissioners have no power to approve acquisitions by exchange because they are not directly providing the assets used to acquire the property. Their right of first refusal, however, arises because they probably did at

---

28. 283 N.C. 165, 217 S.E.2d 650 (1972). The case is discussed in § 307-A, *supra*.

29. *See* § 307-A, *supra*.

some time provide the money the school unit used to acquire the property being conveyed. That fact does not change simply because the conveyance will be done as an exchange rather than for cash, and for that reason there is no ground to exempt exchanges from the county commissioners' right of first refusal.

It should also be noted that the right does apply when a school unit proposes to convey property to some other governmental unit, such as a city.

E. Terms of Sale

The several statutory procedures for disposing of property assume that the local government will establish various terms of sale,[30] but the procedures do not specify the kinds of terms contemplated or permitted. As with many matters, the specific terms associated with any sale will be a matter of discretion. Terms of sale commonly established by North Carolina local governments include

- the nature of the sale (sealed bid, auction, upset bid, etc.);
- a minimum sales price, if any;
- the need for and amount of any deposit;
- in large-scale transactions, a showing by the purchaser of financial responsibility;
- that the buyer be current on property tax payments to the local government;[31]
- whether payment will be by cash or on some other basis;
- whether employees may bid on the property;[32]
- time of closing; and
- whether the property is sold "as is."

---

30. The statutes often require the published notice of the sale to include any terms of sale. *E.g.,* G.S. 160A-270.

31. In Deibler v. City of Rehoboth Beach, 790 F.2d 328 (3d Cir. 1986), the federal court of appeals held that a requirement that candidates for city office be current on tax payments was unconstitutional because the requirement was not related to one's fitness for office. A comparable requirement for eligibility to acquire government property, however, does seem supportable. The selling government is releasing property to the private sector and obviously wants to collect taxes on the property once sold. That someone has not paid property taxes on property already owned is suggestive of whether that person will pay them on the property being acquired.

32. Conflicts of interest that arise when a government conveys property are discussed in § 509, *supra.*

Only if terms of sale might be thought to unreasonably restrict the number of buyers[33] or be thought to pursue goals extraneous to the property transactions involved, are they likely to be found an abuse of discretion.

A unit may establish terms of sale for each separate sale, particularly if sales are irregular and infrequent. But if sales become frequent, the unit may wish to develop and adopt standing policies on terms of sale and other elements of the sale process. By establishing regular and repeated practices, such policies assist persons who regularly bid on public property as well as the government's officials and employees who conduct the sales.

F. Conditions on the Use of Property

The North Carolina Court of Appeals has held that under Article 12's general property disposition procedures a local government may not restrict by deed the uses to be made of property conveyed by the government if the restrictions will depress the price offered for the property. In *Puett v. Gaston County*,[34] the county proposed to subdivide and dispose of twenty-one acres of a seventy-five-acre hospital tract, generally limiting the property's use to medical office buildings. In a suit brought by a taxpayer, the court upheld a preliminary injunction against the sale. The court held that such a restriction on use might well depress the value of the property; if this were so, the commissioners would not be fulfilling their responsibility to obtain the highest price for the property.

The court's opinion assumes that price is the only legitimate interest a local government has when it conveys property under general disposition procedures. Although one could certainly quarrel with this assumption (as Gaston County no doubt would), on the basis of the North Carolina statutory context and what little case law there is from elsewhere, the case was probably correctly decided. A number of separate North Carolina statutes, regulating disposition of property when the government's interest in the end use of the property is clear, expressly

---

33. *E.g.,* in Lieberman v. Township Comm., 141 A.2d 553 (N.J. Super. Ct. App. Div. 1958) the township required a bid deposit in the form of a certified check. The court held it was unreasonable for the township to return a deposit offered in cash.

34. 19 N.C. App. 231, 198 S.E.2d 440 (1973).

permit conveyances subject to conditions or covenants.[35] The absence of such an express permission in the general disposition statutes is telling. Furthermore, the few cases on point from other states agree with the substance of the *Puett* decision: the main goal of the sale procedures is price, and use conditions that depress the market for property are therefore not permitted.[36] Thus, if a local government wishes to dispose of property and by deed or other instrument limit the permissible uses of the property, it must act pursuant to clear authority to impose conditions or covenants on use, either by specific general law or by local act.[37]

G. General Comments on Notice

Many of the statutory procedures described in this chapter require public notice of the conveyance or of a public hearing concerning the conveyance. This section examines three aspects of notice: the meaning of publication, the property's description, and the timing of the notice.

"*Publish.*" Under the general provisions of G.S. Chapter 160A, to *publish* a notice means "insertion in a newspaper qualified under G.S. 1-597 to publish legal advertisements" in the local government, and that shorthand applies to the various procedures in Article 12 and elsewhere in G.S. Chapters 160A and 153A.[38] It also should apply to publication requirements for other procedures found in other chapters of the General Statutes. That the newspaper must be qualified to publish legal advertisements does not mean, however, that the notice must be placed in the legal advertisement columns. A number of local governments publish notice of upcoming sales in display ads placed among the news columns of the

---

35. *E.g.,* G.S. 158-7.1(d) (economic development); 160A-321 (city enterprises); 160A-400.8(3) (historic properties); and 160A-457(4) (community development).

36. The most relevant cases are from New York. *See* Ross v. Wilson, 127 N.E.2d 697 (N.Y. 1955) (improper to accept lower bid because government preferred that bidder's use); Tarshis v. City of New York, 262 N.Y.S.2d 538 (N.Y. App. Div. 1965) (improper to limit bidders to nonprofit corporations and uses to religious or educational purposes); Deed Realty Corp. v. City of Yonkers, 147 N.Y.S.2d 136 (N.Y. Sup. Ct. 1955) (improper to condition title sold at auction by requiring reversion to city if Otis Elevator ceases to operate plant in city).

37. 1983 N.C. Sess. Laws, ch. 224, is an example of such a local act. It permits local governments in McDowell County to dispose of real property, subject to "limitations on the future use of the property."

38. G.S 160A-1(7). G.S 153A-1(6) has a comparable provision that applies throughout that chapter. The details of G.S. 1-597 are discussed in Steven Holt, *Publication of Legal Notices*, Loc. Gov't Law Bull. No. 22 (Institute of Government 1983).

paper, a practice thought more likely to reach possible buyers and one that is permitted by the statute. In addition to published notice, some governments routinely mail invitations to bid to persons who often bid on property or who have made known their interest in a particular parcel or tract.

Property description. Several of the statutory procedures require that the notice describe the property. It is not necessary that such a description be by metes and bounds or courses and distances. Rather, any description that enables ordinary persons reading the notice to locate the property is sufficient, and in many instances references to tax maps, plats, or street addresses will be far more useful than a set of courses and distances.

Timing of the notice. The various sales procedures that require publication of notices require that the notices be published some number of days before an action is taken or that some action be taken within some number of days after publication. These statutes do not, however, include any rules for counting days, nor is there a general rule applicable throughout G.S. Chapter 160A. In these circumstances, the common practice is to rely upon the rules set out in Rule 6 of the North Carolina Rules of Civil Procedure.[39] That rule specifies that in computing time periods one does not count the day of publication but one does count the last day of the required time period. (If the last day is a Saturday, Sunday, or holiday, it is not counted, and the time period ends at the end of the next day that is not a Saturday, Sunday, or holiday.) Thus if a statute requires that a local government give at least ten days' published notice of a public hearing and the hearing will be held on October 22, the latest the notice may be published is October 12. The ten-day period in this instance starts with October 13 and ends on October 22.

§605. Negotiating Procedures

A. Use of Agents

A local government may use its own employees or independent real estate brokers when it disposes of property. The real estate licensing laws state that a corporation—which would include a municipal corporation or other local government[40]—may act in the fashion of a real estate

---

39. G.S 1A-1, Rule 6.

40. Uncertainty about whether "corporation" includes municipal corporations may have led to the 1999 amendment to the real estate licensing laws that

broker in transactions involving its own property without being licensed itself as a broker.[41] Because a corporation may only act through individuals, this perforce means that a corporation's employees may act in the fashion of a real estate broker when dealing with the corporation's property, even if those employees are not licensed as brokers.[42] Of course, a local government may also contract with a broker to help with the selling process, such as locating potential buyers for the property.[43] Some local governments have used brokers to locate and encourage buyers once the upset bid procedure has begun.

Although governing boards may use employees and independent contractors to assist in the disposition process, they may not, without specific statutory authority, delegate to someone else—an individual, a governing board committee, some other board, or some private entity— the decisions of whether to dispose of property at all and what price to accept. Although North Carolina case law on this point is inconclusive,[44]

---

expressly exempts housing authorities and their employees from need of a license when dealing with property owned by an authority. *Id.* § 93A-2(c)(8) (added to by N.C. Sess. Law 1999-409).

41. *Id.* § 93A-2(c)(1) (Cum. Supp.).

42. The Vermont Supreme Court reached this conclusion in interpreting that state's real estate licensing laws, which were, in this respect, essentially identical with North Carolina's. *In re* McGrath, 411 A.2d 1362 (Vt. 1980). *See also* Palkoski v. Garcia, 115 A.2d 539 (N.J. 1955), in which the court appears to have accepted this conclusion, although it went on to hold that the person involved in that case was not an employee of the company whose land was being sold. In Florida Real Estate Comm'n v. Johnson, 362 So. 2d 674 (Fla. 1978), the Florida Supreme Court held that it was unconstitutional to permit individuals and each member of a partnership to act in the fashion of a real estate broker with respect to property owned by the individual or partnership without being licensed as a real estate broker, but only allow one designated employee of a corporation to so act with respect to corporate property. Equal protection mandated that corporations be allowed to work through any of their employees when dealing with their property.

43. Cody Realty & Mortgage Co. v. City of Winston-Salem, 216 N.C. 726, 6 S.E.2d 501 (1940). *Accord* Magnotta v. Gerlach, 93 N.E.2d 569 (N.Y. 1950).

44. In Bowles v. Fayetteville Graded Schools, 211 N.C. 36, 188 S.E. 615 (1936), the school board instructed its property committee to consider offers for a parcel of land, "with power to act." The committee did as it was told, and eventually its chairman executed a contract of sale, which an unsuccessful bidder then challenged in court. The trial held the delegation of all decision making to the committee invalid, but the supreme court affirmed on the narrow ground that the school unit's charter required that all contracts be executed by the chairman of the school board, and that was not done in the case. The court did not com-

the statutes themselves make this clear. Throughout the general disposition statutes basic decision making is expressly the responsibility of the
governing board. In general the board must act to authorize the sale and
later must give final approval of the sales price. In a few instances these
statutes expressly permit delegation of basic decisions to others,[45] exceptions that further prove the general rule that the governing board itself
must act.

B. Open Meetings Law

It was noted in Section 308 that the open meetings law permits closed
sessions to discuss development of negotiating positions for *acquiring*
real property. With one indirect exception, however, no provision of the
law permits closed sessions to discuss any aspect of *disposing* of property, real or personal. The exception permits closed sessions to discuss
matters relating to the location or expansion of industries, "including
agreement on a tentative list of economic development incentives that
may be offered" to a company.[46] One possible incentive is to convey land
or a building to a company, and therefore that limited category of conveyance can be discussed in closed session. Once a tentative incentive
agreement is reached with a company, the local government must hold a
public hearing on the proposed agreement before it can be made final.
(Section 608-C discusses the procedural requirements attendant upon a
conveyance of property for economic development.)

C. Rejection of All Offers

Some disposition statutes give the governing board the right, at any time
in the process, to reject all offers and either seek new offers or cancel the
entire sale.[47] The absence of such an express statutory right in other
statutes, however, is unimportant because the North Carolina courts
have recognized that a governing board may always reject all bids.[48] A
local government cannot be forced to sell its property.

---

ment upon the broader discussion of the trial court. A very old Virginia case
agrees with the trial court. Beal v. City of Roanoke, 17 S.E. 738 (Va. 1893).

45. G.S. 160A-266(c) (Cum. Supp.) (personal property worth less than
$5,000), discussed *infra* § 608-A2; and 160A-272 (short-term leases), discussed
infra § 610-A1.

46. G.S. 143-318.11(a)(4).

47. *E.g., id.* § 160A-269 (upset bids).

48. *See* City of Asheville v. Herbert, 190 N.C. 732, 130 S.E. 861 (1925).

§606. Deeds

G.S. 160A-275 permits any "city, county, or other municipal corporation" to execute and deliver general warranty deeds to real property.[49] The statute also excuses any governing board member of such a government from personal liability because the government executed a general warranty deed, unless the board member acted in "fraud, malice, or bad faith." A few early courts had held that local governments could not give general warranty deeds without specific statutory authority,[50] and those cases, as well as the immunization of board members from liability, may account for this statute. (No North Carolina appellate case seems to have occasioned the statute, first enacted in 1945.)

As a practical matter, most local governments in North Carolina give quitclaim rather than warranty deeds. Governments often acquire property without undertaking a full title search—most commonly when foreclosing liens on property for unpaid taxes under the *in rem* procedure—and in such a case a quitclaim deed may be the only prudent deed to give.

§607. Property and Deed Excise Taxes

A. Payment of Property Taxes

G.S. 105-285(d) deals with the taxability of property conveyed by a local government to an owner in whose hands the property will no longer be exempt from taxation. If the conveyance takes place after January 1 but before July 1, the grantee must list the property for taxation as of the date of conveyance. The property is valued as of the preceding January 1 and is taxed for the fiscal year beginning July 1. If the conveyance takes place in the second half of the calendar year, the property remains unlisted until the succeeding January 1. The parties to the transaction may agree as to which of them will pay the taxes due on the property, although in any event the taxes will constitute a lien on the property in the hands of the purchaser. Many local governments include as a term of sale the requirement that all taxes be paid by the grantee.

---

49. *General warranty deeds* and other forms of deeds are explained in the glossary.

50. *E.g.,* Harrison v. Palo Alto County, 73 N.W. 872 (Iowa 1898).

B. The Excise Stamp Tax on Deeds

G.S. 105-228.30 levies an excise tax on each deed or other instrument by which any interest in real property is conveyed to another person and directs that the tax be paid to the register of deeds by the *grantor* before the deed is recorded. G.S. 105-228.28 provides that the General Statutes article within which this tax is located applies to every person and entity that conveys an interest in North Carolina real estate "other than a governmental unit and instrumentalities thereof." Therefore, when a local government conveys its real estate, no excise stamp tax need be paid on that deed.

§608. Private Negotiation and Sale of Personal Property and of Fee Interests in Real Property

Generally G.S. Chapter 160A, Article 12, requires competitive sales of fee interests in real property. The Article also generally requires competitive sales of personal property when that property is valued at $30,000 or more. The Article does, however, permit privately negotiated sales of personal property worth less than $30,000, and also includes a few narrow authorizations of privately negotiated sales of fee interests in real property or of both real and personal property. In addition, a few other statutes permit privately negotiated sales of real or personal property. This section reviews these various authorizations for private sales. It should be noted that these exceptions permit not only private sales of the fee interest in real property but also private sales of any lesser interest, including long-term leaseholds.

Normally, real property includes not only land but also permanent improvements made to the land, most typically buildings. Occasionally, however, a local government wishes to separate a building from the land and convey the building alone, retaining title to the land. When that occurs, the building has become personal property. By being separated from the land, the building has taken on the nature of a trade fixture, and trade fixtures are personal property.[51]

---

51. George F. Madsen, *Fixtures*, in THE AMERICAN LAW OF REAL PROPERTY § 7.04[1] (Arthur R. Gaudio, general ed., 1994). In Scales v. Wiley, 33 A. 771 (Vt. 1895), the plaintiff agreed to disassemble a barn on her property and then reassemble it on defendant's property. The court wrote that this "clearly was not a contract for the sale of land or of any interest therein. . . . [The building] was to be changed from real to personal estate." *Id.* A number of cases that hold that

A. Personal Property

1. Generally

G.S. 160A-266 permits the private sale of personal property valued at less than $30,000 "for any one item or group of similar items."[52] The procedures that a local government must follow with such a sale are set out in G.S. 160A-267. The governing board begins the process with adoption of an authorizing resolution, which must be adopted at a *regular* meeting. The resolution must identify the property to be sold, and authorize a named official of the government to dispose of the property.

The resolution may, but need not, establish a minimum price for the property. It also may be appropriate to permit the selling official to divide the property and sell it in lots at his or her discretion. (It should be understood that the official in charge of the sale normally has authority not only to conduct the sale but also to execute any necessary documents on behalf of the local government.) Appendix A, in Section II-A, includes an example of such a resolution.

Once the resolution is adopted, the local government must publish a notice that summarizes the resolution. The sale itself may not be concluded until at least ten days after publication of the notice. (Recalling the rule discussed above in Section 604-G, this means that if the notice is published on, say, the 9th of the month, the earliest that the property may be sold is on the 19th of that month.) Appendix A, in Section II-B, includes an example of the notice.

Law Enforcement Officers' Weapons. Local law enforcement agencies are often interested in selling surplus weapons to the officers who have been using those weapons. A local government may do so pursuant to G.S. 160A-266 and 160A-267. Such sales can create public relations concerns, because sometimes citizens assume that officers are receiving

---

contracts for the sale of buildings that have been or will be severed from the land are not contracts involving real property are collected in A.W., Annotation, *Agreement for Sale of Buildings or Material Therein as One for Sale of Interest in Real Property within Statute of Frauds,* 91 A.L.R. 1280 (1934).

52. Obviously, the actual market value of property sometimes is not known until it is sold. If the local government authorizes a private sale of property it believes to be worth less than $30,000 and then receives an offer of $30,000 or more, the better course is probably to convert the process to an upset bid sale of the property, using that offer as the initial bid.

some sort of favorable treatment, but there is no question as to their legality. In addition, G.S. 20-187.2 expressly permits the sale of the person's service side arm to a retiring law enforcement officer.

2. Property Worth Less than $5,000

G.S. 160A-266(c) permits local governing boards to adopt regulations or policies that allow specific administrators, without need of further board action, to dispose of personal property worth less than $5,000 for any one item or group of similar items. These regulations or policies may delegate to one or more named administrators the authority to declare qualifying property to be surplus, set the fair market value of the property, and convey title to the property. The statute does not suggest to which official or officials these powers may be delegated, leaving that decision to each unit. Typical choices include the chief administrative officer, such as a manager or school superintendent; a finance officer or business manager; a purchasing agent; a property officer; or individual department heads. The regulations should specify the method or methods by which the property may be sold; these may include private sale, public sale, or both. Indeed, the method might be one not used for any other form of property, such as through a consignment agent or at a government surplus warehouse. At least one local government has taken its authority to conduct raffles and used surplus automobiles as the property to be raffled off.[53] And a government could exchange property worth less than $5,000 for services, something not permitted for more valuable property. The board may wish to establish some scheme of priority among permissible methods or it may leave the choice to the selling official. The statute also leaves the question of whether there must be public notice of any sale to local choice, and the board could require that notice be part of any selling process or leave that decision to the selling official to make on a case-by-case basis. Finally, although the statute does not mention this point, the board may wish to include guidelines in the regulations concerning purchases of such property by the selling official or her family or by other employees of the local government and their families.[54] The

---

53. G.S 14-309.15 (Cum. Supp.) permits nonprofit organizations to conduct raffles; in S.L. 1993-219, the General Assembly provided that for purposes of the raffle statute, governmental entities are considered nonprofit organizations. Thus local governments may conduct raffles.

54. Purchase of the property by the selling official, and perhaps by members of her immediate family, might violate G.S. 14-234. *See supra* § 509-A.

North Carolina League of Municipalities has prepared a model ordinance authorizing sales pursuant to G.S. 160A-266(c), and these policies are available from the League.

If a governing board does delegate sales power, G.S. 160A-266(c) requires each administrator to whom the delegation is made to keep a record of sales and make a semiannual report to the board. One report is due each February 1, summarizing sales between the preceding July 1 and December 31, and the other is due each August 1, summarizing sales in the period of January 1 to June 30. Each report is to generally describe any property disposed of, list to whom it was conveyed, and state the consideration received for the property.

Law Enforcement Officers' Weapons. Local law enforcement agencies are often interested in selling surplus weapons to the officers who have been using those weapons. G.S. 160A-266(c) is adequate authority for such a sale, subject to the same potential public relations issues noted in the discussion of G.S. 160A-266 and -267.

B. Exchanges

G.S. 160A-271 permits those local governments subject to Article 12 to exchange real or personal property for other real or personal property and sets out a procedure for exchanges. The statutory procedure begins only after the local government has actually negotiated the terms of the exchange with the owner of the other property. At that point the local government must publish a notice that

- describes the properties to be exchanged;
- states the value of the properties and other consideration being exchanged; and
- states the governing board's intention to authorize the exchange at its next regular meeting.[55]

(Appendix A, in Section VI-A, includes an example of this notice.) The statute directs that the notice be published at least ten days before the meeting at which the board will authorize the exchange.[56] (Recalling the

---

55. The notice should include the *date* of the next regular meeting, to avoid confusion.

56. The statutes state that the resolution must be adopted "upon 10 days public notice." This language should be understood to mean *at least* and not *exactly* 10 days. In smaller counties without daily newspapers, a requirement of exactly ten days' notice would often be impossible to meet.

rule discussed above in Section 604-G, this means that for a meeting on, say, the twenty-second of the month, the notice must be published no later than the twelfth of the month.)

Note that the statute requires that the board act at its next *regular* meeting; it may not do so at a special or called meeting.[57] The purpose of the notice is simply to publicize the government's intention to undertake the property exchange; the governing board is not required to hold a hearing on the matter, although it may take public comment if it wishes. The board authorizes the exchange by adopting a resolution to that effect. The statute does not set out any required content for the resolution, but it seems wise to repeat the material included in the published notice. (Appendix A, in Section VI-B, includes an example of this resolution.) Once the resolution is adopted, the exchange may go forward. Although a simultaneous exchange is most common, the statute does not require that. In one instance known to the author, the local government agreed to make certain improvements to the property it owned before conveying the property to the other party, but the other party was willing to convey his property to the local government immediately; the statute has room for such a sequential exchange.

The exchange statute requires that a local government exchanging property receive "a full and fair consideration" for its property.[58] Three points should be made about consideration.

First, "full and fair" does not mean exactly equal. The governing board may, in its discretion, weigh such nonmonetary factors as the need for the particular property being acquired, the savings of both time and money made possible by exchanging rather than purchasing or condemning the

---

57. If events before or at the *next* regular meeting cause the board to delay the authorization, a new notice probably is not necessary, at least if the matter is simply put off until the succeeding regular meeting. The notice stated that the board *intended* to authorize the exchange, and that remains correct. If the authorization will be delayed for more than a single meeting, however, it would be prudent to publish a new notice.

58. The first sentence of G.S. 160A-271 permits a local government to exchange any real or personal property for any other real or personal property. The second sentence goes on to authorize a local government to exchange facilities of a governmental enterprise for "like facilities." The second sentence avoids being redundant because it does not include the additional requirement of "full and fair consideration." The second sentence was included in the statute to facilitate the adjustment of enterprise service areas around the edges of cities, and it was thought that a requirement of full and fair consideration would add unnecessary complications to already complex transactions.

property, and so on. If such factors are included as part of consideration, the board should mention and document them in the resolution authorizing the exchange. As long as no abuse of discretion is shown, the transaction should withstand any legal challenge.[59]

Second, the consideration may consist of more than the property being acquired; the statute's notice requirement talks of the "properties and *other consideration*" being exchanged. Clearly that additional consideration may include cash. (The government may also give up cash, as well as property, in exchange for other property.) There can be no hard-and-fast rule as to how large a percentage of total consideration received may be cash. If cash makes up more than one-half of the total consideration received by the government, it would be wise to document carefully the need for the exchange; but a fifty-fifty split should not be a litmus test. It may be, for example, that the other party insists upon an exchange as a condition of conveying her property. The best that can be said is that on the totality of the circumstances it should appear that an exchange— rather than a concealed sale—lies at the heart of the transaction.

Third, although the statute permits an exchange of real for personal property, or personal for real, it does not permit a government to convey its property and receive services in exchange. That is, a local government may not use the exchange statute to convey property to someone who then agrees to provide services to the government in consideration of the property but conveys no property to the government. While it may be possible that a government could accept services as the make-up consideration when the property it is receiving is slightly less valuable than the property it is conveying, the comment that concluded the last paragraph remains pertinent: the transaction must still be a true exchange of properties, with any other consideration included only to equalize the value of the properties being exchanged.

As was noted in Section 602-B, several special-purpose local governments are not included within Article 12 and thus are not subject to G.S. 160A-271. With the exception of various public hospitals, these special-purpose local governments are not subject to any specific competitive-sale requirements. In that circumstance the case law from elsewhere (there are no relevant North Carolina appellate cases) supports

---

59. *See* Painter v. Wake County Bd. of Educ., 289 N.C. 165, 217 S.E.2d 650 (1975). The school statute in effect at the time required "full" consideration for the exchange, and the court was willing to accept some inequality of value between the two parcels.

the proposition that the power to sell or dispose of property includes the power to exchange property.[60] Although these other governments may devise their own procedures for exchange, the relevant records should fully document the value of the properties and of any other consideration involved. This documentation would be necessary to defend the transaction should it be challenged.

Trade-ins. G.S. 143-129 governs the procedures by which local governments purchase apparatus, supplies, materials, and equipment. Sometimes local governments wish to trade in existing property as part of the process of purchasing new property. Such a trade-in is a disposal of the existing property, however, and at one time the only way to accomplish such a trade-in was to try to fit such transactions into both G.S. 143-129, the purchase statute, and G.S. 160A-271, the exchange statute, and it was not an easy fit. In 1997, however, the General Assembly enacted G.S. 143-129.7 to deal directly with trade-ins associated with purchases of apparatus, supplies, materials, and equipment. That statute allows a local government that is purchasing property through formal bids to consider the amount offered for the surplus property in determining the lowest responsible bidder.[61]

C. Economic Development Property

G.S. 158-7.1(b) permits counties and cities (but not other local governments) to acquire and develop land for an industrial park for industrial or commercial use, to acquire separate parcels of property for industrial or commercial use, to acquire options to purchase such property, and to construct or acquire shell buildings.[62] Subsection (d) of this statute then

---

60. East Chicago Co. v. City of East Chicago, 87 N.E. 17 (Ind. 1909); Brady v. Carlson, 457 N.E.2d 1182 (Ohio Ct. App. 1983); Bobo v. City of Spartanburg, 96 S.E.2d 67 (S.C. 1956). In cases in which the power to sell was held *not* to include the power to exchange, the statutes required competitive (or nonprivate) sales, and it was that requirement that the courts found inconsistent with exchange. *E.g.,* Bowling v. City of El Paso, 525 S.W.2d 539 (Tex. Civ. App. 1975).

61. This statute is discussed in greater detail in BLUESTEIN, *supra* note 1, at 39–40.

62. Section 307-C, *supra*, sets out the special procedural requirements that a county or city must follow before taking any of these steps.

authorizes local governments to convey any property or interest (including options) so acquired or constructed to a private person or entity by private negotiation and sale.[63]

As with exchanges, the statutory procedure begins only after the local government has negotiated the terms of the conveyance with the private person or company. At that point, G.S. 158-7.1(d) requires that the governing body of the county or city hold a public hearing on the conveyance, upon at least ten days' published notice. Once the hearing is complete, the governing body must approve the transaction.

Notice of the Public Hearing. As noted above, the statute requires that the local government give at least ten days' published notice of the public hearing. (Recalling the rule discussed above in Section 604-G, this means that for a meeting on, say, the twenty-second of the month, the notice must be published no later than the twelfth of the month.) The notice must include the following details:

- the interest to be conveyed or leased,
- the value of the interest,
- the proposed consideration for the conveyance or lease, and
- the governing body's intention to approve the conveyance or lease.

Appendix A, in Section I-A, includes an example of a notice for a public hearing to convey land under this statute.

The Wage Determination. Before a county or city may convey an interest in real property pursuant to G.S. 158-7.1, subsection (d) requires the governing body to "determine the probable average hourly wage to be paid to workers by the business to be located at the property to be conveyed." In reaching that determination, the governing body probably should consider only those employees paid on an hourly basis, given the statute's reference to average *hourly* wage.[64] Furthermore, the governing body should follow the practices of the state Employment Security Commission, which is charged by statute with calculating companies' average

---

63. A local government may also convey property under this statute that it acquired for some other purpose but no longer needs for that purpose. The procedures for conveying property for economic development are discussed in considerable detail in DAVID M. LAWRENCE, ECONOMIC DEVELOPMENT LAW FOR NORTH CAROLINA LOCAL GOVERNMENTS, ch. 4 (Institute of Government 2000).

64. This is an important limitation. The Employment Security Commission, in determining the average weekly wage paid at a company, includes all employees, not just those paid on an hourly basis.

weekly wages, and include a company's cash payments to employees but not noncash benefits.[65] Thus wages include regular and overtime pay, vacation and holiday pay, year-end bonuses and profit-sharing, and comparable employee pay incentives; they do not include noncash benefits such as insurance or retirement contributions made by a company on an employee's behalf.

Consideration. Finally, G.S. 158-7.1(d) requires the governing body to determine "the fair market value of the interest [the government is conveying], subject to whatever covenants, conditions, and restrictions the county or city proposes to subject it to." Subsection (d) concludes by requiring that the "consideration for the conveyance may not be less than the value so determined" by the governing body. Subsection (d2) of the section, however, states that in

> arriving at the amount of consideration that it receives, the [governing body] may take into account prospective tax revenues from improvements to be constructed on the property, prospective sales tax revenues to be generated in the area, as well as any other prospective tax revenues or income coming to the [local government] over the next ten years as a result of the conveyance or lease.

Because a local government will receive the various tax and other revenues in any event, this amounts to an authorization to convey the property as an incentive to a company, with the company in fact paying none or only part of the value of the property.

If a local government decides to use the authorization in G.S. 158-7.1(d2) and take various revenues into account in arriving at the amount of consideration received for conveyance of government property, the subsection imposes some additional procedural requirements.

First, the governing body must "determine that the conveyance of the property will stimulate the local economy, promote business, and result in the creation of a substantial number of jobs in the county or city that pay at or above the median average wage in the county or, for a city, in the county where the city is located." Recall that G.S. 158-7.1(d) requires a local government to forecast the probable *average hourly wage* that will be paid by the purchaser or lessee anytime it plans to convey or lease real property pursuant to G.S. 158-7.1. Subsection (d2) imposes an additional

---

65. G.S. 96-8(13) (Cum. Supp.).

requirement that necessitates determining the *median average wage* that the company will pay and comparing that to the county's existing median average wage. The company's forecast average wage must equal or exceed the county's current average wage. That is, if real property is to be used as an incentive, the jobs created must be at least as good as the average level of jobs already present in the county. The statute specifies that the median average wage in a county is the median average wage for all insured industries in the county as computed by the North Carolina Employment Security Commission.[66] Because the statute explicitly references the Employment Security Commission determinations, it intends that in this case governments follow the Commission's practice of including the wages of all employees at a location and not just hourly employees.

Second, the local government and the company must enter into a contract that obligates the company "to construct, within a specified period of time not to exceed five years, improvements on the property that will generate the tax revenue taken into account in arriving at the consideration."

Appendix A, in Section I-B, includes an example of a resolution authorizing conveyance of real property pursuant to G.S. 158-7.1(d) and (d2).

D. Community Development Property

Cities (but not counties or any other local governments) may by private sale "sell, exchange, or otherwise transfer" real property located in a community development project area. The property may be transferred to a redeveloper, subject to covenants, conditions, and restrictions, for some use that accords with the community development plan for the project area.

Although no North Carolina statute defines *community development project area* or *community development plan*, the phrases are terms of art in the Community Development Block Grant (CDBG) program. That fact creates some ambiguity in this authorization for private sales of property. Clearly, if the city is receiving CDBG moneys from the federal government (or from the state as a pass-through), the geographic area in which those moneys are being expended is a community development project area;

---

66. Actually, the Employment Security Commission determines the "average weekly insured wage" for each county. *Id.* § 96-8(22) (Cum. Supp.). Presumably this is the figure meant in G.S. 159-7.1(d2).

and the city will have prepared a community development plan as part of the grant process. But the introductory paragraph to G.S. 160A-457 states that a city may exercise the powers authorized by the section "either as a part of a community development program or independently thereof," which suggests that the definitions of the CDBG program are not binding on activities undertaken pursuant to the section but not using CDBG moneys. But how else give meaning to the words? The statute's introductory language, just quoted, was part of the statute as originally enacted; the authorization for private sales of property was added some years later. Perhaps, given that sequence, the language in the introductory paragraph should be given less weight. At the least, in defining an area as a community development project area and in establishing a plan for the area, a city should respect the policies underlying the CDBG program. The pervasive purpose of the CDBG program is improving the lives of persons of low and moderate income. These purposes shape the areas that might reasonably be designated as community development project areas and the kinds of redevelopers and redevelopments that might be assisted within such an area. Conveying property for an economic development project, for example, that provides only high-skill jobs and that locates at some remove from low- and moderate-income residential areas seems incompatible with the goals of community development.

The statute requires that the property be appraised before it is conveyed, although apparently this can be done by qualified city employees as well as by independent appraisers. Although the statute does not state this, presumably the appraisal may take into account any restrictions to be placed on the property by covenant, condition, or otherwise. The sale price may not be less than this appraised value.

Once an agreement of conveyance has been reached, the city must publish notice of a public hearing on the transaction. The statute requires the notice to be published once a week for two successive weeks, with the first publication occurring not less than ten days nor more than twenty-five days before the hearing. (Recalling the rule discussed above in Section 604-G, this means that for a meeting on, say, September 22, the first notice must be published no later than September 12 and no earlier than August 28.) The statute directs that the notice disclose the terms of the transaction, although it also should identify the property being conveyed, state the city's intention to convey the property, and give the date, time, and place of the public hearing. (Appendix A, in Section X-A, includes an example of a notice for this public hearing.) At the hearing itself, the city must disclose the value of the property based on the appraisal discussed above. Once the hearing is concluded, at the same meeting if the city council wishes, and before closing the transaction, the council must approve the transaction. (Appendix A, in Section X-B, includes an example of a resolution approving a conveyance under this section.)

E. Property for Nonprofit Agencies Carrying Out Public Purposes

1. In General

G.S. 160A-279 provides that whenever a statute permits a county or city to appropriate money to a nonprofit organization, the county or city may also convey real or personal property to the organization and may do so by private sale. (This section is quite plain that it does not apply to any other local governments that are otherwise subject to Article 12 of G.S. Chapter 160A.)[67] Although a number of separate statutes authorize counties or cities to appropriate funds to nonprofit organizations, those separate statutes are unnecessary in this context. Rather, G.S. 153A-449 and 160A-20.1 permit counties and cities, respectively, to "contract with and appropriate money to any person, association, or corporation, in order to carry out any public purpose that the county [or city] is authorized by law to engage in." That is, if a county or city has statutory authority to engage in a particular activity, these statutes allow it to appropriate money to a private organization for that activity. And therefore, under G.S. 160A-279, the county or city may convey real or personal property to the same organization by private sale.[68]

There is one limitation on use of G.S. 160A-279 and one special procedural requirement. First, a county or city may not use the authorization to convey property that it acquired through exercise of the power of eminent domain.[69] Second, the county or city must attach to the conveyance covenants or conditions that will ensure that the property will be put to some public use by the recipient. As was noted in Section 508-B above, the constitution permits a local government to convey property without monetary consideration, if the recipient agrees to use the property for a public

---

67. G.S. 160A-279(b) reads: "Notwithstanding any other provision of law, this section applies only to cities and counties and not to any other entity which this Article otherwise applies to."

68. It is not necessary that the county or city have appropriated money to the organization, only that it has statutory authority to do so.

69. G.S. 160A-279(a) ("provided no property acquired by the exercise of eminent domain may be conveyed under this section").

use. The requirement of covenants or conditions ensuring such public use demonstrates that the General Assembly expected that in most cases local governments would use G.S. 160A-279 to make conveyances that were supported by continued public use of the property rather than by monetary payments.

A county or city conveying property pursuant to G.S. 160A-279 must follow the procedures set out in G.S. 160A-267, which generally deals with private sales of personal property. The governing board begins the process by adopting a resolution or order authorizing conveyance of the property. (There is no notice required before the resolution or order is adopted nor any statutory requirement of a public hearing.) The board must adopt this resolution or order at a *regular* meeting. The document must identify the property being conveyed and authorize a named official of the government to dispose of the property. In addition, the document may, but need not, specify a minimum price. Because most often the consideration will be the recipient's promise to use the property for a public use, a minimum price is usually irrelevant. If continued public use is the consideration, though, it is a good idea for the resolution or order to indicate that fact. In addition, although G.S. 160A-267 does not require identifying the grantee in the resolution, a government conveying property pursuant to G.S. 160A-279 will usually want to include that information as well. Appendix A, in Section IX, includes an example of a resolution authorizing a conveyance under G.S. 160A-279.

Once the resolution or order has been adopted, the statute requires that the local government publish a notice summarizing the contents of the document. The conveyance may not be concluded until at least ten days after publication of this notice. (Recalling the rule discussed in Section 604-G, this means that if the notice is published on, say, the 9th of the month, the earliest that the property may be conveyed is on the 19th of the month.)

2. Motor Vehicles for Work First Recipients

The 1998 General Assembly added a proviso to G.S. 160A-279 permitting counties and cities to convey surplus automobiles to public or private entities that would in turn give the vehicles to Work First participants. The proviso requires that the Work First recipients of the automobiles be selected by the county department of social services. Constitutionally, local governments may give cash to persons eligible for public assistance, and indirectly giving them a used government vehicle is no different functionally from giving them the cash to buy such a vehicle. If a local government exercises the authority granted by this proviso, it must still follow the procedures for using G.S. 160A-279 set out above.

F. Property for Affordable Housing Projects

1. Counties

G.S. 153A-378 includes two paragraphs that authorize counties to convey real property by private sale to developers of or residents of housing for persons of low or moderate income. First, paragraph (4) authorizes counties to "convey residential property by private sale to persons of low or moderate income in accordance with G.S. 160A-267." The procedures of the cited statute are found in Section 608-A. The board of commissioners may attach any terms and conditions it deems appropriate to conveyances made pursuant to this first authorization.

Second, paragraph (3) authorizes counties to "convey property by private sale to any public or private entity that provides affordable housing to persons of low or moderate income." The paragraph requires the county to include as part of such a conveyance covenants or conditions that assure that the property will be developed by the grantee for sale or lease to the target population. Other than that, however, the paragraph imposes no procedural requirements on the county, and therefore there is no requirement of public notice or of a public hearing before the conveyance is made. Because the conveyance is to an entity that provides housing for persons of low or moderate income, it need not be supported by monetary consideration; the promise of public use—provision of housing—is adequate.

2. Cities

Through a linkage of statutes, G.S. 160A-279 authorizes cities to convey property by private sale to nonprofit entities for construction of low- or moderate-income housing.[70] The statutory trail begins with G.S. 160A-456(b). This statute authorizes a city council to "exercise directly

---

70. G.S. 160A-278 authorizes the local governments subject to Article 12 to lease land to persons who will use the land to construct housing for persons of low or moderate income. This statute was enacted at the same legislative session as G.S. 160A-279, although earlier in time, and is essentially redundant to the latter statute.

those powers granted by law to . . . housing authorities." That is, a city may undertake any activity that may be undertaken by a housing authority and need not act through such an authority. These initial authorizations necessitate reference to G.S. 157-9, which sets out the powers granted by statute to housing authorities. A basic power included in this section is to "prepare, carry out, and operate housing projects." *Housing project*, in turn, is defined in G.S. 157-3(12) and includes programs that assist developers of multifamily housing and developers and owners of owner-occupied housing. From here, the trail turns to G.S. 160A-20.1, which authorizes cities to appropriate money to private organizations to carry out any activity that a city may carry out directly; therefore a city may appropriate money to private organizations that develop multifamily or owner-occupied housing for persons of low or moderate income. Because a city may appropriate money to such organizations, G.S. 160A-279 authorizes private sales of property to them. And because the recipients will use the property to provide low-or-moderate income housing, the conveyance need not be supported by monetary consideration; the promise of public use—provision of housing—is adequate.

G. Fire Department and Rescue Squad Properties

G.S. 160A-277 authorizes counties, cities, and sanitary districts[71] to lease, sell, or otherwise convey *land* by private sale to a volunteer fire department or volunteer rescue squad.[72] (This statute was enacted eight years before G.S. 160A-279. The enactment of the latter statute has made G.S. 160A-277 redundant for counties and cities, but it is still useful authority for sanitary districts.) The recipient must be providing fire protection or rescue squad services to the conveying unit and must use the property for constructing or expanding its fire protection or rescue facilities. In

---

71. G.S. 160A-277 itself speaks only of cities, but of course Article 12 applies to several other types of local governments. G.S. 160A-277, however, requires that the recipient of the land provide fire protection or rescue services to the conveying government, and the entire framework of the statute implies that the lease or conveyance is made as a part of the government's responsibility to provide those services. Because only cities, counties, and sanitary districts have the authority (or responsibility) to provide those services, only those three kinds of local governments may use G.S. 160A-277.

72. The statute does not extend to personal property and, by its use of the word *land*, apparently does not apply to improved real estate either.

recognition that the property will continue in public use, the statute permits the conveyance to be made "with or without monetary consideration."

Although the statute does not require it, if the local government conveys title to the land rather than leasing it, and does so without monetary consideration, the government should add covenants or conditions to the deed to ensure continued public use of the property. That public use is, after all, the consideration supporting the conveyance, and if the public use stops, the consideration has failed. In a comparable case, the North Carolina Supreme Court suggested that any fee interest so conveyed should be subject to a condition that returns the property to the conveying government if the use for which the property was conveyed is abandoned.[73]

The statutory procedure for leases or conveyances to fire departments or rescue squads begins once the terms of the transaction have been agreed to by the parties. The local government publishes a notice that

- describes the property to be leased or conveyed,
- states the value of the property,
- states the proposed monetary consideration (or lack thereof), and
- states the governing board's intent to authorize the lease or conveyance at its next regular meeting.[74]

The statute directs that the notice be published at least ten days before the meeting at which the board will authorize the exchange.[75] (Recalling the rule discussed above in Section 604-G, this means that for a meeting on, say, the twenty-second of the month, the notice must be published no later than the twelfth of the month.)

Note that the statute requires that the board act at its next *regular* meeting; it may not do so at a special or called meeting.[76] The purpose of the notice is simply to publicize the government's intention to convey

---

73. Brumley v. Baxter, 225 N.C. 691, 36 S.E.2d 281 (1945) (city conveyance to veterans' recreation authority). *See also* the discussion *supra* § 508-B.

74. The notice should include the date of the next regular meeting, to avoid confusion.

75. The statute states that the resolution must be adopted "upon 10 days' public notice." This language should be understood to mean *at least* and not *exactly* 10 days. In smaller counties without daily newspapers, a requirement of exactly 10 days' notice would often be impossible to meet.

76. If events before or at the *next* regular meeting cause the board to delay the authorization, a new notice probably is not necessary, at least if the matter is

land to the fire department or rescue squad; the governing board is not required to hold a hearing on the matter, although it may take public comment if it wishes. At the meeting, the board authorizes the conveyance by adopting a resolution to that effect. Once the resolution is adopted, the conveyance may go forward.

H. Historically, Architecturally, or Scenically Significant Properties

A long proviso to G.S. 160A-266(b) permits the local governments that are subject to Article 12 to dispose of real or personal property by private sale when the property is significant because of its

- architectural, archaeological, artistic, cultural, or historical associations; or
- relationship to other property significant for architectural, archaeological, artistic, cultural, or historical associations; or
- natural, scenic, or open condition.

A local government may make such a sale only to a nonprofit corporation or trust whose purposes include the preservation or conservation of such properties. In addition, the deed must include a preservation or conservation agreement. Such an agreement, which is defined in G.S. 121-35, protects the characteristics of the property that make it significant and justify its private sale. The association or trust may use the property itself or dispose of it.[77] In either case the property must be subject to covenants or other restrictions that promote and protect its significant characteristics. These covenants should, when appropriate, secure rights of some public access to the property.[78]

---

simply put off until the succeeding regular meeting. The notice stated that the board *intended* to authorize the exchange, and that remains correct. If the authorization will be delayed for more than a single meeting, however, it would be prudent to publish a new notice.

77. There is no requirement that the nonprofit organization dispose of the property to some other nonprofit organization. Indeed, it is common for historical properties to be reconveyed to individuals, to be used for private residences, or to developers, who can take advantage of the tax credits available for rehabilitation of certified historic structures. *See* I.R.C. § 47 (West 1999); G.S. 105-129.35 through -129.37 (as added to by S.L. 1999-39).

78. If the property is ultimately sold as a private residence, for example, public access would not be appropriate.

The statute does not require any procedural steps before a private sale may be made pursuant to its authorization.

I. Open Space

Article 19, Part 4, of G.S. Chapter 160A authorizes counties and cities to preserve open space. One of the techniques that G.S. 160A-403 permits is for a county or city to acquire the fee to property and then convey it either back to the original owner or to a new owner, subject to covenants or other arrangements that limit the future use of the property and thereby preserve it as open space. If the government's conveyance is to the original owner, G.S. 160A-403 permits the conveyance to be made by private sale. In addition, the government may privately sell the property subject to conditions to a nonprofit corporation or trust pursuant to G.S. 160A-266(b), discussed just above in Section 608-H.[79] A sale to any other grantee, however, must be competitive, pursuant to the standard procedures of Article 12.[80]

J. City Enterprises

G.S. 160A-321 prohibits the sale (or lease or discontinuation) of certain city-owned enterprises, unless the transaction is first approved by the voters.[81] (There is no comparable requirement of voter approval for county-owned enterprises, or for enterprises owned by more special purpose local governments.) The enterprises subject to the prohibition are electrical systems, gas systems, water systems, sewer systems, public transportation systems, cable television systems, and stormwater and

---

79. G.S. 160A-403 states that the property may be conveyed by private sale to the original person "but to no other person." The proviso to G.S. 160A-266(b), however, was enacted after enactment of G.S. 160A-403, and its authorization presumably permits an exception to the flat prohibition of the earlier statute.

80. Because G.S. 160A-403 requires imposition of covenants to guarantee continuation of the property in open space, a competitive sale under Article 12 would not be subject to the general rule prohibiting imposition of covenants on property sold competitively. See supra § 604-F.

81. The voter approval requirement only applies to the lease, sale, or discontinuance of the entire enterprise. Sale of some assets because of changes in operating policies does not activate the requirement. Mullen v. Town of Louisburg, 225 N.C. 53, 33 S.E.2d 484 (1945) (sale of electrical generating facilities, but with continued operation of distribution system, not subject to voter approval requirement).

drainage systems.[82] This requirement of voter approval has been the law since 1907,[83] and in a 1919 case the North Carolina Supreme Court held that when an enterprise was sold with voter approval, pursuant to the predecessor statute of G.S. 160A-321, the general property sales statute did not apply.[84] The court thereby reached the very practical conclusion that the conveyance of an entire enterprise system could be privately negotiated. Because the relationship between the enterprise statute and property disposition statutes remains as it was in 1919 (although the details have changed), that case presumably remains good law.

A negative implication from the above discussion is that enterprise systems that are not subject to G.S. 160A-321 may not be sold privately. These enterprises are city airports, parking facilities, and solid waste collection and disposal facilities, and any enterprises owned by a county, sanitary district, or regional solid waste management authority.[85]

K. Miscellaneous Private Sales

1. Tax-foreclosed Property

Although in general property purchased by local governments through tax foreclosure must be resold pursuant to Article 12 of G.S. Chapter 160A, G.S. 105-376(c) does permit private sale of such property in limited circumstances. The government may privately sell the property to the former owner or to any other person, such as a mortgagee, who formerly held an interest in the property. The minimum consideration for such a sale is an "amount not less than the taxing unit's interest" in the property if the unit is sole owner, or "not less than the total interests of all taxing units" if the seller holds the property for the benefit of other units.

The only procedural requirement for such a sale is that the governing board must approve private sale of the property. Presumably the board could approve each parcel sold or adopt a general resolution applicable to all such properties currently held or subsequently acquired.

---

82. G.S. 160A-321 simply states that the voter approval requirement does not apply to airports, parking facilities, and solid waste facilities. Deleting these three from the list of enterprises set out in G.S. 160A-311 results in the list in the text.

83. It was added to by ch. 978, 1907 N.C. Pub. Laws.

84. Allen v. Town of Reidsville, 178 N.C. 513, 101 S.E. 267 (1919).

85. These last three kinds of local government are those enterprise-operating local governments that are subject to Article 12 of G.S. 160A. *See supra* § 602-A.

2. Other Foreclosed Property

G.S. 153A-163 permits a local government to purchase real property at a judicial sale, an execution sale, or a sale made pursuant to a power of sale, in order to secure a debt due the local government. The statute goes on to permit private sale of such property (as well as exchange or sale pursuant to Article 12), as long as the local government receives at least the amount it paid for the property. The statute does not require any procedural steps before such a private sale is made.

3. Donated Property

If property is donated to a local government for a specific purpose set out in the instrument of conveyance, and if the governing board determines that the property will not be used for that purpose, G.S. 153A-177 permits the local government to reconvey the property, without consideration, to the grantor or his heirs or assigns. The governing board's determination of nonuse should be set out in the board's minutes.

Before a reconveyance is made, the unit must publish notice of its intention to make the reconveyance. The notice must be published once a week for two successive weeks, but the statute does not set out a time period during which the first notice must be published. The statute does require that the notice precede governing board action, and therefore the notice may be published either before or after the board authorizes the reconveyance, as long as it appears before the transaction is closed.

4. Eminent Domain Property

If a local government has acquired property through exercise of eminent domain and has subsequently decided the property is not needed for the purpose for which it was condemned (or is no longer needed for that purpose), G.S. 40A-70 permits it to reconvey the property to the original owner. If the property was part of a larger lot or tract, the original owner must still own the remainder of that lot or tract. To gain the return of the property, the original owner must pay the government the full price paid when the property was condemned, the cost of any improvements the government has made to the property, and interest on both the original price and the cost of improvements at the legal rate of interest. If a local government decides to offer the property to the original owner on the statutory terms, it must send written notice to the owner to that effect, giving a date by which the owner must make payment. That date may not be less than thirty days after the notice is sent to the owner.

5. Cemeteries

G.S. 160A-342 permits a city that operates a cemetery to transfer the cemetery, together with accumulated perpetual care funds, to a religious organization or other licensed private cemetery operator. The transferee must covenant to continue to operate the cemetery, to maintain it perpetually, and to use transferred perpetual care funds only for maintenance of the cemetery.

§609. Competitive Sale of Fee Interests in Real Property and of Personal Property

A. Introduction

Article 12 offers three methods by which the local governments subject to the Article may, in the usual course, sell the fee interest in real property or sell personal property that is valued at $30,000 or more—public auction, sealed bid, and negotiated offer and upset bid.[86] Before discussing each of the three methods, a few preliminary comments are in order, applicable to all three methods.

First, it is a matter of the governing board's discretion whether to sell property and which method to use. If a board wishes to sell property by private sale, pursuant to one of the procedures described in Section 608, another interested buyer cannot force the government (in the absence of some clear abuse of discretion) to sell to her or to sell competitively, even if the unhappy buyer is willing to pay more for the property than the government will receive from the private sale. After all, the private sale authorizations recognize policy goals other than realizing the highest price for the property, and a government will frequently be willing to accept a lower price (or no cash consideration at all) in order to further those other goals.

Second, when the government is selling real property, each of the three methods requires that the local government's governing board approve the high bid for the property, and each permits the board to reject all bids

---

86. A government that owns land with a building sometimes wishes to separate the building from the land and sell the building only. In that situation the building is personal property, and the government should follow the procedures for sale of personal rather than real property. *See* the discussion *supra* at the beginning of § 608.

and start again. Deciding whether to accept the high bid is a matter of the board's discretion, and therefore its decision will stand unless abuse can be shown.

Third, the government is sometimes asked to give a buyer an option to purchase the government's property.[87] If the property must be sold by competitive methods, the government and the optionee will have to comply with one of those methods before the sale can be completed. The most sensible time for that is probably when the optionee is ready to exercise the option and acquire the property. At that point, the government should begin one of the three competitive methods.

Fourth, the statutes expressly permit the selling government to establish terms and conditions of sale. They are silent, however, about whether a high bidder may establish conditions on her bid, such as the availability of financing or a title examination by the buyer's attorney. The prudent course is to assume that such bidder conditions are invalid unless permitted by the seller's terms and conditions of sale, and that the bid itself is unresponsive and therefore should be ignored. The best course is to include in the seller's terms and conditions a statement about whether buyer's conditions will be permitted; if so, what conditions are permitted; and what the effect will be if unpermitted conditions are attached to a bid.

Finally, sometimes the high bidder wishes to assign her bid to another party, so that the government actually conveys the property to someone who did not bid. The statutes do not address the propriety of bid assignments, but in general they present no problem. As the *Puett* case made clear, the government's interest in a competitive sale is to realize the highest price it can, and it does not matter who the buyer is.[88] If the government has attached reasonable conditions to the sale, such as the buyer demonstrating financial responsibility or being current on existing property taxes, the bid assignee will have to meet those conditions. But if that is done, the statutes create no bar to an assignment of the highest bid.

---

87. *See supra* § 506-B, for a discussion of whether local governments may grant options to purchase their property.

88. *See* the discussion in *supra* § 604-F.

B. Public Auction

One of the three methods by which Article 12 permits the competitive sale of property is the public auction. The procedure for auction sales of real property is slightly different from that for auction sales of personal property, and the differences will be noted below.

An initial question in any auction sale involves selection of the auctioneer. First, a local government may ask one or more of its employees to conduct the sale. The auctioneer licensing law does not require a licensed auctioneer when a sale is conducted "by or under the direction of any public authority."[89] Second, a local government may decide to employ a professional auctioneer. Doing so takes advantage of a professional's expertise in marketing and in conducting the sale. Employing an auctioneer is a service arrangement, and so the contract is not subject to competitive bidding; the local government may select and contract with the auctioneer in the same manner it does with other service providers.

The statutory procedure for an auction sale, regulated by G.S. 160A-270, begins when the governing board adopts a resolution or (with personal property) an order. When the sale is of real property, this resolution

- authorizes the sale;
- describes the property to be sold;
- specifies the date, time, and place of sale;
- sets out any terms of sale; and
- notes that the governing board must accept the high bid before the sale is complete.

Appendix A, in Section V-A, includes an example of this resolution.

The statute permits but (unlike the other two procedures discussed below) does not direct the board to require a bid deposit from the highest bidder. If the board decides to require a deposit, it should set the amount of the deposit, the permissible forms of deposit, the time by which the deposit must be made, and the conditions under which the deposit will be forfeited. All these details must then be included in the resolution authorizing the sale. If no deposit will be required, it is helpful to note that fact in the resolution as well. (A board may wish to adopt a standing rule on deposits for auction sales, which could then be used automatically and referenced in the resolution.)

---

89. G.S. 85B-2(2).

Once the resolution is adopted, the local government publishes a notice of the sale. The notice, which must be published once, at least thirty days before the sale

- describes the property;
- sets out the terms of sale;
- gives the date, time, and place of sale; and
- refers to the authorizing resolution.

(Appendix A, in Section V-B, includes an example of this notice.) Because the notice refers to the resolution, it is not necessary to repeat the resolution in full in the notice. Nevertheless, the statute requires that the notice describe the property and set out the terms of sale; although the statute does not say so, obviously the date, time, and place of sale must be included as well. It is also helpful to include in the notice the name of the unit employee or official who can answer inquiries about the property. If for any reason the auction cannot be held on the date specified in the resolution and notice, the local government must begin the proceeding again with a new resolution and a new notice.

After the auction is held, the high bid is reported to the governing board. The board then has thirty days from the day the bid is reported to it to accept or reject that bid. If the board wishes to accept the bid, it should do so by motion or resolution; if the board decides to reject the bid, the best method is again by motion or resolution. A rejection can be implicit, however, either because the board allows the thirty-day period to expire without taking any action or because it begins the procedure for a new sale of the property. (Appendix A, in sections V-C and V-D, includes examples of resolutions accepting the bid and rejecting the bid.)

The basic difference between auction sales of personal property and auction sales of real property is that the local government's governing board need not confirm sales of personal property after the auction. Title and possession to personal property can, therefore be transferred on the day of the auction, as soon as the sale is completed and payment made, and this difference is reflected in the resolution (or order) and notice that begin the process. Therefore, when the government is selling personal property, the board's resolution or order

- identifies the property to be sold;
- sets out the date, time, and place of the auction;
- sets out any terms of sale; and

- authorizes a specific official to dispose of the property of the auction.[90]

This resolution, or a notice summarizing its contents, must then be published at least once, not fewer than ten days before the date of the auction.

C. Sealed Bid

G.S. 160A-268 simply states that a local government may sell property by advertisement for sealed bids "in the manner prescribed by law for the purchase of property." (The statute does modify that basic statement in one respect when the government is selling real property, by requiring at least thirty days' public advertisement of the sale.) The purchase statute is G.S. 143-129, and the procedures and comments set out below are drawn from that statute.

Although the purchase statute begins with a published advertisement, it is preferable to begin a sealed-bid sale with a governing board resolution much like that required for auction sales. The resolution should

- identify the property;
- authorize the sale;
- set out any terms and conditions of sale;
- specify the date, time, and place of bid opening;
- describe deposit requirements; and
- set out the date by which the highest bid will be accepted or rejected.

Appendix A, in Section III-A, includes an example of such a resolution.

G.S. 143-129 requires a bid deposit of at least 5 percent; the governing board may, however, require a larger deposit. The governing board may also waive the deposit when it is purchasing personal property, which suggests that a local government may waive the deposit when it is

---

90. The named official is responsible for executing any documents necessary to transferring title to property sold at the auction; she need not be the person who actually conducts the auction. As the earlier discussion noted, that person could be an employee of the local government or a professional auctioneer.

As was also noted above, the auction statute makes no mention of a bid deposit. If payment is made at the auction itself, no deposit is necessary. If the local government, as a term of sale, allows a short period within which payment may be made (even as short as 48 hours), then a deposit requirement is appropriate (although not mandatory) and may be included among the terms of sale.

disposing of such property. The purchasing statute sets out four permissible forms of deposit, and therefore each of these is also permissible when property is being sold. The four forms are cash, cashier's check, certified check, or surety bond. Although the bond is standard for deposits when the government is acquiring property, the other three are much more likely to be offered when the government is selling.

Once the board has authorized the sale, it should cause the advertisement of the sale to be published. The advertisement must be published at least once. For real property, the first advertisement must appear at least thirty days before the day bids will be opened. For personal property, the advertisement must appear at least seven days before bids are opened.[91] Drawing again on G.S. 143-129, the advertisement must

- describe the property;
- identify the person to whom inquiries about the property and sale should be directed;
- state the time and place at which bids will be opened; and
- note the board's right to reject all bids.

Appendix A, in Section III-B, includes an example of the advertisement.

The bids must be opened in public and then reported to the governing board and recorded in its minutes. Unless it chooses to reject all bids, the board must sell the property to the highest "responsible bidder." The purchasing statute gives some content to the meaning of *lowest* responsible bidder for purposes of that statute (quality, performance, and the time specified for performance), but those factors do not seem relevant to sales of government property to the *highest* responsible bidder. The highest responsible bidder should almost always be the bidder who submitted the highest bid; only in extraordinary circumstances should the board pass over the high bidder on the ground she is not responsible. Certainly the board may not reject the high bidder simply because another bidder plans a use of the property more attractive to the board.[92] The purchasing

---

91. G.S. 160A-268 specifically requires 30 days' notice for sales of real property. The seven-day period for sales of personal property is based on the requirement in G.S. 143-129 that advertisements for purchase of personal property be published at least one week before the bids are opened.

92. *Cf.,* Porsh Builders, Inc. v. City of Winston-Salem, 302 N.C. 550, 276 S.E.2d 443 (1981) (city selling urban development property to highest responsible bidder may not select second high bidder because his bid was "more nearly" in compliance with development plan than that of high bidder).

statute does not specify how long bids remain good, but bid specifications routinely do so, and that practice should be followed as well when property is being sold.

One provision of G.S. 143-129 does not fit into the property sale context. That statute requires forfeiture of the bid deposit if the successful bidder does not execute a contract or give satisfactory surety within ten days after the contract is awarded. If the contract is executed or sureties given within the ten days, the conditions of the deposit have been met and the bidder is entitled to a return of the deposit or release of her sureties. These requirements, however, are not directly transferable to the sale of property, and therefore the authorizing resolution should adjust them as necessary. The basic concern for the selling government is to be protected against buyer default until the sale is closed.[93] Releasing the deposit upon execution of a contract of sale does not meet that concern.[94] Therefore the resolution and the advertisement should specify that the deposit will be retained until closing, regardless of whether and when a contract of sale is executed.

D. Upset Bid

Since the enactment of G.S. Chapter 160A in 1971 the upset bid procedure has become the most common method used by local governments selling their real property; it is much less frequently used for personal property. The procedure, set out in G.S. 160A-269, is staged over several weeks, which may allow more bidders to participate than would be possible with a one-day auction, the former method of choice.

The procedure begins when the local government receives an offer to purchase property. The offer may be unsolicited, may be the product of negotiations between government officials and the offeror, or may be in direct response to solicitations from the government. Indeed, some local

---

93. When a government is *purchasing* property, it can protect itself against seller default, after contract execution, by requiring a performance bond. There is no comparable bond to protect the government when it sells property.

94. If the buyer defaults on the contract, the government may bring an action for damages, but the costs and delays of litigation make that route a pale substitute for forfeiture of a deposit.

governments have combined the upset bid procedure with one of other sales procedures by treating the high bid received at an auction or from sealed bids as the opening offer of an upset bid procedure.[95]

Whatever the circumstances, the offer is reported to the governing board. If the board "proposes to accept" the offer, the upset bid procedure begins. Although the statute does not require it at this stage, the board typically adopts a resolution proposing to accept the offer and setting out the details of the sale. This resolution

- describes the property;
- describes the amount and terms of the initial offer;
- establishes the terms of the deposit requirement;
- details the upset bid procedures that will be followed;[96]
- states the time period within which the final bid will be accepted or rejected; and
- sets out any other relevant details.

Appendix A, in Section IV-A, includes an example of such a resolution.

The statute requires, as a condition of beginning the procedure, that the initial offeror submit to the local government's clerk a bid deposit in the amount of 5 percent of her bid. Furthermore, each bidder who submits an upset bid must also submit a 5 percent bid deposit. The statute does not, however, specify the form of the deposit nor the circumstances under which the deposit is forfeited or may be released. Presumably the deposit should be forfeited if the current offeror attempts to withdraw her offer and should be released if an offer is upset; similarly, a deposit submitted with an unsuccessful bid should be released once it is clear the bid was unsuccessful. The board must establish these details and should then include them in the originating resolution.

Once the governing board has acted and the offeror's deposit has been received, the local government publishes notice of the upset sale. The statute requires that the notice

- describe the property,
- set out the amount and terms of the offer, and
- specify the requirements for submission of an upset bid.

---

95. Using the high bid from an auction or sealed bid process may be necessary because the earlier procedure suffers from procedural flaws. Rather than start that other procedure all over, the government can, with the bidder's consent, take the high bid it has in hand and begin the upset bid procedure.

96. *See* the discussion on the two possible methods of selecting the successful upset bidder *infra* at notes 97 and 98.

It is useful to also include in the notice the name of the person (or office) to whom upset bids should be submitted. In addition, the other details of sale established in the board's resolution should be summarized, or the notice should refer to the resolution and state where it can be examined. Appendix A, in Section IV-B, includes an example of this notice.

The statute requires that an upset bid be received within ten days from the date the notice is published. Recalling the rule discussed in Section 604-G, in counting the ten days the day of publication should not be counted. Thus if the notice is published on the fourteenth of the month, the first day is the fifteenth, and the tenth day is the twenty-fourth of the month; any upset bid, that is, must be received by the end of business on the twenty-fourth. (The notice is most useful if it states the final date by which bids must be received rather than simply stating that bids must be received within ten days from publication.) To qualify as an upset bid, the bid must raise the original (or current) offer by an amount at least 10 percent of the first $1,000 of that offer and 5 percent of the remainder. Two examples illustrate these rules:

1. Original offer: $ 900
     Minimum upset bid
        Original offer   900
        + 10% of first $1,000   90
        + 5% of remainder   0
                                                $ 990

2. Original offer: $ 9,000
     Minimum upset bid
        Original offer   9,000
        + 10% of first $1,000   100
        + 5% of remainder ($8,000)   400
                                              $ 9,500

When a bid has been successfully raised—that is, upset—the new bid becomes the current offer, and the local government conducts another upset sale, on the same terms and under the same procedures as the first sale. The local government continues this process until a ten-day period passes without receipt of a qualifying upset bid.

Confusion is possible over the method of selecting the qualifying upset bid. Under the upset bid procedure used in a number of other statutes,[97] the upset period remains open only until a qualifying upset bid is submitted, whether that is on the first day, the fifth day, or the tenth day. Once that first qualifying bid is received, it becomes the new offer, and a new sale is held. Many local governments, however, follow a different procedure. They leave the upset period open the entire ten days specified in the statute and require that bids be submitted in sealed form. Only at the end of the ten days are the bids examined, and the highest of these (rather than the first qualifying) becomes the new offer. The potential difference between the two methods is illustrated by this example:

> The original offer is $9,000, and therefore the minimum upset bid is $9,500. Under the first method, if a $9,500 bid is received on day 3, that concludes the upset period and a new upset sale is held. At that sale, the offer is $9,500 and the minimum upset bid is $10,025 ($9,500 + $100 + $425). Under the second method, however, if a $9,500 bid is received on day 3 and a $9,600 bid on day ten, the latter bid prevails and becomes the new offer. (Note that a $9,600 offer would not successfully upset an earlier $9,500 offer under the first method of upset bidding.) The minimum offer on the new sale under this second method is $10,130 ($9,600 + $100 + $430).

The language of G.S. 160A-269 is compatible with either of these methods. Nevertheless, to avoid confusion among potential buyers, the selling government should make clear in the board's resolution and in the notice which of the two methods it will follow. (If the board decides to follow the second method, it should require that potential upset bids be submitted in writing and be sealed, and bids should not be opened until the ten-day period has ended.[98] The requirement for sealed bids should also be set out in the resolution and notice.)

---

97. *E.g.,* G.S. 1-339.1 through -339.40 (Cum. Supp.) (judicial sales); *id.* §§ 1-339.41 through -339.71 (Cum. Supp.) (execution sales); and *id.* §§ 45-21.1 through -21.33 (sales under a power of sale).

98. If the second method is used, there is a possibility of identical high bids. The sale procedure could specify a method of selecting from identical bids, such as picking the one submitted earliest. If that method is used, then bids must be stamped with time and date when they are submitted.

Once a final qualifying offer has been received, that offer is reported to the governing board, which must decide whether to accept or reject it. (If the local government wishes to expedite the final sale of the property, particularly if no upset bids are expected, the governing board could accept the original offer (or any higher, upsetting offer), subject to upset, in the original resolution. Then, once a ten-day upset period has passed without any new bids, the government's officials could proceed immediately to execute the necessary documents and close the sale.) The statute does not set out a maximum time within which the board must decide and act; therefore the board itself should establish (back in that original resolution) that period as one of the terms of sale. Doing so is clearly preferable to doing nothing, from both a legal and a business standpoint. Not doing so would require that the board act within a "reasonable" time, and the uncertainty of what is reasonable and the potential inconvenience that delay creates for the offeror argue for establishing the period at the beginning.

§610. Leases of and Easements and Profits in Real Property

A. Leases

Leases of real property are governed by G.S. 160A-272.[99] (If the local government leases its property, with the lessee holding an option to purchase, the transaction amounts to a sale rather than a lease. The government should follow the procedures regulating sale of the fee interest rather than the lease procedures.) The lease statute requires, as a condition of any lease entered into pursuant to it, that the governing board determine that the property will not be needed by the local government during the term of the lease. That is, the statute is concerned with leases of temporarily *surplus* property. If a local government wishes to enter

---

99. G.S. 160A-272.1 provides, in its entirety, that "[s]ubject to G.S. 160A-321, a city-owned utility or public service enterprise, or part thereof, may be leased." This section probably should be understood as a cross-reference to G.S.160A-321, which concerns the sale, lease, or abandonment of city-owned enterprises. *See supra* § 608-J. As such, the reference to any "part thereof" probably refers to an operating segment of such an enterprise and not to the isolated lease of surplus property of the enterprise. After all, G.S. 160A-321 does not itself refer to disposition of surplus property. *Id.* Leases of surplus enterprise property should be made pursuant to G.S. 160A-272.

into an arrangement with someone who will make a public use of the government's property, this may not be an appropriate statute, inasmuch as the property in such an arrangement is really not surplus. Rather, the local government should proceed under one of the statutes that permits a private sale of fee interests in real property; these perforce also permit privately negotiated leases of such property. Alternatively, the government might enter into some kind of arrangement respecting the property that is not a lease but is rather an operating contract or a license, as discussed in Section 510-A.

The procedure to be followed for those transactions that are subject to G.S. 160A-272 depends on the length of the lease: a simple procedure for leases of up to one year; a more formal procedure for leases up to ten years; and an even more formal procedure for leases longer than ten years. In determining the length of a proposed lease and therefore which procedure to follow, the local government must count any periods of renewal permitted by the lease. Thus a three-year lease that permits the lessee to renew for up to three additional three-year periods has a total term of twelve years.

1. Leases of One Year or Less

The statute allows a governing board to authorize leases of up to one year or less in two different ways. First, the board may itself approve each such lease by adopting a separate resolution finding that the property is surplus and authorizing the appropriate officials to execute the lease. If the board acts in this way, the statute provides that "no public notice need be given" for the resolution. Second, the board may delegate to the manager or some other administrative official authority to lease the government's property for terms of one year or less. This delegation can include authority to decide which parcels to lease, to determine that these parcels of property are surplus for the period of the lease, and to establish the terms of the lease itself. Appendix A, in sections VII-A and VII-B, includes examples of a resolution approving a one-year lease of a specific parcel of property and of one delegating to an administrative official authority to enter into short-term leases.

The statute does not require any specific procedure beyond the board resolution or delegation for a short-term lease, and therefore the local government may negotiate such a lease privately or use a competitive procedure of its own design.

2. Leases of Ten Years or Less

The statutory procedure for a lease of ten years or less begins once the government has selected a lessee and agreed on the terms of the lease. Although in most cases the lease terms will have been developed through private negotiation with the lessee, it is also possible for a local government to establish the lease terms itself and then competitively seek the lessee willing to pay the highest rent for the leasehold. The statutory procedure begins with publication of a notice stating the governing board's intention to authorize the lease. This notice, which must be published at least ten days before the meeting to which it refers,[100] must

- describe the property;
- state the annual rental or lease payments; and
- announce the board's intention to authorize the lease at its next regular meeting.[101]

Appendix A, in Section VII-C, includes an example of this notice.

The procedure concludes with the board's adoption of a resolution authorizing the lease. The statute requires that this resolution be adopted at a *regular* meeting of the board. Besides specifically authorizing the lease, the resolution should identify the property and include (or refer to) the board's determination that the property will not be needed during the term of the lease. Appendix A, in Section VII-D, includes an example of such a resolution.

3. Leases of Longer Than Ten Years

G.S. 160A-272 provides that a local government may lease its property "for such terms and upon such conditions as the [governing board] may determine, but not for longer than ten years (except as otherwise provided herein)." The quoted language does not, as a quick reading sometimes causes some to think, prohibit leases of longer than ten years. Rather, the parenthetical exception refers to the last sentence of G.S. 160A-272, which reads, "Leases for terms of more than ten years shall be treated as a sale of property and may be executed by following any of the procedures

---

100. The statute states that the resolution must be adopted "upon ten days' public notice." This language should be understood to mean *at least* and not *exactly* ten days. In smaller counties without daily newspapers, a requirement of exactly ten days' notice would often be impossible to meet.

101. The notice should include the date of the next regular meeting, to avoid confusion.

authorized for sale of real property." That is, a local government may enter into a lease for longer than ten years, but to do so it must follow one of the three procedures for sales of fee interests in real estate: public auction, sealed bid, or negotiated offer and upset bid.[102] The details of each of these procedures are discussed in Section 609.

There are a couple of difficulties with using the competitive sale procedures for leases of ten years or more, and those lie in comparing bids. First, bidders might include escalation clauses in their bids, offering a higher rent in later years of the lease, or they might otherwise offer different amounts for different years of the lease period. These differences are best handled by comparing all bids based on the present value of these future rent payments. In addition, and more difficult, local governments renting property for commercial purposes sometimes wish to negotiate lease terms that include, as rental payments, some percentage of the gross receipts of the lessee. Because the amount of any lessee's gross receipts is speculative, the local government lessor cannot compare bids from different possible lessees. With such leases the better path is to enter into them pursuant to G.S. 158-7.1(d), which permits local governments to privately negotiate leases (as well as sales) of their property for commercial purposes.

The second difficulty involves the deposit required of bidders in the sealed bid and upset bid procedures. This deposit must be 5 percent (or more with the sealed bid procedure) of the bid amount, but what is the bid amount? A local government probably has at least two choices: first, use the actual dollar amount of the total rental payments over the period of the lease; or second, use the present value of those rental payments. Whichever it selects, the various notices required by the procedures should state clearly what is required.

B. Leases at Public Airports

G.S. 63-53 contains three paragraphs that authorize leases of property and space at a public airport. Paragraph (3) authorizes counties and cities to lease "space, area, improvements, or equipment" at such an airport to public and private lessees. Paragraph (4) authorizes counties and cities to lease (or sell) surplus airport property. And paragraph (6) authorizes

---

102. In an appropriate situation, the local government may also follow one of the procedures for private sales of real property. It might, for example, grant a long-term lease of property to a nonprofit corporation pursuant to G.S. 160A-279.

counties and cities to lease improved real estate at an airport to public
or private commercial or industrial enterprises. Of these three paragraphs, the only one that mentions procedures is paragraph (4), the
paragraph that authorizes leases of surplus property. That paragraph
directs that any leases (or sales) be "in accordance with the laws of this
State . . . governing the sale or leasing of similar municipally owned
property." That is, in leasing surplus airport land, a local government
should follow the procedures of Article 12. The silence about procedures
in the other two paragraphs suggests that there are no mandatory procedures for leases under those paragraphs and that therefore a county or
city may privately negotiate those leases. Given the nature of those
leases—space within an airport for airport purposes, and leases for
industrial or commercial projects—it makes sense that the law permits
private negotiation.

C. Easements and Air Rights

1. Easements When the Local Government Owns the Fee or Easements Over or within a City Street

G.S. 160A-273 authorizes those local governments subject to Article
12 to grant easements "over, through, under, or across" any property of
the government.[103] Cities may, in addition, grant an easement in a street
or alley that is within the city and not maintained by the Department of
Transportation, as long as the easement does not "substantially impair or
hinder" use of the street or alley as a way of passage.[104] The statute does
not establish any procedural requirements for the grant of these easements (except some grants of air rights, discussed in the next paragraph),
and such a grant may consequently be made through private
negotiation.[105]

G.S. 160A-273 also speaks to the granting of air rights over local government property. With the exception noted below, the statute requires
that transfers of air rights be treated as sales of real property, therefore

---

103. G.S. 115C-518 authorizes school administrative units to grant utility
easements and to dedicate street and sidewalk easements. These authorizations
duplicate that of G.S. 160A-272.

104. *Id.* § 160A-296(a)(6) also permits cities to "license . . . pipes, poles, wires,
fixtures, or appliances" on or under city streets. Most cities license utility use of
their streets rather than granting easements for that purpose.

105. Use of the word *grant* does not block a local government from receiving
fair consideration for any easement it conveys, including easements for air rights.

requiring use of one of the competitive procedures discussed in Section 609 or of an appropriate private sale procedure. The exception permits a city to grant air rights over a street right-of-way in order to permit construction of a bridge or passageway between buildings on each side of the street, and to do so in the same manner it grants other easements. That is, the statute permits private negotiation of such grants and requires no procedural steps before the grant is made.

2. Easements When the Local Government Owns Only the Easement

G.S. 160A-273 clearly is concerned with the grant of easements by a local government when it owns more than the easement. But what if the government owns only an easement and it wishes to convey that interest to someone else? Section 506-C discusses whether a city might sell a street easement and concludes that the only way to convey such an easement is through the street vacation procedure. But there is no comparable statute applicable to utility easements, and there is no procedure set out in Article 12 for conveying utility easements. How, then, might a local government convey a utility easement it no longer wants or needs?

In answering that question, it is important to begin with a reminder of what it is the local government owns: an easement for utility lines, and nothing more. If the local government no longer needs a utility easement and no other utility operator needs it, that easement has become essentially worthless. In such a situation, a common practice is for the governing board to note the facts, declare that the local government is abandoning the easement, and direct the administrative staff to give a quitclaim deed to the easement to the owner of the underlying fee simple estate.

If the easement will still be used, however, and the local government wishes to convey it to some other utility operator, there are two statutes that might fit the circumstances. If the new user is another local government, the easement can be conveyed pursuant to G.S. 160A-274.[106] If the new user is a nonprofit utility operator, the easement can be conveyed pursuant to G.S. 160A-279.[107] But if the new user is a for-profit entity, the only apparent statutory authority for the conveyance is one of the three competitive sale methods included in Article 12—public auction, sealed bid, or private negotiation and upset bid.[108]

---

106. *See infra* § 613-A.
107. *See supra* § 608-E.
108. *See supra* § 609.

D. Profits à Prendre

A profit à prendre (profit) is a right to remove oil, minerals, sand and gravel, timber, and comparable materials from someone else's land. Occasionally local governments might have reason to convey such an interest in real property, and the question arises as to the proper procedure for doing so. Article 12 does not specifically mention profits, but profits are frequently characterized as being closely related to easements.[109] May a local government, therefore, use the procedures available for easements when it conveys a profit, or must it use the procedures used for fee interests?

The best answer is that a local government must use the procedures set out for fee interests—that is, it must use competitive procedures rather than a negotiated sale. G.S. 160A-273 permits private sale of easements because the property interests likely to be involved are of minimal value. A local government is most likely to use this authority to convey a utility easement of one kind or another, and such easements frequently cost very little. In addition, with utility easements there is often only a single potential buyer, and so competitive sales make no sense. Neither of these characteristics is true of profits. First, with a profit, the buyer is removing material from the land, material that is likely to have significant value. Second, there will almost always be more than one buyer interested in the subject matter of the profit; therefore, competitive sales are realistically possible. For these reasons, it makes more sense to follow the procedures for conveying fee interests in real property than that for conveying easements.

E. Cemetery Lots

North Carolina law permits cities and sanitary districts to operate cemeteries, and an integral part of cemetery operation is the sale of cemetery lots.[110] When a cemetery lot is sold, the selling government usually gives a deed for the lot, and often the deed purports to convey a fee simple interest in the lot to the buyer. (The deed normally does limit use of the

---

109. "A profit à prendre, though similar to and sometimes called an easement..." Builders Supplies Co. v. Gainer, 282 N.C. 261, 266, 192 S.E.2d 449, 453 (1972). See JON W. BRUCE & JAMES W. ELY, JR., THE LAW OF EASEMENTS AND LICENSES IN LAND § 1.04 (rev. ed. 1995) [hereinafter BRUCE & ELY] (easements and profits are distinct but closely related interests in land).

110. City authority is found at G.S. 160A-341 through -348. Sanitary district authority is found at *id.* § 130A-55(19).

lot to cemetery purposes.) Although the North Carolina courts do not appear to have considered the nature of the buyer's title to cemetery lots, the courts of many other states have. Their consistent response is that the buyer of a cemetery lot, even when she holds a deed that purports to grant her fee simple title, has at most an easement, permitting a right of burial and no more.[111] Indeed some courts, noting that the cemetery operator normally may discontinue use of the ground as a cemetery and convert it to other uses, hold that the cemetery lot "owner" has only a license.[112] Whether she holds an easement or a license, the holder clearly does not hold any kind of fee.

The statutes create no special requirements for the sale of cemetery lots, probably because the interest being conveyed is only an easement or license, and therefore the local governments operating cemeteries may design whatever procedures they wish.

§611. Sale of Timber

Local governments sometimes own land holding commercially valuable timber that they wish to sell. In addition, when they prepare sites for their own projects or otherwise cut trees on their own land, there is often timber on the property that might have commercial value. This section discusses the procedures that must be followed when timber, either growing or already cut, is sold.

A. Cut Timber

When timber is cut—either by its owner or by a contractor—and then sold in cut form, it is personal property.[113] Therefore, if a local government sells cut timber, it should follow the procedures appropriate for personal property, which are discussed in Section 609.

---

111. *E.g.,* Whitesell v. City of Montgomery, 355 So. 2d 701 (Ala. 1978); Willows v. City of Lewiston, 461 P.2d 120 (Idaho 1969).

112. *E.g.,* Carter v. Town of Avoca, 197 N.W. 847 (Iowa 1924); Mansker v. City of Astoria, 198 P. 199 (Or. 1921).

113. "The cutting of the timber into logs . . . would constitute a conversion of the standing timber from real property into personalty." Walston v. Lowry, 212 N.C. 23, 25, 192 S.E. 877, 877 (1937); Harry W. Falk, Jr., Timber and Forest Products Law 26 (1958) [hereinafter Falk].

B. Standing Timber

The Traditional Understanding

When timber is sold while still standing (to be cut by the buyer), the North Carolina courts and the courts of most other states have traditionally characterized it as real property.[114] In North Carolina, standing timber is most commonly sold through a timber deed, which in this state has conveyed a fee simple title to the timber. Typically, the grantee of a timber deed must cut and remove the timber within a specified period of time; once that period passes, title to any uncut timber reverts to the fee simple owner of the land itself.[115] Although timber can also be sold through a profit à prendre, the North Carolina Supreme Court has made that an unlikely vehicle for commercial sales of timber. In *Builders Supplies Co., Inc. v. Gainey*, the court described a profit as nonexclusive, allowing the owner of the land to convey simultaneous profits in the same land to more than one buyer.[116] Buyers of commercial timber, however, will want an exclusive right to the timber and so are unlikely to accept a profit rather than a timber deed.[117] In either case, a timber deed or a profit, a local

---

114. *E.g.,* Williams v. Parsons, 167 N.C. 529, 83 S.E. 914 (1914); Haw River Land & Timber Co., Inc. v. Lawyers Title Insurance Co., 152 F.3d 275 (4th Cir. 1998); FALK, *supra* note 113, at 28.

115. "We have held in numerous cases that these deeds for standing timber, as ordinarily drawn, convey a fee-simple interest in such timber as realty, determinable as to all such timber as is not cut and removed within the time specified in the deed and that, while such estate lasts, it is clothed with the same attributes and subject to the same laws of devolution and transfer as other interests in realty." Williams v. Parsons, 167 N.C. 529, 531, 83 S.E. 914, 915 (1914).

116. "Customarily, at least, the grant of a profit à prendre does not preclude the grantor from exercising a like right upon the land or granting such right to others also." 282 N.C. 261, 267, 192 S.E.2d 449, 453 (1972).

117. The North Carolina court's understanding of a profit is not shared elsewhere. *See* HERBERT THORNDIKE TIFFANY, THE LAW OF REAL PROPERTY § 839 (3d ed. 1939) (profit may be exclusive). Indeed, the notion that a timber deed conveys a fee simple title to the timber has been the subject of a good deal of academic criticism, and often these critical commentators suggest that the profit à prendre is a much more suitable category of property to fit timber deeds into. *E.g.,* Eugene C. Luccock, *Timber Deeds—A Case for the Restatement of the Law of Property*, 20 WASH. L. REV. 199 (1945); Ralph W. Johnson, *Washington Timber Deeds and Contracts*, 32 WASH. L. REV. 30 (1957). The latter author wrote: "The property concept that does fit the ordinary timber transaction, without the need of stretching or warping definitions, and through which some logical treatment can be given to this area is that of *'profit à prendre,'* the right to take a part of the soil or produce of the land." 32 WASH. L. REV. at 38.

government selling its timber in standing form under this traditional understanding should follow the procedures for disposing of fee interests in real property.

The Effect of the Uniform Commercial Code

The original version of the Uniform Commercial Code (U.C.C.) defined transactions in goods under Article 2 to include the sale of timber only when the timber was to be cut by the seller. If the timber was to be cut by the buyer, it was treated as if it were real property. The same distinction was drawn in Article 9, which deals with security interests in goods. Thus, this original version treated standing timber in the same manner as the traditional understanding explained above. In 1972, however, the U.C.C. was changed. In order to facilitate financing of timber sales, both Article 2 and Article 9 were amended to treat contracts for the sale of standing timber as goods regardless of who was to cut the timber.[118] The North Carolina General Assembly adopted these changes in 1975. Therefore, G.S. 25-2-107(2) now states that any contract for the sale of timber, apart from the land, is a contract for the sale of *goods* under Article 2 of the U.C.C., and G.S. 25-9-105 includes such timber as *goods* under Article 9. There is some uncertainty about the effect of this statutory change on the traditional characterization of standing timber as real property.

The courts in at least two states have suggested that these changes in the U.C.C. change the general property law characterization of standing timber from real to personal. The strongest statement comes from the Washington State Court of Appeals, which has written that the U.C.C. definition "now defines the test for determining the real or personal character of 'timber, minerals, or the like.'"[119] The Idaho Supreme Court has commented that "it is true that, under Idaho's version of the Uniform Commercial Code, a contract for the sale of timber converts standing timber into personalty."[120] If these judicial suggestions are correct, then

---

118. "Financing of timber requires that it be capable of treatment as chattels, without running into the restrictions applicable to banks governing loans on real estate." *Integrated Statement of the Proposals of the Reporters for Changes in Article 9 and Related Changes in Other Articles*, 7 UNIFORM COMMERCIAL CODE CONFIDENTIAL DRAFTS 378 (Elizabeth Slusser Kelly & Ann Puckett, compilers, 1995).

119. Clarke v. Alstores Realty Corp., 527 P.2d 698, 701 (Wash. Ct. App. 1974).

120. *In re* Estate of Howard, 732 P.2d 275, 277 (Idaho 1987).

Another case that might be cited here is Georgia-Pacific Corp. v. Department of Revenue, 410 So. 2d 550 (Fla. Dist. Ct. App. 1982). Although in that case the

when a North Carolina local government sells standing timber, it is selling personal property, not real property. The opposing argument is that the U.C.C. definition does not in fact change the nature of growing timber from real to personal property in *all* contexts. The U.C.C. itself provides that the definitions in Article 2 and Article 9 apply only to those articles; it makes no claim for a broader effect of the definitions.[121] Moreover, commentators both on property interests and on the Uniform Commercial Code take a narrower view of the effect of the Code's definition. One treatise on the U.C.C. quotes the Washington state court statement set out just above and then comments:

> A more accurate statement would be that U.C.C. Section 2-107 determines *the applicability of the Code* to transactions in things to be severed by calling them by name without attempting to classify them as being either real or personal property. . . . It is to be noted that goods are defined differently in Article 2 on sales than in Article 9 on secured transactions.[122]

Another treatise, on secured transactions under the Code, characterizes the effect of the Article 2 and Article 9 definitions of goods on timber to be cut as follows:

> So long as the timber is not subject to a contract or conveyance that contemplates that it will be cut, the timber must be dealt with under the law of real property: no Article 9 security interest is possible. But once the timber is subject to a contract of sale, *a fiction is created. Though the timber remains real*

---

court held that timber sales were sales of real property for purposes of Florida's deed stamp tax, the opinion emphasized that a Florida statute, adopted concurrently with the U.C.C. provisions on timber sales, provided that the deed tax was to remain applicable to transactions as if the U.C.C. had not been enacted. It is not clear, however, that the court would have reached an opposite conclusion in the absence of the tax statute. The opinion also noted that the U.C.C. definition was limited, by its own terms, to the Code and that the purpose of the U.C.C. change was fairly narrow.

121. G.S. 25-2-107(2) (1995) provides that a "contract for the sale . . . of timber to be cut is a contract for the sale of goods *within this article*"; and *id.* § 25-9-105 (Cum. Supp.)

122. 1A Ronald A. Anderson, Anderson on the Uniform Commercial Code § 2-107:4 (3d ed. 1996) (emphasis added).

property for other purposes, it is treated as goods under the U.C.C., so that an Article 9 security interest may be created in the standing timber and its proceeds.[123]

That is, these authors argue that the U.C.C. definitions are not an attempt to change the law of property in all contexts but rather a characterization of sales of timber (and other products of the land) solely for purposes of Article 2 and Article 9 of the Code.[124] When Article 2 or Article 9 deal with a particular legal issue—such as, the conditions of a valid contract, what constitutes adequate performance of a contract, the remedies available in event of a breach, or perfecting a security interest—sales of standing timber are treated as sales of goods and the U.C.C. sets out the legal rules to resolve the issue. But if the U.C.C. does not deal with a particular issue, under this narrower understanding its definitions of goods are not controlling. G.S. 25-2-107 itself lends some support to this narrower understanding. Paragraph (3) affirms that a timber deed or other document conveying interests in standing timber "may be executed and recorded as a document transferring an interest in land," thereby giving notice to third parties of the buyer's rights under the document.[125]

---

123. Julian B. McDonnell, *Article 9 and the Law of Real Estate Financing,* in Peter F. Coogan et al., 1C Secured Transactions Under the Uniform Commercial Code § 16.05 (1999) (emphasis added).

Ray Andrews Brown, The Law of Personal Property 608 (3d ed., Walter B. Raushenbush ed., 1975), in summarizing the effect of the U.C.C. provisions on timber in Article 9 (the latter regulates security interests in goods and, like Article 2, characterizes timber to be cut as goods), states that the provisions "would analogize timber to be cut to crops for purposes of creation of a security interest, *but would continue to recognize timber's character as real estate* for purposes of perfection by filing" (emphasis added).

See also Ronald W. Polston, *Profits à Prendre,* in 8 Thompson on Real Property, Thomas Edition § 65.04(b) (David A. Thomas ed. 1994), who writes: "The [U.C.C.] would therefore seem to classify timber as goods, *for purposes of all transactions involving it*" (emphasis added).

124. That the U.C.C. definitions are specific to the U.C.C. and indeed to each article of the U.C.C. is indicated by the Code's treatment of contracts for minerals. Although Article 2 and Article 9 each treat contracts for timber to be cut in the same way, the two articles have slightly different definitions of when minerals are to be treated as goods. In G.S. 25-2-107(1), a contract for the sale of minerals becomes a contract for the sale of goods only if the minerals are to be severed by the seller and without regard for when they are severed. In G.S. 25-9-105(1)(h) minerals do not become goods until they are extracted from the ground, but whether they are extracted by buyer or seller is irrelevant.

125. G.S. 25-2-107(3).

Two appellate cases decided since the definition was added to the North Carolina version of the Code are consistent with this narrower understanding of the definition of goods in G.S. 25-2-107(b). In *Mills v. New River Wood Corporation*[126] the grantor of a timber deed sued the grantee, alleging that the grantee had damaged the grantor's remaining trees while cutting and removing the timber covered by the deed. The grantee defended the suit, in part, on the ground that the plaintiff was barred by the three-year statute of limitations in G.S. 1-52. The court rejected the defense, however, holding that the timber deed merely "evidenced the underlying contract of sale,"[127] and that contract was a sale of goods under the U.C.C. As such, the contract was subject to the four-year statute of limitations included in G.S. 25-2-725, and the suit was timely brought. In this case the Article 2 definition was relevant because Article 2 includes a statute of limitations for claims arising under contracts for the sale of goods. In the more recent Fourth Circuit case of *Haw River Land & Timber Co., Inc. v. Lawyers Title Insurance Company*[128] the plaintiff acquired a timber deed to 712 acres in Wake County. When it turned out that 179 of the acres were in a watershed and could not be cut, the plaintiff sued the company that had insured its title, arguing that the watershed regulations made its title unmarketable. In characterizing the plaintiff's property interest, the federal court relied entirely on traditional North Carolina law: plaintiff had acquired a fee simple title to the timber. Article 2 was not relevant to the coverage of the title insurance policy and so there was not a word about the Code's definition of goods in the opinion.[129]

---

126. 77 N.C. App. 576, 335 S.E.2d 759 (1985).

127. *Id.* at 577, 335 S.E.2d at 760.

128. 152 F.3d 275 (4th Cir. 1998).

129. *See also* United States v. 3,035.73 Acres of Land, 650 F.2d 938 (8th Cir. 1981). In that case the United States brought an eminent domain action shortly after the owners of the fee had entered into an arrangement with a timber company. The district court held that the document memorializing the arrangement was indistinguishable from a timber deed and that therefore, under Arkansas law, the document conveyed an interest in real property, which was entitled to compensation in the eminent domain action. The court of appeals affirmed, with two of the judges accepting the analysis of the trial court. The third judge dissented, arguing that the Arkansas version of the U.C.C. had changed the character of timber and that it was no longer real property and therefore no longer entitled to compensation in the eminent domain suit. The majority ignored the argument, apparently believing that the U.C.C. was irrelevant to the characterization of property in the law of eminent domain.

Furthermore, a 1974 case from the North Carolina Supreme Court involving another provision of the U.C.C. also supports this narrower understanding. In *Szabo Food Service, Inc. v. Balentine's, Inc.*[130] the defendant had sold its cafeteria operation to the plaintiff in 1966. Three years later the two parties entered into an agreement, which they called a lease, under which the defendant resumed operation of the cafeteria; as part of the agreement, the defendant had use of the cafeteria equipment. If defendant continued to operate the cafeteria until the end of the agreement's term, ten years later, plaintiff agreed to transfer title to the equipment to defendant. After two more years, a dispute arose between the two companies over which one was responsible for listing the cafeteria equipment for taxes. Although the trial court held that the plaintiff was responsible, the state court of appeals reversed.[131] The appellate court based its decision on the definitions in the U.C.C. At the time, G.S. 25-1-201(37) stated that if an agreement provided that upon compliance with its terms the "lessee" of property becomes owner of the property, then the agreement is not a lease but rather a conditional sale. When property is the subject of a conditional sale, the property tax laws direct that it should be listed by the buyer, not the seller. The supreme court then reversed the court of appeals. The higher court rejected the relevance of the U.C.C. definition, because the legal issue involved was not governed by the Code.[132] The U.C.C. definition was not made universal.

In a case decided in December 1999, the North Carolina Supreme Court might be thought to have adopted the first position—that the changes in the U.C.C. have changed the nature of standing timber from real to personal property, even in contexts separate from the Code—but that reads too much into the case. In *Fordham v. Eason*[133] the question was whether the buyer under a "timber purchase and sales agreement"

130. 285 N.C. 452, 206 S.E.2d 242 (1974).

131. Szabo Food Serv., Inc. v. Balentine's, Inc., 19 N.C. App. 654, 199 S.E.2d 736 (1973).

132. "G.S. 25-1-201(37), then, defines 'security interest' without reference to whether title is in the vendor or the vendee under the security agreement. The applicable taxing statutes, however, specify that ad valorem taxes will be paid by the vendee of personal property where 'title to the property is retained by the vendor as security for the payment of the purchase price. . . .' The proper listing and payment of taxes therefore depends upon the location of title, *and the Code provides no guidance in this search.*" 285 N.C. at 460–61, 206 S.E.2d at 248–49 (emphasis added).

133. 351 N.C. 151, 521 S.E.2d 701 (1999).

owned real property or personal property for purposes of bringing an action for trespass against a third party who had cut the timber in question. The court stated that "we must determine whether it is appropriate to evaluate this particular cause of action and claim for timber rights as a trespass to realty or a trespass to chattel. Essential to this decision is the determination of whether timber should be classified as realty or as goods."[134] In answer, the court held that when "North Carolina adopted the Uniform Commercial Code in 1965, it changed the classification of timber when timber is *the subject of a contract for sale*" and therefore "we conclude that timber is classified as goods under North Carolina law when it is *the subject of a contract for sale*."[135] Actions for trespass are not an issue addressed by the U.C.C., yet the court relied on the U.C.C. provision to resolve the issue. It is important to note, however, that this case does not appear to have involved a timber deed or other instrument including language of conveyance. Rather, it involved a contract for sale. Clearly, if timber is sold under such a contract, this case holds that it is personal property. Therefore, if a local government sells standing timber under such a contract, it apparently may use personal property procedures. The case does not address, however, the situation in which standing timber is conveyed by timber deed. In such a situation, it remains possible that the courts will adopt the narrower understanding of the U.C.C. changes.

The author believes that the U.C.C. definitions do not modify, in non–U.C.C. contexts, the real-property character of standing timber conveyed by a timber deed. At the least, the issue is still undecided. The U.C.C. does not address the procedures that a local government must follow before it enters into a timber deed. In that circumstance, local governments wishing to convey standing timber by such a deed are safer if they continue to treat the timber as real property and follow the procedures appropriate to real rather than personal property.

C. Contracts to Clear Land

In addition to selling timber, cut or standing, local governments undertake construction projects that require clearing land that contains timber. In addition, they sometimes contract to have particular trees cut from their property. If the contract to clear the land or cut the trees

---

134. *Id.* at 153–54, 521 S.E.2d at 703.
135. *Id.* at 154–55, 521 S.E.2d at 703-4.

allows the contractor to keep and dispose of some or all of the timber, does the transaction become a sale of timber or is it still a service contract? (If it is a service contract, the law does not require that it be bid.)[136]

This issue has not been directly decided by this state's appellate courts, but a number of North Carolina cases involving contracts to cut trees and those cases from other states more directly on point suggest that characterization of the transaction is a matter of the underlying intentions of the local government and its contractor. If the local government is primarily interested in clearing land preparatory to a construction or improvement project, it is a service contract and need not be bid (unless it is part of the construction contract). If the local government is primarily interested in having certain diseased trees cut or in making specific landscape improvements, it is a service contract and need not be bid. But if the local government is primarily interested in selling the timber, it is a sale of property and the property disposal procedures must be followed. The following cases, from North Carolina and elsewhere, support these general statements.

North Carolina Cases

In *Ives v. Atlantic & N.C. Railroad Co.*,[137] the plaintiff agreed under an oral contract to cut 3,000 cords of timber from his property and 12,000 cords from the railroad's, and to deliver all the timber to the railroad. When the plaintiff sued for breach of the contract, the railroad defended on the grounds that this was a sale of timber and, under the Statute of Frauds, had to be in writing to be enforceable. The court rejected the railroad's argument, holding that the transaction was not a sale of standing timber but rather a contract "for the conversion of trees growing on the defendant's land into cord wood and the delivery of the same."[138] In *Johnson v. Wallin*,[139] the plaintiff agreed under an oral contract to cut down trees on the defendant's land, to mill some of the trees into lumber and deliver these to the defendant, and to keep the remaining wood as compensation. As in *Ives*, the defendant argued that the contract was unenforceable, because it was for the sale of timber and was not in writing. The defendant particularly pointed to the plaintiff's right to keep some of the

---

136. BLUESTEIN, *supra* note 16, at 21–23.
137. 142 N.C. 131, 55 S.E. 74 (1906).
138. *Id.* at 134, 55 S.E. at 76.
139. 227 N.C. 669, 44 S.E.2d 83 (1947).

timber he had cut. But again, as in *Ives*, the court rejected the argument, holding that the contract was not for the "sale of growing timber. It is a contract for employment for the conversion of trees growing on defendant's land into logs and for manufacture of the logs into lumber for the primary benefit of defendant."[140]

Cases from Elsewhere

In *Stagner v. Staples*,[141] the plaintiff agreed under an oral contract to take out trees, including stumps, from the defendant's land, to pick up roots and limbs, and to disk the cleared land. The defendant intended to construct a shopping center on the land after it was cleared. As compensation, the defendant agreed to pay the plaintiff $6,750 plus any timber on the ground. When the plaintiff sued for breach of the contract, the defendant made the usual argument that this was a contract for sale of timber and, as such, was required to be in writing. In finding for the plaintiff, the Missouri Court of Appeals wrote as follows:

> The object which the defendant had in mind was to obtain the plaintiff's services and the use of his heavy earth-moving machinery in clearing the land. It is true enough that the clearing process involved the severance of timber, but there is nothing before us to indicate that it was either party's intention for the plaintiff to acquire any right to use the land simply for the purpose of severance, or to acquire any right or title to the timber until after it was felled and had become personalty. . . . [T]he agreement here seems to us to be a contract for hire for services in clearing the land . . . and the fact that the plaintiff was to receive a small part of his compensation in fallen timber would not, in our opinion, convert the contract into an agreement for the sale of standing trees.[142]

In *Dobson v. Masonite Corporation*[143] the plaintiff agreed under an oral contract to cut all the oak on the defendant's 9,200-acre tract, to sell as much of the cut timber as possible, to pay the defendant a set price for each 1,000 feet of timber cut, and to keep all other proceeds from the sale of the cut timber as compensation under the contract. The Fifth

---

140. *Id.* at 671, 44 S.E.2d at 84.
141. 427 S.W.2d 763 (Mo. Ct. App. 1968).
142. *Id.* at 766.
143. 359 F.2d 921 (5th Cir. 1966)

Circuit Court of Appeals held that whether this was a service contract or a contract for the sale of timber was a question of fact—of the parties' intentions—and upheld the jury's verdict that it was a service contract.

If the notion that intention is crucial is accepted, there are a number of objective indicators of the parties' primary intention. Perhaps most important, if the local government is paying the contractor for the cutting, rather than being paid, the primary purpose is more likely to be land clearance or tree cutting and not sale of timber. If there is no separate contract for land clearance but rather the task is part of the responsibilities of the general contractor for a construction or improvement project, the primary purpose is land clearance. (Of course, in that context, the construction or improvement contract would have to be bid under G.S. 143-129.) If the contract calls for the removal of all trees, not just merchantable trees (or trees larger than a specified trunk size), the primary purpose is land clearance. If the contract calls for the removal of stumps as well as trees, so that the land is truly being cleared, the primary purpose is land clearance. Anytime a local government enters into such a contract, however, it should be cognizant of the potential value of any timber on the land; if that value exceeds the value of the services provided by the contractor, the local government may wish to limit the contract to cutting the timber and deal separately with disposing of the cut logs, or it may simply wish to treat the transaction as a sale of timber and follow the appropriate procedures.

§612. Disposing of Special Categories of Personal Property

A. Securities

Sometimes a local government receives stocks, bonds, or other securities as a bequest or gift or through other circumstances. G.S. 160A-276 permits the government to convert those securities into cash in the same way anyone else would—on an established market through a broker—without need of complying with the sale procedures applicable to other forms of personal property.[144]

---

144. Local governments may also acquire certain types of securities as part of their investment programs. Transactions that are part of the investment program are governed by the investment statutes—G.S. 159-30 (local governments and public authorities); G.S. 115C-443 (school administrative units); and G.S. 115D-58.6 (community and technical colleges)—and not by G.S. 160A-276.

Specifically, the statute permits a local government to sell, through a broker, "shares of common and preferred stock, bonds, options, and warrants or other rights with respect to stocks and bonds and other securities." To qualify for sale under this statute, the security must have an established market and be traded on a regular basis on a national stock exchange or over the counter by reputable brokers and dealers.[145] These requirements may preclude use of this statute for sales of stock in some closely held corporations, which may have no established market for their stock. This kind of stock would either have to be sold in the same manner as other personal property, or the government would need to secure special legislative authority for a private sale of the stock.

Before securities are sold under G.S. 160A-276, the governing board should adopt a resolution authorizing the sale and naming an appropriate official to execute any instrument of sale on the government's behalf.[146] The board may want to establish a minimum price in the resolution or simply direct sale at the market price, whatever that happens to be. (Appendix A, in Section VIII, includes an example of such a resolution.) There is no requirement of any sort of public notice in conjunction with the sale.

B. Abandoned Property and Forfeited Property

Article 2 of G.S. Chapter 15 requires that sheriffs and chiefs of police keep records of all property their departments seize or confiscate and of all property that they "become possessed [of] in any way in the discharge of [their] duty." Thus these records include not only confiscated property but also property that has been lost or stolen and then not claimed, such as a bicycle found in the woods by a police officer. The article permits the sheriff or police chief to sell any property so held, setting out a lengthy and somewhat cumbersome method for doing so, and that method is detailed below.

Because sales under this procedure invariably include some lost or abandoned property, as well as property that has been seized as part of a law enforcement investigation, many counties and cities turn all lost or abandoned property coming into their possession over to the sheriff or

---

145. The term *national stock exchange* probably includes any exchange regulated by the Securities Exchange Commission and thereby includes regional stock exchanges.

146. The statute does not require a resolution or order, but one is necessary as a practical matter for the board to delegate authority to sell the securities.

police chief. All such property is then disposed of in accordance with G.S. Chapter 15, Article 2. The statute itself, however, mandates this treatment of abandoned and lost property only if the property has come into a law enforcement agency's possession as part of the agency's responsibilities— only, that is, if the property has been picked up by law enforcement officers. If the property has been picked up by employees of other agencies or departments, such as by maintenance employees after a public meeting or recreation employees at a public park, the local government is free either to turn the property over to a law enforcement agency (thus triggering application of G.S. Chapter 15, Article 2) or to design some other method of disposing of the property. Abandoned or lost property is almost always worth $5,000 or less, and therefore the local government could design procedures for disposing of it pursuant to G.S. 160A-266(c), discussed in Section 608-A2. The principal difference that separate procedures would make is that the net proceeds of sale would not be subject to G.S. 15-15 and could therefore be retained by the selling local government.

If a law enforcement agency has property that is subject to Article 2 of G.S. 15, it must first wait at least 180 days after obtaining the property, in order to give time for claimants to come forward. (With bicycles the agency need wait only sixty days.) It then publishes a notice in a newspaper published in the county that

- describes the property being held;
- notes that the property is being held by the law enforcement agency;
- requires any persons with a claim to or interest in the property to come forward within thirty days;
- notes that the property will be sold if not claimed; and
- includes any other information that will help in reasonably informing the public about the property being held.[147]

If the property is not claimed within thirty days, the agency may proceed to sell the property by auction, either at the courthouse door or at the office of the agency itself.[148] Before doing so, the agency must publish a second notice, at least ten days before the actual sale. This notice is also published in a newspaper published in the county; in addition, the agency must post the notice at the courthouse door and at three other public places in the county. The notice sets out the time and place of the

---

147. G.S. 15-12 (Cum. Supp.).
148. *Id.* § 15-13 (Cum. Supp.).

auction, and a descriptive list of the items that will be sold.[149] Once the sale is complete, the agency must turn over the net proceeds to the treasurer of the county board of education.[150]

Bicycles. The statute allows an alternative for disposing of abandoned or lost bicycles. G.S. 15-12(b) permits the agency to donate the bicycles to a charitable organization instead of selling them. If the agency plans to use this alternative, the first notice it publishes must state so.

C. Worthless Property

If property has been used to the point that it no longer has any value, none of the statutory sales procedures are relevant, and no statute mandates procedures for determining that such property is in fact worthless and for disposing of it. As a practical matter, individual employees make such determinations every day for very small items, such as worn-out pens, obsolete publications, and broken equipment. With items that were originally more costly, such as calculators, personal computers, or other office equipment, more formal procedures may be appropriate. Some local governments have adopted policies requiring approval of specific officials, such as department or division heads, before property originally costing more than a specific amount (such as $100) is tossed away as worthless.

§613. Disposition to Other Governments

A. Generally

When a local government proposes to convey property to another government, many of the concerns that frame the law of local government property transactions do not apply. Concerns about favoritism, about giving away property, about possible conflicts of interest—all are generally absent when the property transaction is between governments rather than between a government and a private buyer or seller. Recognizing this, G.S. 160A-274 permits property transactions—leases, dispositions, exchanges, joint-use agreements—among governments without imposing the formal procedural requirements that condition other dispositions of

---

149. *Id.* § 15-14.
150. *Id.* § 15-15.

government property.[151] In addition, the statute recognizes that the recipient government will put the property to public use and so expressly permits a conveyance to be made with or without monetary consideration.[152]

The statute applies to transactions between *governmental units*, defined to include the State of North Carolina and its agencies and institutions and all types of local governments and their agencies in the state. There are important exclusions from the definition, however. It does not include the federal government or any federal agency, nor does it include any state government agency or local government agency outside North Carolina. Property transactions with these excluded governments must comply with the same procedural and substantive requirements as transactions with private parties. In addition, the definition does not include nonprofit agencies, no matter how close or dependent their relationship to a county, city,

---

151. *Id.* § 153A-158.1 (Cum. Supp.) permits about 60 counties and the school administrative units in those counties to transfer property between the county and the school unit; *id.* §§ 153A-158.2 and 115D-15.1 extend comparable authorizations to counties and community and technical colleges. These authorizations are intended to facilitate financing of school and college facilities by counties. Because the school or college property is owned by the county (and therefore the county can give a security interest in the property), the county can finance improvements to the property under G.S. 160A-20.

152. G.S. 160A-274(b) permits a governmental unit to "exchange with, lease to, lease from, sell to, purchase from, or enter into agreements *regarding the joint use* by any other governmental unit of any interest in real or personal property that it may own" (emphasis added). In Carter v. Stanly County, 125 N.C. App. 628, 482 S.E.2d 9 (1997), the state court of appeals seemed to read the italicized language as modifying all the quoted language coming before it and not just the word "agreements," so that the statute only applied to property transactions that resulted in the joint use of the property by both governments. Under this reading, the statute does not authorize one government to convey property to another when only the recipient government will use the property. Perhaps the court's reading can be characterized as dicta, because the court went on to approve the property transaction at issue in that case. If not, the reading is manifestly wrong. It makes no sense grammatically—if the italicized language modifies all that comes before, then so does the phrase "by any other governmental unit," and such a series of modifiers doesn't work as English in that statute. Furthermore, such a reading makes no sense logically. If one governmental unit sells property to another, how are they to end up jointly using the property? The statute's caption makes clear that it authorizes sales, leases, exchanges, *and* joint use, and not just sales, leases, and exchanges incident to joint use.

school unit, or other local government. For disposition of property to nonprofit agencies, G.S. 160A-279 remains the most appropriate statutory authority.

G.S. 160A-274 sets out no procedural requirements for transactions between qualifying governmental units, except that any transaction must be authorized by the governing board. At one time the Attorney General's Office argued that this statutory silence meant that such transactions must follow the procedural steps established in other sections of Article 12,[153] but that opinion has since been reversed.[154] Unfortunately, the first opinion continues to be cited in the codified annotations to G.S. 160A-274, while the reversing opinion is unmentioned. For that reason, the second opinion is set out below in an addendum to this chapter. The second opinion is clearly correct. If transactions under G.S. 160A-274 are required to follow the procedures of other sales under Article 12, there would be no need for special statutory mention of transactions between governmental units; the general provisions of Article 12 would suffice. This conclusion and the second opinion from the Attorney General's Office conform to the judicial interpretation of similar statutes in other states.[155] Therefore governments acting pursuant to G.S. 160A-274 may follow any procedure with which they feel comfortable.

B. School Property

G.S. 160A-274 permits transactions upon whatever terms and conditions the two governmental units consider wise, with or without monetary consideration. Section 508-B3 of this book, however, discusses the need for consideration when *school* property is sold, even to another government, and the general authorization in G.S. 160A-274 to sell property without monetary consideration should be understood to be modified by that constitutional rule. A school unit must receive monetary consideration when it sells its property. But G.S. 160A-274 does contain a specific provision permitting *leases* of school property for nominal consideration.

---

153. 49 N.C. A.G. 91 (1980).

154. Opinion to George T. Rogister, Jr., and Ann L. Majestic, Oct. 13, 1983, copy on file with author.

155. Tynatishon v. Herbert, 291 N.E.2d 51 (Ill. Ct. App. 1972); County of Hennepin v. City of Hopkins, 58 N.W.2d 851 (Minn. 1953). *See also* Martin v. Board of Pub. Instruction, 42 So. 2d 712 (Fla. 1949) (in the absence of special statutory authority for intergovernmental property transactions, sales to other governments must follow regular sales procedures).

The proviso permits a school administrative unit to lease surplus property to another governmental unit for one dollar per year. Presumably this authorization represents a legislative judgment that the case law requiring full consideration when a school board sells school property is inapplicable to leases of such property. One might argue with the logic of such a distinction, but as long as the parties do not use the proviso's authorization to evade the rule on sales of school property, the statute is entitled to a presumption of validity and may be relied upon.

§614. Local Governments and Local Government Properties Not Subject to Article 12

Section 602-B noted that certain local governments are not covered by Article 12, while two categories of local government property—property acquired for urban redevelopment purposes and hospital facilities—are subject to special disposition procedures. This section discusses these exceptions to Article 12.

A. Redevelopment Properties

1. Introduction

G.S. chapters 160A and 153A permit any of four agencies to exercise urban redevelopment powers, which are set out in G.S. Chapter 160A, Article 22.[156] First, a city (or, less likely as a practical matter, a county) may establish a redevelopment commission.[157] This is the traditional choice and was for many years the only choice. Second, a city or county may decide not to establish a redevelopment commission (or may abolish an existing redevelopment commission) and instead designate the city or county's housing authority as the agency to exercise redevelopment powers.[158] Third, a city or county may decide to do without a separate agency and instead delegate redevelopment powers to the governing board itself.[159] Finally, since 1975 city councils and boards of county commissioners have been authorized to "exercise directly" the powers of

---

156. Urban redevelopment involves determining that certain areas are "blighted" and then taking steps to remove the blight. One traditional set of steps involves the redevelopment agency acquiring blighted property, clearing it, and then selling it to new users for uses that will prevent the blight from returning.

157. G.S. 160A-504.

158. *Id.* § 160A-505.

159. *Id.*

redevelopment commissions.[160] Because a city or county could already exercise those powers under the third option set out above, the 1975 statute meant that a city or county could act even if it already had and intended to retain a separate agency exercising redevelopment powers.[161] Whichever organizational choice is made, each of these bodies—redevelopment commission, housing authority, city council, or board of county commissioners—when it disposes of property acquired for urban redevelopment purposes, must do so in accordance with the special provisions of the urban redevelopment law.

One of the unique characteristics of redevelopment property transactions is that the property is acquired and disposed of in order to implement a redevelopment plan. Such a plan is a required condition of any redevelopment activity and, regardless of how a city's or county's redevelopment function is organized, must be approved by the city or county governing board.[162] The property disposition statute (G.S. 160A-514) requires that property be conveyed for uses that accord with the redevelopment plan, and the statute includes express authority to encumber property with covenants and conditions to ensure such uses.

Two other special requirements that condition conveyances of redevelopment property must be mentioned. First, before a 1985 revision, G.S. 160A-514 required that any disposition of redevelopment property be approved by the city or county's governing board. (Of course, if the governing board is the agency exercising redevelopment powers, this requirement is redundant.) The 1985 revision generally deleted the specific requirement of governing board approval from G.S. 160A-514. That requirement, however, was also found in G.S. 160A-512(6), and that section was not changed in 1985. Therefore, despite its removal from G.S. 160A-514, the requirement of governing board approval remains in force.

The other special requirement also originates in G.S. 160A-512(6), and it applies to each of the agencies that might dispose of redevelopment property. This provision requires that if property within a redevelopment area is sold in parts to more than a single redeveloper—certainly a common occurrence—the selling agency must "find that the sale or other transfer of any such part will not be prejudicial to the sale of other parts

---

160. *Id.* §§ 153A-376(b) (Cum. Supp.) (counties) and 160A-456(b) (Cum. Supp.) (cities).

161. In 1987 the General Assembly made this point explicit for cities. *Cf. id.* § 160A-456(b) (Cum. Supp.).

162. G.S. 160A-513.

of the redevelopment area, nor in any other way prejudicial to the realization of the redevelopment plan." This finding should be included in the minutes of the selling agency whenever such a partial sale is made.

2. Private Sale or Exchange of Real Property

G.S. 160A-514(e) permits four categories of private sale of redevelopment property:[163]

(1) Property may be conveyed to the city or county in which the project is located for streets, alleys, or public ways.
(2) Easements or rights-of-way may be conveyed to an appropriate public or private agency for "public utilities, sewers, streets, and other similar facilities."
(3) Property may be conveyed to an appropriate public body for parks, schools, and other public buildings and facilities.
(4) Property may be conveyed to a nonprofit organization organized and operated exclusively for educational, scientific, literary, cultural, charitable, or religious purposes.[164]

Because conveyances in the first three categories are to agencies that will continue the property in public use, the statute expressly permits each to be made with or without monetary consideration. Continued public use will not necessarily occur, however, with conveyances to nonprofit organizations, and therefore the statute requires that the selling agency receive full consideration for the property. The selling price may be no less than the "fair value" of the property, as determined by a committee of three professional North Carolina real estate appraisers, appointed by the selling agency. Finally, the statute specifically requires that the city's or county's governing board approve a private sale to a nonprofit organization.[165]

---

163. Several cities have received local authority from the General Assembly to dispose of all redevelopment property by private sale. *E.g.,* Act of July 21, 1971, ch. 1060, 1971 N.C. Sess. Laws 1623.

164. If a local government conveys redevelopment property to a nonprofit organization pursuant to this authorization, G.S. 160A-514(e)(4) requires that the conveyance be subject to restrictive covenants that assure continuation of the specific use to which the property is to be put.

165. In Campbell v. First Baptist Church, 298 N.C. 476, 259 S.E.2d 558 (1979), the North Carolina Supreme Court held that exchanges of real property with nonprofit organizations, as well as sales to such organizations, were subject to

The statute imposes no procedural requirements on private sales in the first three categories listed above. Before property may be privately sold to a nonprofit organization, however, the selling agency must hold a public hearing on the transaction. The agency must publish notice of the hearing once a week for two successive calendar weeks in a newspaper published in the city or county where the project is located, with the first publication at least fifteen days before the day of the hearing.[166] The statute does not specify the content of the notice, but at the least it should

- identify the property;
- state the selling agency's intention to convey the property to the nonprofit organization; and
- set out the date, time, and place of the hearing.

G.S. 160A-514(c) permits the exchange of redevelopment property, and the statute provides that the conveying agency may undertake an exchange pursuant to G.S. 160A-271, the exchange procedure of Article 12.[167]

3. Competitive Sale of Real Property

Any other sale of real property acquired for redevelopment must be made by one of the three competitive methods of Article 12: upset bid, public auction, or sealed bid.[168]

4. Personal Property

G.S. 160A-514(d) permits a redevelopment agency to convey personal property valued at less than $500 by private sale. The subsection does not detail how personal property worth more than $500 should be sold, but property of this value should be sold competitively, either by upset

---

the requirement of governing board approval and to the public hearing requirement discussed below.

166. G.S. 160A-514(e)(4), -513(e). If no newspaper is published in the city or (if the project is outside a city) county in which the project is located, the statute requires that the notice be posted at least 15 days before the hearing in four public places in the city or county.

167. This statutory procedure, enacted in 1987, reverses that part of Campbell v. First Baptist Church, 298 N.C. 476, 259 S.E.2d 558 (1979) that held that exchanges of redevelopment property must follow competitive procedures. The exchange procedure is detailed in § 608-B, *supra*.

168. These three procedures are detailed in § 609, *supra*.

bid, public auction, or sealed bid. The explicit authorization for private sale for property of lesser value implies that competitive procedures are required for more valuable personal property, and that understanding certainly comports with the general structure of G.S. 160A-514.

5. Temporary Leases

G.S. 160A-514(g) permits a redevelopment agency to lease temporarily real property in a redevelopment area until the property can be disposed of in accordance with the redevelopment plan. A temporary lease may be privately negotiated without meeting any procedural conditions, and the property may, during the lease, be put to uses that are inconsistent with the redevelopment plan.

B. Hospital Facilities

1. Introduction

Historically, community hospitals were predominantly owned by local governments or other nonprofit entities.[169] Recent years, however, have witnessed considerable upheaval in the delivery of health care, and many local governments have conveyed or are considering conveying their hospitals to other agencies, both public and private. Several sections of G.S. Chapter 131E regulate conveyances of publicly owned hospitals.[170]

This legislation demonstrates a strong legislative concern that a local government's disposal of its hospital facility or facilities not result in any loss of important hospital services to the community in general or to the medically indigent in particular. The legislation also reflects a concern about ensuring payment of any hospital-related debt still outstanding when a public hospital is leased or sold and about protecting the state's investment in local facilities constructed with capital grants from the Area Health Education Centers program (AHEC). The legislation addresses these concerns by requiring that any lease or sale be accompanied by conditions that ensure the continuation of hospital services and

---

169. This section discusses the lease or sale of an entire hospital facility. Disposition of surplus hospital property, real or personal, is subject to other statutes. Counties, cities, and city or county agencies operating hospitals are subject to Article 12 of G.S. Chapter 160A. Hospital authorities are expressly subject to no statutory procedure, G.S. 131E-23(d), while the hospital district statute is silent as to disposition of hospital property.

170. The sections are G.S. 131E-7(d), -8, -8.1, -13, and -14.

the payment of hospital debt and by requiring that such a lease or sale be accomplished through procedures that ensure public notice and, in some cases, the opportunity for competitive sale. Furthermore, if any facility proposed for lease or sale was constructed with an AHEC grant, the local government must notify the director of AHEC of the proposed conveyance and arrange either to continue the local AHEC program or reimburse AHEC.[171] The extensiveness of other conditions and procedures depends on the nature of the lessee or buyer of the hospital facilities, the most extensive being required when that other party is a for-profit entity.[172]

2. Lease or Sale to Nonprofit Corporations Associated with the Local Government

A common arrangement for operation of publicly owned hospitals has been for the local government that owns the facility to lease it to a nonprofit corporation whose board of directors is appointed, in whole or in large part, by the local government. A nonprofit corporation with that sort of relationship to the government that owns the hospital normally has other ties with the government as well, ties that in total make the nonprofit corporation essentially an agency of the local government.[173] Recognizing this, the statutes permit *leases* to this kind of nonprofit corporation and impose neither procedural requirements nor operating conditions.[174]

G.S. 131E-8 governs *sales* to such a controlled nonprofit corporation and requires somewhat more formality than a lease. The statute permits the continued operation of the hospital to be full consideration for the

---

171. *Id.* § 131E-8.1.

172. Lease or sale of hospital facilities is both complicated and specialized. For that reason this section merely summarizes the conditions and procedures required for these transactions. A more comprehensive discussion is found in JOSEPH S. FERRELL, *Organization and Powers of County and City Hospitals*, 9–14 (1985), a chapter in HOSPITAL LAW IN NORTH CAROLINA (Anne M. Dellinger ed., Institute of Government 1985).

173. A representative example of a nonprofit corporation with close ties to a local government is described in News & Observer Publ'g Co. v. Wake County Hosp. Sys., Inc., 55 N.C. App. 1, 284 S.E.2d 542 (1981). *See also* Coats v. Sampson County Mem'l Hosp., Inc., 264 N.C. 332, 141 S.E.2d 490 (1965), *and* Sides v. Cabarrus Mem'l Hosp., Inc., 287 N.C. 14, 213 S.E.2d 197 (1975). These relationships are discussed in detail in Ferrell, *supra* note 172, at 14–18.

174. G.S. 131E-7(d). This hospital statute is silent as to procedures. G.S. 131E-13(g) provides that G.S. Chapter 131E is the exclusive authority for leases and sales of hospital facilities, and therefore Article 12 procedures do not apply.

sale but requires that the nonprofit corporation be legally bound to continue operation of the facility as a community general hospital and to provide such services to the medically indigent as the corporation and the selling government agree to. If the corporation ceases to operate the facility or dissolves without arranging for a successor to operate the hospital, the statute directs that the facility revert to the local government. Finally, the statute requires that the corporation, at the time of sale, place moneys or obligations in escrow that, with accumulated interest, will be sufficient to retire any debt of the selling government related to the facility and outstanding at the time of sale. The statute concludes by requiring that the selling government's governing board approve the sale at a regular meeting upon ten days' public notice.[175]

3. Lease or Sale to For-profit Corporations or to Independent Nonprofit Corporations

G.S. 131E-13 sets out detailed provisions governing the sale or lease of hospital facilities to for-profit corporations. This statute imposes more rigorous conditions upon these sales or leases than are required for sales to nonprofit corporations controlled by a local government,[176] reflecting the much greater independence of the buyer or lessee under G.S. 131E-13, as well as the differing objectives of a for-profit organization. The statute imposes a set of conditions that seek the same result as the conditions imposed on a sale to a controlled nonprofit corporation. Additionally, it imposes the same requirements for payment of the seller or lessor's hospital-related debt as does the statute dealing with sales to controlled nonprofit corporations. But G.S. 131E-13 goes far beyond the other statute when it establishes the procedures that a lease or sale must follow. It does not simply impose a variety of steps to ensure public knowledge of and opportunity to comment on the sale or lease. It also requires that the final arrangement be the product of a competitive process, with proposals being solicited from at least five prospective lessees or buyers.[177]

---

175. G.S. 131E-8(c).

176. For example, the for-profit hospital is required to continue specific listed hospital services, while the controlled nonprofit hospital is required only to maintain a "community general hospital."

177. G.S. 131E-13(d).

G.S. 131E-14 requires that if a local government sells or leases a hospital facility to an *independent* nonprofit corporation,[178] it must follow the *procedural* requirements for sales or leases to for-profit corporations. This statute, however, does not require that all the conditions of for-profit sales or leases be imposed on an independent nonprofit corporation. Rather, transactions with these corporations apparently are to be accompanied by the same *conditions* that accompany sales to controlled nonprofit corporations.[179]

C. Units and Agencies Not Subject to Article 12

Section 602-B contains a list of local governments that either possess express authority to convey property through private sale or operate under statutes that say nothing whatsoever about property disposition procedures. This latter group therefore may probably also sell by private sale.[180]

Governments in either group may also sell, in their discretion, through competitive procedures, either using one of the Article 12 procedures or a procedure of their own design. Although this point has not arisen in any reported North Carolina litigation, cases from other states do require that any locally designed competitive procedures be fair to all potential bidders.[181] Thus, while the selling government may in its discretion decide to deal with only one potential buyer by selling through private negotiation, if the government decides to open the sale up to competition, it must do so in a way that does not unduly favor or disfavor any bidder or potential bidder.

---

178. In this context an *independent* nonprofit corporation is one whose governing body (or a majority thereof) is *not* appointed by the local government selling or leasing the hospital facility.

179. Strictly speaking, G.S. 131E-8 speaks only to *sales* to independent nonprofit corporations, arguably leaving leases to such corporations to the simple authorization of G.S. 131E-7(d). The policy of the statute, however, is otherwise so clear that a lease to an independent nonprofit should certainly include the same conditions required for a sale.

180. Kranjec v. City of West Allis, 66 N.W.2d 178 (Wis. 1954) (when no statute requires competitive leases of city property, city may privately negotiate such leases).

181. Irwin Marine, Inc. v. Blizzard, Inc., 490 A.2d 786 (N.H. 1985) (court invalidates sale because high bidder after first sale was not notified that its bid was rejected nor that a new sale was being held; court argues that these failures placed the bidder at an unfair disadvantage).

Addendum
Opinion of the Attorney General's Office Regarding
Property Transactions Pursuant to G.S. 160A-274

13 October 1983

Mr. George T. Rogister, Jr.
Ms. Ann L. Majestic
Attorneys at Law
P.O. Box 1151
Raleigh, North Carolina 27602

Dear Mr. Rogister and Ms. Majestic:

On 9 January, 1980 our office issued a formal opinion (49 N.C.A.G. 91) that published notice and hearing requirements contained in Article 12 of Chapter 160A must be followed where real or personal property is disposed of between governmental units pursuant to N.C.G.S. 160A-274. *For reasons which follow, the 1980 opinion is overruled.* Where governmental units enter into agreements pursuant to N.C.G.S. 160A-274 for the use of real or personal property, the published notice and hearing requirements of Article 12 need not be complied with.

Article 12 of Chapter 160A deals generally with the sale and disposition of property by cities and towns. N.C.G.S. 160A-266 through 160A-272 set forth with specificity how cities and towns may dispose of real or personal property. Included within these statutes are requirements for notice, advertisements, and hearings depending upon the property involved and its disposition. It should be noted that N.C.G.S. 160A-266 through 160A-272 contemplate the sale or lease of property to other than governmental units.

N.C.G.S. 160A-274 specifically speaks to the disposition of real or personal property between governmental units (city, county, school administrative unit, sanitary district, fire district, the State, or any other public district, authority, department, agency, board, commission, or institution) and does not include any published notice or hearing requirements. The language used in N.C.G.S. 160A-274 allows much latitude and

continued on next page

is most broad, allowing disposition of "any interest in real or personal property" owned by a governmental unit "upon such terms and conditions as the unit deems wise, with or without consideration." It appears that the Legislature purposefully used such broad language to encourage transactions between governmental units and did not intend to require public notice and hearing prior to approval of such agreements. Had the Legislature so intended, it could easily have made clear its intention to require public notice and hearing. In this regard, N.C.G.S. 160A-277, which is also a part of Article 12, is instructive. This statute authorizes a city, "upon such terms and conditions as it deems wise, with or without monetary consideration," to lease or convey real property to a volunteer fire department. That statute specifically requires the city to give ten days' public notice "by publication describing the property to be leased or sold, stating the value of the properties, the proposed monetary consideration or lack thereof, and the (city) council's intent to authorize the lease, sale or conveyance." No such notice is required or set forth in N.C.G.S. 160A-274. Had the General Assembly so intended, it would have set forth its intent within that statute, as it did in N.C.G.S. 160A-277.

Should you have any further questions, please advise.

Very truly yours

RUFUS L. EDMISTEN
Attorney General

/s/ Andrew A. Vanore, Jr.
Senior Deputy Attorney General

[The italics in the first paragraph were added in this transcription.]

Appendix A:
Forms for Disposing of Property

I. Economic Development Property (G.S. 158-7.1)
A. Notice of Public Hearings Pursuant to G.S. 158-7.1(d)

NOTICE OF PUBLIC HEARING

XYZ County proposes to convey land in the Eastside Industrial Park, owned by the county, for an economic development project pursuant to North Carolina General Statute § 158-7.1. The Board of County Commissioners intends, subject to public comment at the public hearing for which notice is hereby given, to approve conveyance of a fee simple interest in a 17-acre tract of land at the industrial park. This tract is Parcel 6 at the industrial park, as shown on a plat of the park that is available at the offices of the county Department of Economic Development, Room 241, XYZ County Office Building in the city of ABC. [The conveyance will be made to Michigan Industries, Inc., which will construct a surgical instrument manufacturing facility on the tract.][1] The Board of County Commissioners has determined that the value of the tract is $11,400 an acre, for a total value of $193,800. The purchaser of the tract intends to pay the county the full value of the tract at closing. The Board of Commissioners believes this project will stimulate and stabilize the local economy and result in the creation of a substantial number of new, permanent jobs in the county.

---

1. The name of the purchaser of the land is included in the notice, because in most instances the local government will want to identify the purchaser and thereby allow a more informative public hearing. That sentence is set in brackets, however, because the statute does not require that the notice include this information, and there may be instances in which the information is not yet public. [author's note]

The XYZ County Board of Commissioners will hold a public hearing on the county's proposed conveyance of this tract of land at 7:30 P.M. on Monday, March 10, 200x, in the Commissioners' Room in the XYZ County Office Building, 100 Court Street, ABC, N.C. The commissioners invite all interested persons to attend and present their views.

B. Resolution Authorizing Sale of Real Property for Economic Development

WHEREAS, North Carolina General Statute § 158-7.1 authorizes a county to undertake an economic development project by conveying property to a company in order to cause the company to locate or expand its operations within the county; and

WHEREAS, XYZ County is the owner and developer of the Eastside Industrial Park, Parcel 6 of which is a 17-acre tract; and

WHEREAS, XYZ County and Michigan Industries, Inc. have engaged in private negotiations for the conveyance of Parcel 6, to the end that Michigan Industries, Inc., may construct a surgical instrument manufacturing facility on the tract and have reached tentative agreement on the terms for conveyance; and

WHEREAS, the Board of Commissioners of XYZ County has held a public hearing to consider whether to approve conveyance of the tract to Michigan Industries, Inc.;

THEREFORE, THE BOARD OF COMMISSIONERS OF XYZ COUNTY RESOLVES THAT:

1. The chairman of the Board of Commissioners is authorized to execute the necessary documents to convey to Michigan Industries, Inc., the real property more particularly described below:

[Description][2]

2. The conveyance of the property to Michigan Industries, Inc., will stimulate the local economy, promote business, and result in the creation of a substantial number of jobs in XYZ County that pay at or above the median average hourly wage in the county. The median average hourly

---

2. The description should be adequate to identify the property. If a surveyed description exists, it should be used, but other forms of description will adequately identify the property. [author's note]

wage in XYZ County, as determined by the North Carolina Employment Security Commission, is $x.xx per hour. The probable average hourly wage at the facility to be constructed by Michigan Industries, Inc., is $x.xx, which is above the current median hourly wage in the county. This determination of the probable average hourly wage at the facility is based upon materials provided to the county by Michigan Industries, Inc. [upon testimony from officials of Michigan Industries, Inc., at the public hearing, and materials provided at that time to the county by Michigan Industries, Inc.].

3. The fair market value of the property, subject to the covenants and conditions associated with the Eastside Industrial Park, is $193,500. This determination of fair market value is based upon an appraisal of the property by London Appraisal Company, a copy of which is on file in the office of the XYZ County Economic Development Department, XYZ County Office Building. [This determination of fair market value is based upon the sales prices of comparable tracts of land in XYZ County, as reported to the Board of Commissioners.]

4. As consideration for the conveyance of the property, Michigan Industries, Inc., has agreed to construct on the property a surgical instrument manufacturing facility at a cost of at least $13,500,000. A copy of the contract is attached to this resolution. This facility will generate property tax revenues over the next 10 years in an amount at least sufficient to return to the county the fair market value of the property.

[4. As consideration for the conveyance of the property, Michigan Industries, Inc., will pay $195,000 at closing.][3]

Adopted June 23, 200x.

II. Sale of Personal Property Worth Less Than $30,000 (G.S. 160A-266)

A. Resolution Authorizing Sale

WHEREAS, XYZ County owns certain items of personal property that have become surplus for its current needs; and

---

3. The first version of paragraph (4) assumes that the property is being given to the company as an incentive; the second version, in brackets, should be used if the company is paying monetary consideration for the property. [author's note]

WHEREAS, North Carolina General Statute § 160A-266 permits the county to sell such property by private sale, upon authorization by the Board of Commissioners at a regular meeting and notice to the public; and

WHEREAS, the Board of Commissioners is convened in a regular meeting;

THEREFORE, THE BOARD OF COMMISSIONERS OF XYZ COUNTY RESOLVES THAT:

1. The Board of Commissioners authorizes the county purchasing agent to sell by private sale the following items of surplus personal property:

[Description]

2. The clerk to the Board of Commissioners shall publish a notice summarizing this resolution, and no sale may be executed pursuant to this resolution until at least 10 days after the day the notice is published.

Adopted July 12, 200x.

B. Notice of Authorization of Sale

PUBLIC NOTICE
SALE OF COUNTY-OWNED PERSONAL PROPERTY

The Board of Commissioners of XYZ County has authorized the county purchasing agent to sell by private sale the following items of county-owned personal property:

[Description]

Any persons interested in purchasing any of these items may apply to the county purchasing agent at Room 44, Courthouse Annex, 44 Main Street, ABC, N.C., or may telephone during normal business hours at 123-4567.

III. Sale by Sealed Bid (G.S. 160A-268)

A. Resolution Authorizing Sealed Bid Sale

WHEREAS, XYZ County owns a 4-acre tract located along the north side of Cornel Road, about 1,350 feet southeast of the intersection of Cornel Road and Skyline Drive, and known as Lot XX, Tax Block XXXX, XYZ County Tax Maps; and

WHEREAS, North Carolina General Statute § 160A-268 permits the county to sell real property by advertisement and sealed bid;

THEREFORE, THE BOARD OF COMMISSIONERS OF XYZ COUNTY RESOLVES THAT:

1. The Board of Commissioners hereby authorizes the sale of the following described tract of land by sealed bid:

[Description]

2. The county will accept sealed bids for the property until 3:00 P.M., Wednesday, March 24, 200x. Bids shall be delivered to the office of the county manager, Room 210, County Office Building, 100 Court Street, ABC, N.C.

3. At 3:00 P.M., Wednesday, March 24, 200x, all bids received shall be opened in public and the amount of each bid recorded. The record of bids shall be reported to the Board of Commissioners at their regular meeting on Monday, March 29, 200x.

4. The Board of Commissioners will determine the highest responsible bidder for the property and will award the bid by its regular meeting on April 12, 200x. Bids will remain open and subject to acceptance until the Board of Commissioners awards the bid.

5. To be responsible a bid must be accompanied by a bid deposit of five percent (5%) of the amount of the bid. A bid deposit may take the form of cash, a cashier's check, a certified check, or a surety bond. The deposit of the bidder to whom the award is made will be held until sale of the property is closed; if that bidder refuses at any time to close the sale, the deposit will be forfeited to the county. The deposits of other bidders will be returned at the time the Board of Commissioners awards the property to the highest responsible bidder.

6. In addition, to be responsible, a bidder must be current on payment of all property taxes owed to the county.

7. The county reserves the right to withdraw the property from sale at any time and the right to reject all bids.

Adopted February 18, 200x.

B. Advertisement for Sealed Bids

ADVERTISEMENT FOR SEALED BIDS

SALE OF COUNTY PROPERTY

The Board of Commissioners of XYZ County has authorized the sale by sealed bid of the following parcel of real property:

[Description]

The county will accept sealed bids for the property until 3:00 P.M., Wednesday, March 24, 200x, at the office of the county manager, Room 210, County Office Building, 100 Court Street, ABC, N.C. At 3:00 P.M., Wednesday, March 24, 200x, all bids received shall be opened in public and the amount of each bid announced and recorded. The record of bids shall be reported to the Board of Commissioners at their regular meeting on Monday, March 29, 200x.

The Board of Commissioners will determine the highest responsible bidder for the property and will award the bid by its regular meeting on April 12, 200x. Bids will remain open and subject to acceptance until the Board of Commissioners awards the bid.

Each bid must be accompanied by a bid deposit of five percent (5%) of the amount of the bid. A bid deposit may take the form of cash, a cashier's check, a certified check, or a surety bond. The deposit of the bidder to whom the award is made will be held until sale of the property is closed; if that bidder refuses at any time to close the sale, the deposit will be forfeited to the county. The deposits of other bidders will be returned at the time the Board of Commissioners awards the property to the highest responsible bidder.

In order for a bid to be considered, the bidder must be current on payment of all property taxes owed to the county.

The county reserves the right to withdraw the property from sale at any time and the right to reject all bids.

Inquiries about the property and the sale may be made to the XYZ county manager, Room 210, County Office Building, 100 Court Street, ABC, N.C.

IV. Negotiated Offer and Upset Bid (G.S. 160A-269)

A. Resolution Authorizing Upset Bid Process

WHEREAS, the City of ABC owns certain property, [property description]; and

WHEREAS, North Carolina General Statute § 160A-269 permits the city to sell property by upset bid, after receipt of an offer for the property; and

WHEREAS, the City has received an offer to purchase the property described above, in the amount of $17,000, submitted by E. D. Boyer of ABC; and

WHEREAS, E. D. Boyer has paid the required five percent (5%) deposit on his offer;

THEREFORE, THE CITY COUNCIL OF THE CITY OF ABC RESOLVES THAT:

1. The City Council authorizes sale of the property described above through the upset bid procedure of North Carolina General Statute § 160A-269.

2. The city clerk shall cause a notice of the proposed sale to be published. The notice shall describe the property and the amount of the offer, and shall state the terms under which the offer may be upset.

3. Persons wishing to upset the offer that has been received shall submit a sealed bid with their offer to the office of the city clerk within 10 days after the notice of sale is published. At the conclusion of the 10-day period, the city clerk shall open the bids, if any, and the highest such bid will become the new offer. If there is more than one bid in the highest amount, the first such bid received will become the new offer.[4]

4. If a qualifying higher bid is received, the city clerk shall cause a new notice of upset bid to be published, and shall continue to do so until a 10-day period has passed without any qualifying upset bid having been received. At that time, the amount of the final high bid shall be reported to the City Council.

5. A qualifying higher bid is one that raises the existing offer by not less than ten percent (10%) of the first $1,000.00 of that offer and five percent (5%) of the remainder of that offer.

---

4. If the local government wishes to use the other method of upset bid (as discussed in Section 609-D), paragraph (3) should be written as follows:

3. Any person may submit an upset bid to the office of the city clerk within 10 days after the notice of sale is published. Once a qualifying higher bid has been received, that bid will become the new offer. [author's note]

6. A qualifying higher bid must also be accompanied by a deposit in the amount of five percent (5%) of the bid; the deposit may be made in cash, cashier's check, or certified check. The city will return the deposit on any bid not accepted, and will return the deposit on an offer subject to upset if a qualifying higher bid is received. The city will return the deposit of the final high bidder at closing.

7. The terms of the final sale are that
  — the City Council must approve the final high offer before the sale is closed, which it will do within 30 days after the final upset bid period has passed, and
  — the buyer must pay with cash at the time of closing.

8. The city reserves the right to withdraw the property from sale at any time before the final high bid is accepted and the right to reject at any time all bids.

9. If no qualifying upset bid is received after the initial public notice, the offer set forth above is hereby accepted. The appropriate city officials are authorized to execute the instruments necessary to convey the property to E. D. Boyer.

Adopted May 14, 200x.

B. Notice of Sale by Upset Bid

PUBLIC NOTICE

SALE OF CITY PROPERTY

An offer of $17,000 has been submitted for the purchase of certain property owned by the City of ABC, more particularly described as follows:

[Description]

Persons wishing to upset the offer that has been received shall submit a sealed bid with their offer to the office of the city clerk, Room 17, City Hall, 118 4th Street, ABC, N.C., by 5:00 P.M., May 28, 200x. At that time the city clerk shall open the bids, if any, and the highest qualifying bid will become the new offer. If there is more than one bid in the highest amount, the first such bid received will become the new offer.

A qualifying higher bid is one that raises the existing offer to an amount not less than $17,900.

A qualifying higher bid must be accompanied by a deposit in the amount of five percent (5%) of the bid; the deposit may be made in cash, cashier's check, or certified check. The city will return the deposit on any bid not accepted, and will return the deposit on an offer subject to upset if a qualifying higher bid is received. The city will return the deposit of the final high bidder at closing.

The buyer must pay cash at closing.

The City Council must approve the final high offer before the sale is closed, which it will do within 30 days after the final upset bid period has passed. The city reserves the right to withdraw the property from sale at any time before the final high bid is accepted and the right to reject at any time all bids.

Further information may be obtained at the office of city clerk, Room 17, City Hall, 118 4th Street, ABC, N.C., or at telephone 123-4567 during normal business hours.

V. Public Auction (G.S. 160A-270)

A. Resolution Authorizing Auction Sale

WHEREAS, the City of ABC owns five parcels of land indicated on Attachment A that are surplus to its needs; and

WHEREAS, North Carolina General Statute § 160A-270 permits the city to sell real property at public auction upon approval of the City Council and after publication of a notice announcing the auction;

THEREFORE, THE CITY COUNCIL OF THE CITY OF ABC RESOLVES THAT:

1. The City Council authorizes the sale at public auction of the five parcels of land indicated on Attachment A.

2. The auction will be conducted at 10:00 A.M., Wednesday, October 12, 200x, in the Council Chamber, City Hall, 118 4th Street, ABC, N.C.

3. The terms of the sale are that the buyer must present at the auction a bid deposit of five percent (5%) of the amount of the bid, either in cash or with a certified check. This deposit will be held by the city until either the City Council rejects the high bid for the property or, if the City Council accepts the high bid, the closing of the sale. The deposit will be forfeited to the city if the high bidder refuses to close the sale after the bid has been approved by the City Council.[5]

---

5. If no bid deposit is to be required, as is likely with an auction sale of personal property, the term of sale paragraph might read:

4. After the auction, the high bid for each parcel shall be reported to the City Council. The council will accept or reject the bid within 30 days after the bid is reported to it. No sale may be completed until the council has approved the high bid.[6]

5. The city reserves the right to withdraw any listed property from the auction at any time before the auction sale of that property.

Adopted September 5, 200x.

ATTACHMENT A

Parcels Available for Public Auction
[Property descriptions]

B. Notice of Auction Sale

PUBLIC NOTICE OF AUCTION SALE

The City Council of the City of ABC, at its meeting of September 5, 200x, authorized the sale by public auction of the following five parcels of city-owned real estate:

[Description]

The auction is scheduled to be held at 10:00 A.M., Wednesday, October 12, 200x, in the Council Chamber, City Hall, 118 4th Street, ABC, N.C.

The high bidder for each parcel must present at the auction a bid deposit of five percent (5%) of the amount of the bid, either in cash or a certified check. This deposit will be held by the city until either the City Council rejects the high bid for the property or, if the City Council

---

3. The terms of sale are:
   — that the property is sold in its current condition, as is, and the City gives no warranty with respect to usability of the property; and
   — that the buyer will pay the full amount of his or her bid before the conclusion of the auction, either in cash or with a certified check. Failure to make payment on the day of the auction cancels the buyer's bid.

   Also, with an auction of personal property, paragraph (4) of the resolution is unnecessary. [author's note]

6. *Ibid.*

accepts the high bid, the closing of the sale. The deposit will be forfeited to the city if the high bidder refuses to close the sale after the bid has been approved by the City Council.

After the auction, the high bid for each parcel will be reported to the City Council. The council will accept or reject the bid within 30 days after the bid is reported to it. No sale may be completed until the council has approved the high bid.

The city reserves the right to withdraw any listed property from the auction at any time before the auction sale of that property.

C. Resolution Accepting High Bid for Property

WHEREAS, the City of ABC conducted an auction sale of five parcels of property on October 12, 200x; and

WHEREAS, high bids were submitted for each of the five parcels as shown on Attachment A;[7]

THEREFORE, THE CITY COUNCIL OF THE CITY OF ABC RESOLVES THAT:

The high bid is accepted for each parcel of property shown on Attachment A, and the appropriate city officials shall execute the documents necessary to transfer title to the properties.

Adopted October 17, 200x.

ATTACHMENT A

[Property description and high bid for each parcel]

D. Resolution Rejecting High Bid for Property

WHEREAS, the City of ABC conducted an auction sale of a tract of land located at 515 S. Main Street in ABC on October 12, 200x; and

WHEREAS, the high bid for the tract was $7,500; and

WHEREAS, the City Council believes this is well below the market value of the tract;[8]

---

7. If only one parcel is sold at auction, the *whereas* clauses might describe the property and give the amount of the high bid. [author's note]

8. This statute does not require that the governing board give any reason for rejecting the bid. Doing so, however, undercuts any allegation that the board rejected the bid for a legally improper reason. [author's note]

THEREFORE, THE CITY COUNCIL OF THE CITY OF ABC RESOLVES THAT:

The high bid for the tract of land located at 515 S. Main Street, City of ABC, is hereby rejected.

Adopted October 17, 200x.

VI. Exchanges (G.S. 160A-271)

A. Notice of Board's Intention to Authorize Exchange

PUBLIC NOTICE

EXCHANGE OF REAL ESTATE

Pursuant to North Carolina General Statute § 160A-271, the Board of Commissioners of XYZ County states its intention to authorize the exchange of certain county-owned property for certain property owned by John Shatto, of the City of ABC, N.C.

The exchange involves the following unimproved tracts of land:

The county's land is a 4-acre tract located along the north side of Cornel Road, about 1,350 feet southeast of the intersection of Cornel Road and Skyline Drive. The tract is known as Lot XX, Tax Block XXXX, XYZ County Tax Maps; and the tract is valued at $15,600.

The land to be acquired by the county is comprised of lots 6, 7, and 8 of Johnston's Addition to the Town of Qville, which are known as tracts 15, 16, and 17, Tax Block XXXX, XYZ County Tax Maps. The three lots collectively contain 2.24 acres and are collectively valued at $15,900.

The exchange will be an even trade.

All persons interested in this exchange are invited to attend the meeting of the Board of Commissioners to be held in the Commissioners Room, XYZ County Office Building, 100 Court Street, ABC, N.C., at 7:00 P.M., on Monday, May 10, 200x. At that time the board intends to authorize the exchange of the properties described above.

B. Resolution Authorizing Exchange of Property

WHEREAS, XYZ County owns a 4-acre tract of land, known as Lot XX, Tax Block XXXX, XYZ County Tax Maps, located along the north side of Cornel Road, about 1,350 feet southeast of the intersection of Cornel Road and Skyline Drive, and valued at $15,600; and

WHEREAS, Mr. John Shatto of the City of ABC, N.C., owns three lots in the Johnston Addition to the Town of Qville, known as tracts 15, 16, and 17, Tax Block XXXX, XYZ County Tax Maps, and valued at $15,900; and

WHEREAS, the County and Mr. Shatto wish to make an even exchange of the two described properties; and

WHEREAS, North Carolina General Statute § 160A-271 authorizes the county to make such an exchange if authorized by the Board of Commissioners by a resolution adopted at a regular meeting of the board upon at least 10 days' public notice; and

WHEREAS, the county has given the required public notice, and the board is convened in a regular meeting.

THEREFORE, THE BOARD OF COMMISSIONERS OF XYZ COUNTY RESOLVES THAT:

1. The exchange of properties described above is authorized.

2. The appropriate county officials are directed to execute the appropriate instruments necessary to carry out the exchange.

Adopted May 10, 200x.

VII. Leases (G.S. 160A-272)

A. Resolution Leasing Property for One Year or Less

WHEREAS, the City of ABC owns a vacant, unimproved lot located on the corner of 10th and East Jefferson streets that it does not currently have use for; and

WHEREAS, Rock Island Leather Co. (Rock Island) owns the adjoining lot and building; and

WHEREAS, the City and Rock Island have agreed upon a lease, under which Rock Island will lease the city's lot for the term of one year beginning October 1, 200x, for a consideration of $4,000, payable in advance; and

WHEREAS, North Carolina General Statute § 160A-272 authorizes the city to enter into leases of one year or less upon resolution of the City Council adopted at a regular meeting; and

WHEREAS, the City Council is convened in a regular meeting;

THEREFORE, THE CITY COUNCIL OF THE CITY OF ABC RESOLVES
THAT:

The City Council hereby approves lease of the city property described
above to Rock Island Leather Co. and directs the appropriate city
employees to execute any instruments necessary to the lease.

Adopted September 24, 200x.

B. Resolution Delegating Leasing Authority to Manager

WHEREAS, XYZ County owns various parcels of property that it has
no current need for; and

WHEREAS, North Carolina General Statute § 160A-272 authorizes the
Board of Commissioners to delegate to the county manager the authority
to determine that specific parcels are temporarily surplus to the county's
needs and to lease such parcels for periods of up to one year;

THEREFORE, THE BOARD OF COMMISSIONERS OF XYZ COUNTY
RESOLVES THAT:

1. The county manager is authorized to determine that specific parcels of county-owned property are surplus to the county's current needs
and to enter into leases of such parcels for periods of up to one year,
upon such terms and conditions as the manager shall determine.

2. The county manager shall report to the Board of Commissioners at
the first meeting of each quarter as to any leases of county-owned property entered into during the preceding quarter.[9]

Adopted March 5, 200x.

C. Notice of Intended Lease of Ten Years or Less

PUBLIC NOTICE
LEASE OF CITY PROPERTY

The City Council of the City of ABC intends to enter into a lease of
the following city-owned property:

[Description]

The city intends to lease the property to Rock Island Leather Co. (Rock
Island) for a term of three years; Rock Island Leather Co. will also have

---

9. The statute does not require any reporting to the board by the official to
whom leasing authority is delegated, and so a local government may, if it wishes,
delete this requirement. [author's note]

the option to renew the lease for one additional term of three years. In consideration of the lease, Rock Island Leather Co. will install asphalt paving on the city property and will pay the city an annual rent of $4,000. If Rock Island renews the lease, the annual rent during the second term will be $4,500.

All persons interested in this lease are invited to attend the meeting of the City Council to be held in the Council Chambers, City Hall, 118 4th Street, ABC, N.C., at 7:00 P.M., on Monday, May 10, 200x. At that time the board intends to authorize the lease of the property described above.

D. Resolution Leasing Property for a Term of up to Ten Years

WHEREAS, the City of ABC owns a vacant, unimproved lot located on the corner of 10th and East Jefferson streets that the council finds is currently surplus to the city's needs; and

WHEREAS, Rock Island Leather Co. (Rock Island) owns the adjoining lot and building; and

WHEREAS, the city and Rock Island have agreed upon a lease, under which Rock Island will lease the city's lot for the term of three years, beginning May 15, 200x, with the right to renew the lease for one additional term of three years; and

WHEREAS, in consideration of leasing the city's lot, Rock Island has agreed to install asphalt paving on the lot and pay annual rent of $4,000, with the rent rising to $4,500 in the second three-year term; and

WHEREAS, North Carolina General Statute § 160A-272 authorizes the city to enter into leases of up to 10 years upon resolution of the City Council adopted at a regular meeting after 10 days' public notice; and

WHEREAS, the required notice has been published and the City Council is convened in a regular meeting;

THEREFORE, THE CITY COUNCIL OF THE CITY OF ABC RESOLVES THAT:

The City Council hereby approves lease of the city property described above to Rock Island Leather Co. for three years, with the lessee holding a right to renew for an additional three-year period, and directs the appropriate city employees to execute any instruments necessary to the lease.

Adopted May 10, 200x.

VIII. Securities (G.S. 160A-276)

Resolution Authorizing Sale of Securities

WHEREAS, the City of ABC has been given 4,000 shares of stock in Rock City Semiconductor; and

WHEREAS, the city wishes to convert the stock into cash; and

WHEREAS, North Carolina General Statute § 160A-276 authorizes the city to sell stock that has an established market and that is traded on a national stock exchange; and

WHEREAS, the stock of Rock City Semiconductor is traded on the NASDAQ stock exchange;

THEREFORE, THE CITY COUNCIL OF THE CITY OF ABC RESOLVES THAT:

The City of ABC finance director shall sell the city's 4,000 shares of stock in Rock City Semiconductor on the NASDAQ stock exchange during the week following adoption of this resolution.[10]

Adopted February 22, 200x.

IX. Conveyance to a Nonprofit Organization (G.S. 160A-279)

Resolution Approving Conveyance of Property Pursuant to G.S. 160A-279

WHEREAS, the City of ABC owns a 2-acre tract of land with a vacant building on the land, located at 2345 S.E. Division Street, between 23rd and 24th streets; and

WHEREAS, North Carolina General Statute § 160A-279 authorizes a city to convey real property by private sale to a nonprofit corporation, if the city is authorized by law to appropriate money to the corporation; and

---

10. If the local government wants to set a minimum price for the stock, the resolution might read:

The City of ABC finance director shall sell the city's 4,000 shares of stock in Rock City Semiconductor on the NASDAQ stock exchange, for no less than $45 per share. [author's note]

WHEREAS, North Carolina General Statute § 160A-497 authorizes a city to undertake programs for the assistance and care of its senior citizens and to contract and appropriate funds to private organizations in order to carry out such programs; and

WHEREAS, the City of ABC has negotiated with the Eastside Community Preservation Association [hereafter, Association] to convey the 2-acre tract described above to Association, in order that Association may improve the building and then operate a senior citizens' center in the building; and

WHEREAS, the operation of a senior citizens' center on Division Street will assist the city in meeting the needs of its senior citizens;

THEREFORE, THE ABC CITY COUNCIL RESOLVES THAT:

1. The mayor of ABC is authorized to execute all documents necessary to convey fee simple defeasible title to a 2-acre tract of land located at 2345 S.E. Division Street between 23rd and 24th streets, more particularly described as follows:

[Description][11]

2. The consideration for the conveyance is the following set of conditions, covenants, and restrictions, which shall be incorporated in the deed given by the city to Association:

    a. Association will renovate, rehabilitate, and improve the building located on the property, in accordance with general plans submitted to the city by Association and incorporated as a part of this resolution. Association will expend at least $25,000 in this renovation, rehabilitation, and improvement project, and will complete this work by July 1, 200x.

    b. Once the renovation, rehabilitation, and improvement project is complete, Association will operate a senior citizens' center in the building, offering programs for the benefit of senior citizens of the city.

    c. Association shall submit an annual report to the city summarizing the senior citizen programs that it offers at the center.

---

11. * The description should be adequate to identify the property. If a surveyed description exists, it should be used, but other forms of description will adequately identify the property. [author's note]

3. The deed given by the city to the 2-acre tract of land shall convey a title in fee simple determinable. The fee simple interest of Association in the property shall terminate if at any time during the next 25 years Association shall cease to use the property to operate a senior citizens' center.

4. The city clerk shall publish a notice summarizing the contents of this resolution, and the property may be sold at any time after 10 days after publication of the notice.

Adopted October 12, 200x.

X. Community Development Property (G.S. 160A-457)

A. Notice of Public Hearing Pursuant to G.S. 160A-457

NOTICE OF PUBLIC HEARING

The City of ABC proposes to convey land located on Killingsworth Road for a community development project pursuant to North Carolina General Statute § 160A-457. The ABC City Council intends, subject to public comment at the public hearing for which notice is hereby given, to consider approval of the conveyance of a fee simple interest in a 5-acre tract of land that the city acquired on February 19, 1999. This tract fronts on Killingsworth Road, approximately 200 yards south of its intersection with Prescott Street. It is bounded by Killingsworth Road on the west, property owned by Fremont Manufacturing Co. on the north and east, and property owned by Sandy Ceramics on the south. A map of the tract and its environs is available at the office of the city Planning and Development Department, Third Floor, ABC City Hall. The conveyance will be made to Harvey Scott, Inc., which has committed to construct a broom manufacturing facility on the tract. Harvey Scott, Inc., will pay $30,000 for the site, which is the appraised value of the property.

The ABC City Council will hold a public hearing on the city's proposed conveyance of this tract of land at 7:30 P.M. on Monday, March 10, 200x, in the Council Chambers, ABC City Hall. The council invites all interested persons to attend and present their views.

B. Resolution Approving Conveyance of Property Pursuant to G.S. 160A-457

WHEREAS, North Carolina General Statute § 160A-457 authorizes a city to convey by private sale real property located in a community development project area; and

WHEREAS, the ABC City Council has designated the Killingsworth Road district as a community development project area and has adopted a community development plan for the area; and

WHEREAS, the City of ABC owns a 5-acre tract on Killingsworth Road that is zoned for industrial use; and

WHEREAS, the City of ABC and Harvey Scott, Inc., have engaged in private negotiations for the conveyance of the 5-acre tract, to the end that Harvey Scott, Inc., may construct a broom-manufacturing facility on the tract, and have reached tentative agreement on the terms for conveyance; and

WHEREAS, the ABC City Council has held a public hearing to consider whether to approve conveyance of the tract to Harvey Scott, Inc.;

THEREFORE, THE ABC CITY COUNCIL RESOLVES THAT:

1. The city is authorized to convey to Harvey Scott, Inc., the 5-acre property more particularly described below:

[Description][12]

2. The appraised value of the property, as determined by an appraisal made by London Appraisal Company and on file with the city clerk, is $30,000, and Harvey Scott, Inc., has agreed to pay this price to the city upon closing.

3. The mayor of ABC is authorized to execute all documents necessary to conveying the property.

Adopted May 15, 200x.

---

12. The description should be adequate to identify the property. If a surveyed description exists, it should be used, but other forms of description will adequately identify the property. [author's note]

Appendix B.
Index of Statutes

Other North Carolina Laws

North Carolina Constitutional Provisions

Federal Statutes, Codes, and Regulations

Constitutional Provisions from Other Jurisdictions

Appendix C.
Index of Cases

Glossary

This glossary defines a number of technical terms of law, particularly property law, that are used in this book. The definitions are meant to assist the lay reader in understanding the discussion in the text. They are not intended to be satisfactory in all respects for the practicing lawyer, inasmuch as the terms and concepts are often complex and subtle. Bold-face words in the definitions are themselves defined.

Adverse possession—a method by which a person in possession of land, but without title to the land, acquires title. If a person is in open and actual possession of property that she does not own, without permission from the record owner, and if the record owner does not bring an action to eject the possessor within the period of the statute of limitations, then at the end of the limitation period title to the land vests in the possessor. At that time the former record owner's title is extinguished. In North Carolina, the period of limitation is twenty years if the possessor has no deed at all and seven years if she possesses under a deed that is inferior to the deed of the record owner.

Bequest—a gift of personal property made by will.

Charitable trust—a **trust** that normally has no definite beneficiary. In that respect it differs from a private trust. A charitable trust typically devotes the trust property to purposes that benefit or are thought to benefit the community rather than specific persons or groups of persons.

Condemnation—*See* **eminent domain**.

Consideration—in the context of property transactions, the purchase price or other benefit going to the seller of property to compensate her for the conveyance of the property.

Cy-pres—a doctrine used when a gift made for a particular charitable purpose cannot, for some reason, be carried out as directed by the donor. It permits a court to apply the gift to some other purpose that is as close as possible to the underlying charitable intent. The doctrine of cy-pres is accepted into North Carolina law in G.S. 36A-53.

Deed—the most familiar method of transferring title to an interest in property. A deed transfers title between parties living at the time of transfer.

Deed of trust—the typical document involved in a **mortgage** transaction in North Carolina. A deed of trust conveys property owned by debtor to a trustee, who then holds the property for the benefit of the creditor as security for the debt. As with any mortgage, the deed of trust is automatically void if the underlying debt is paid by a specified date.

Defeasible fee—*See* **fee simple defeasible**.

Determinable fee—*See* **fee simple determinable**.

Devise—a gift of real property made by will.

Easement—a right to use (as opposed to possess) the land of another for a specific purpose. The easement exists concurrently with the **fee simple** estate in the property. Governments frequently hold easements for such purposes as streets and utility lines.

Eminent domain—the power to take title to private property without the consent of the owner, as long as the property is taken for a public use and just compensation is paid the owner. Governments exercise the power of eminent domain through a process called "condemnation."

Equity of redemption—the interest retained by a **mortgagor** under a **mortgage**. An inseparable part of any mortgage, it is the mortgagor's right (or the right of her heirs or assigns) to recover her original title to the property through payment of the mortgage debt.

Estate—a possessory interest in land. The nature of the particular estate establishes what rights the holder of the estate has in the land. The two most common estates are the **fee simple** and the estate for years (or common lease). Nonpossessory interests in land, such as **easements**, **licenses**, and **restrictive covenants**, are not estates.

Fee—*See* **fee simple**.

Fee simple—the full ownership of land. The holder of this estate is the person we normally consider the "owner" of the land. The fee simple is also known as the "fee" and, to distinguish it from the **defeasible fee**, as the **fee simple absolute**. The fee simple is the most extensive estate possible in land. It is potentially perpetual in duration, and its holder enjoys an unconditional power to dispose of it, by deed or by will, during her lifetime.

Fee simple absolute—*See* **fee simple**.

Fee simple defeasible—a **fee simple** estate that is subject to a limitation by which the estate may be terminated because of the happening of some event, at which time title passes to the **grantor**, her **heirs or assigns**, or some other person designated by the grantor. It is also known as a "defeasible fee." The three specific types of fee simple defeasible are the **fee simple determinable**, the **fee simple subject to a condition subsequent**, and the **fee simple subject to an executory interest**. These three differ in the nature of the **future interest** held by the grantor or her heirs or assigns or in who holds the future interest.

Fee simple determinable—one category of **fee simple defeasible**. It is also known as the "determinable fee." The fee simple determinable is subject to automatic termination upon the happening of some stated event, at which time title reverts to the **grantor** or her **heirs or assigns**. (The grantor's interest in the property is called a **possibility of reverter**.) An example is a conveyance of property to a city for as long as the property is used as a park, with a statement that if the property should ever stop being used as a park title will revert to the grantor.

Fee simple subject to a condition subsequent—one category of **fee simple defeasible**. The fee simple subject to a condition subsequent may (but need not) be ended by the **grantor** or her **heirs or assigns** upon the happening of some stated event. (The grantor's interest in the property is called a **right of entry for condition broken**.) An example is a conveyance of property to a city on condition that the property be used as a park, with a statement that if the property should ever stop being used as a park the grantor may re-enter and assume ownership and possession, thereby ending the city's title.

Fee simple subject to an executory interest—one category of **fee simple defeasible**. The fee simple subject to an executory interest is like a **fee simple subject to a condition subsequent** but with the following difference: when the event occurs that gives rise to the **right of entry for condition broken**, that right is held by a third party rather than by the **grantor** or her **heirs or assigns**. This estate is not often created.

Fixture—an item of personal property (such as the wood and bricks that constitute a house) that has become more or less permanently attached to real property. The fixture is considered to be part of the real property and to be owned by the owner of the real property.

Future interest—an interest in land or other property in which the right of possession or of enjoyment lies in the future rather than in the present. Examples of future interests include **remainders, reversions,** and **rights of entry**.

Grantee—the person to whom an interest or estate in property is conveyed. He or she receives title to the interest or estate.

Grantor—the person from whom an interest or estate in property is conveyed. He or she surrenders title to the interest or estate. The term has no reference to the **consideration** paid for the property; it includes both gifts of land and transfers fully supported by consideration.

Heirs or assigns—a phrase that encompasses all those persons and entities who eventually come to own a particular piece of property, by whatever method of conveyance. The common phrase "X and his heirs and assigns" refers to X, the owner of the property, and all those who own that property after X.

Inverse condemnation—an action brought by a person whose property has been taken or appropriated by a government agency without the agency compensating the owner or bringing a condemnation action against the owner.

Lessee—the tenant (or person in possession) under a lease.

Lessor—the landlord (or owner of the property) under a lease.

License—a permission to do specific things on the lands of another. Without a license, the acts would be trespasses. The term covers a multitude of activities: a guest in one's home is a licensee, as is a vendor of hot dogs at a city park. The owner of property may give a license orally or in writing and normally may revoke it at will. In addition, a license is personal to the licensee, in that it cannot be assigned to someone else without the licensor's permission. A license does not create an estate or an interest in land.

Lien—a claim to or charge on property, which provides certain classes of creditors with a security interest in the property to secure payment of a debt chargeable to the property's owners. If the debt is not paid in due time, the property can be subjected to the lienholder's claim, usually by sale of the property. Liens attach to both real and personal property and can be created by contract—as, for example, a mortgage lien—or by statute—as, for example, liens for laborers and material-men, for judgment creditors, or for local governments levying property taxes or special assessments.

Life estate—an **estate** in land for the life of the holder of the estate (called the life tenant) or for the life of some other person or persons.

Marketable Title Act—legislation (found in G.S. Chapter 47B) that generally shortens to thirty years the period for which a title attorney must search the land records to determine the title to land. Various burdens on the title, such as nonpossessory interests or old covenants, that do not appear in any chain of title discoverable during the thirty-year period are canceled. The purpose of the Marketable Title Act is to enhance the marketability of land.

Mortgage—a document granting a creditor a security interest in land of his debtor. It takes the form of a conveyance of the land in question from the debtor to the creditor (or to a trustee for the creditor), with the conveyance automatically void if the debt is paid by a specified date. In most North Carolina mortgage transactions, the document involved is a **deed of trust**.

Mortgagee—the creditor in a **mortgage** transaction. She receives title to the debtor's property as security for the money she loans to the debtor. The mortgage represents her interest in the property.

Mortgagor—the debtor in a **mortgage** transaction. He conveys his property as security for the debt to the creditor or, with a **deed of trust**, to a trustee for the creditor.

Option to purchase—a continuing offer to sell a parcel of property, usually at a fixed price and within a specified time. The option is given by the property's owner (the optionor) to a prospective purchaser (the optionee). The optionee is not obligated to exercise the option and purchase the property. The option is a contract and in North Carolina law creates no interest in the land.

Option to repurchase—a contractual right retained by the seller of land, under which she may repurchase the land from the buyer at some time in the future. A frequent example occurs when a seller conveys land to another for a specific use and retains the option to repurchase the land if that use is later discontinued.

Quitclaim deed—a deed in which the **grantor** conveys whatever title she may have (and she may have none) to the property; she makes no warranties of title in the deed. Despite the absence of warranties, the quitclaim deed (sometimes called a "release deed") is completely adequate to convey whatever title is held by the grantor, including a **fee simple** estate.

Possibility of reverter—*See* **reversion**.

Preemptive right—permits the holder of the right to purchase property if and when the owner of the property decides to sell it. This right, which is also called a right of first refusal, is most often given to the seller of property at the time of sale.

Prescription—a method of acquiring title to an **easement** through longtime use of the easement. It is very similar to **adverse possession**, requiring a twenty-year period of open usage without the owner's permission in order for title to the easement to vest in the user. Because the property interest involved is an easement, a nonpossessory interest in land, prescription differs from adverse possession in that it requires use of the property for the statutory period rather than exclusive possession for that period. Local governments have gained title through prescription to streets and roads and, less often, to utility line easements.

Purchase money deed of trust—*See* **purchase money mortgage**.

Purchase money mortgage—a **mortgage** given to the **grantor** of property by the **grantee** when the grantor is not paid in full for the property at the time of sale. It secures the balance of the purchase price due to the grantor.

Release deed—*See* **quitclaim deed**.

Remainder—*See* **reversion**.

Restrictive covenant—a promise restricting the use of land made by the **grantee** of land to her **grantor** as a condition of conveyance. A restrictive covenant may be personal, so that it runs in favor of only the grantor. Alternatively, it may be effective against the grantee's own grantees, in which case the covenant is said to "run with the land." If restrictive covenants are imposed on all lots in a subdivision, they are enforceable against each lot in the subdivision by the owners of any other lot in the subdivision. A restrictive covenant is enforced by payment of damages or by injunction; in this respect it differs from a condition imposed on a **fee simple defeasible**, where a violation of the condition may lead to loss of the property itself.

Reversion—created when the holder of **fee simple** title conveys an interest of limited duration in the land to someone else; the grantor's remaining **estate** in the land, which resumes immediately upon the termination of the estate being conveyed, is called a reversion. A reversion is created, for example, when the owner conveys an estate for years or a **life estate**. The estate held by the grantor of a **fee simple determinable** is very similar but for old reasons is called a "possibility of reverter." A reversion is also similar to a "remainder." If the owner of fee simple title conveys an estate of limited duration and provides that when that estate ends someone other than the grantor is to become owner, that third person's interest is known as a **remainder**.

Right of entry for condition broken—the interest in land held by the **grantor** of a **fee simple subject to condition subsequent**. When the condition upon which the property was conveyed is broken, the holder of the right of entry may, but need not, exercise her right, enter the property, and reclaim ownership and possession.

Right of first refusal—*See* **preemptive right**.

Rule Against Perpetuities—a legal rule intended to limit the ability of current owners of land to make that land nontransferable for long periods of time in the future. Although the details of the Rule are complicated, it basically prohibits creation of any interest in land that need not vest (that is, become fixed, whether the owner of the interest is in possession or not), if it will ever vest, within twenty-one years after the death of any person or persons living when the interest is created. For example, if an individual **grantor** of property retains for herself an **option to repurchase** the property under specified circumstances, the option does not violate the Rule. It can only be exercised by the grantor, who obviously is living at the time the option is created. But if the grantor attempted to retain the option not only for herself but also for her **heirs or assigns**, that option would violate the Rule. It could vest—that is, be exercised—far in the future, well beyond the twenty-one years plus "lives in being" permitted by the Rule.

Security interest—an interest in property that secures payment or performance of an obligation. If the obligation is not met, the property may be sold to satisfy the obligation. Both **liens** and **mortgages** are security interests.

Tenancy in common—a form of concurrent ownership of property. Each co-owner has a separate undivided interest in the property, which she can convey to others and which passes by will or descent to her heirs. The interests of the co-owners need not be established at the same time or by the same instrument, and it is not necessary that each co-owner have an equal share of the property. The tenancy in common is the most common type of concurrent ownership in North Carolina among persons who are not husband and wife. (A married couple normally holds title to property through a form of concurrent ownership known as a "tenancy by the entirety.")

Trade fixtures—**fixtures** that have been attached to the land by a tenant (or other person holding less than a **fee simple absolute** title) for use in that person's trade or business. Generally a person may remove trade fixtures from the property once her tenancy or other use is over.

Trust—an arrangement under which title to property is held by one person who is under a duty to manage the property for the benefit of someone else. The person with title to the property is called the trustee, while the person who benefits from the trust is called the *cestui que trust* or, more simply, the beneficiary.

Warranty deed—a deed in which the **grantor** warrants—or guarantees—the title she is conveying to the **grantee**. If the deed is a general warranty deed, the grantor warrants against defects that arose both before and after she acquired title. If the deed is a special warranty deed, the grantor warrants only against defects that arose while she held title.

Subject Index

www.ingramcontent.com/pod-product-compliance
Lightning Source LLC
Chambersburg PA
CBHW061151220326
41599CB00025B/4442